D1239435

Politics and Policy in the New Korean State

Politics and Policy in the New Korean State

≪ FROM ROH TAE-WOO ≫

TO

≪ KIM YOUNG - SAM ≫

EDITED BY JAMES COTTON

ST. MARTIN'S PRESS
NEW YORK

 LONGMAN

Longman Australia Pty Ltd
Longman House
Kings Gardens
95 Coventry Street
Melbourne 3205 Australia

Offices in Sydney, Brisbane, Adelaide, Perth, and associated companies throughout the world.

Set in 11.5/13.5 Garamond
Produced by Longman Australia Pty Limited
Printed in Singapore

National Library of Australia
Cataloguing-in-Publication data

Politics and policy in the new Korean state : from Roh
    Tae-Woo to Kim Young-Sam.

    Bibliography.
    Includes index.
    ISBN 0 582 80291 1.

    1. Roh, Tae Woo, 1932- . 2. Kim, Young-Sam, 1927- .
    3. Korea (South) – Politics and government – 1988- .
    I. Cotton, James, 1949- .

951.95043

Library of Congress
Cataloguing - in - Publication Data
Politics and Policy in the New Korean State: From Roh Tae-Woo to Kim Young-Sam/
edited by James Cotton.
    p. 256, cm. 234 x 15.6.
    Includes bibliographical references and index.
    ISBN 0-312-12549-6 (cloth)
    1. Korea (South)--Politics and government--1988- I. Cotton.
James. 1949- ,
JQ1729.A15P65   1995
320.95195'09'049--cc20

First published in the United States of America 1995 by
Scholarly and Reference Division,
ST. MARTIN'S PRESS, INC.,
175 Fifth Avenuw,
New York, N.Y. 10010

Contents

Acknowledgements

This collection had its origins in a conference held in Melbourne in September 1992, the joint sponsors of which were the Northeast Asia Program of the Australian National University, the Asia Research Centre of Murdoch University, and the Monash Asia Institute of Monash University. Thanks are due to those institutions and especially to Professors Stuart Harris, David Goodman, and John McKay for their support. The Australia–Korea Foundation is also to be acknowledged for meeting the cost of bringing Professors Manwoo Lee and Sung Chul Yang to Australia. Thanks are due to the University of Tasmania for facilitating the editing of the papers, and to Bae Sun-kwang, Liz Clark, Lynne Payne and Nick Thomas for their research assistance. The editor is also obliged to Professors Ahn Byung-joon, Chang Dal-joong, Kim Hak-joon, Lee Sung-duk and Sohn Hak-kyu, as well as to the contributors, for so generously sharing with him their knowledge of the politics of Korea.

James Cotton
Hobart, Australia
March 1994

Contributors

Bae Sun-kwang is a research student in the Research School of Pacific and Asian Studies, Australian National University, Canberra.

James Cotton is Professor of Political Science, University of Tasmania, Hobart, Australia, and editor of *Korea under Roh Tae-woo: Democratisation, Northern Policy and Inter-Korean Relations.*

Kang Mun-Gu is Assistant Professor of Political Science, Kyungnam University, Masan, and research fellow at the University's Institute for Far Eastern Studies in Seoul.

Young Whan Kihl is Professor of Political Science, Iowa State University, and author of *Politics and Policies in Divided Korea. Regimes in Contest.*

Manwoo Lee is Professor of Political Science, Millersville University of Pennsylvania, and author of *The Odyssey of Korean Democracy. Korean Politics, 1987–1990.*

Chung-in Moon is Associate Professor of Political Science, University of Kentucky, and co-editor of *Alliance Under Tension. The Evolution of South Korean–U.S. Relations.*

Peter J. Rimmer is Senior Fellow in Human Geography, Australian National University, and author of *From Rickisha to Rapid Transit: Urban Public Transport Systems and Policy in Southeast Asia.*

Meredith Woo-Cumings is Assistant Professor of Political Science at Northwestern University, Evanston, Illinois, and author (as Woo Jung-en) of *Race to the Swift. State and Finance in Korean Industrialisation.*

Yang Gil-hyun is a Research Fellow in the Institute for Far Eastern Studies, Kyungnam University, Seoul.

Sung Chul Yang is Professor of Political Science, Kyunghee Unversity, Seoul, and author of *Korea and Two Regimes.Kim Il Sung and Park Chung Hee.*

1

Introduction

James Cotton

This collection of essays examines the role of politics, policy instruments and policies in the transition from the Roh Tae-woo administration to the administration of Kim Young-sam in the Republic of Korea (South Korea). This transition in itself has been a major turning point. Korean politics was dominated for three decades from 1961 by military figures. Though political parties played a role, the parties themselves were mostly dependent upon the holders of power, disappearing in realignments or dissolutions with the departure of their patrons from the scene. Successive constitutions were readily made and unmade, and Korea's booming economy was superintended by an often unsubtle government bureaucracy.

These conditions have changed. The constitution adopted in 1987 has remained in force. The political party formed in 1990 under Roh Tae-woo (through a major realignment of factions) bridged the gap to the new administration, propelling Kim Young-sam to electoral victory in 1992. Not only was Kim a civilian, who had been a champion of democracy in the darkest days of authoritarianism, but his party incorporated a significant number of individuals from the political machines of all three of his military predecessors.

When Kim Young-sam assumed the presidency of South Korea on 25 February 1993, he pledged to follow policies designed to create a 'New Korea'. In his inaugural address he stressed the need to eliminate official corruption, reinvigorate the flagging economy and restore a sense of national discipline. His first 100 days saw an uneven movement towards these goals, although accompanied by sufficient change to demonstrate that a new era in Korean politics had begun.

Appointments to the first executive broke with a number of traditions. The prime minister, Hwang In-sung, was from a part of the country (Cholla province in the south-west) long thought to harbour oppositionists. The cabinet included three women, an extremely daring innovation in this still-patriarchal country. And such sensitive posts as head of the Agency for National Security Planning (the national intelligence agency) and minister in charge of unification affairs (and concurrently deputy prime minister) were given to political outsiders.

Kim vowed that he would not accept funds from business while in office. He also inveighed against the common practice of accepting favours in exchange for cash or other benefits. In pursuit of cleaner politics, he then required all cabinet members and members of the ruling Democratic Liberal Party in the National Assembly to publicly declare their personal assets. In a political system in which influence and office buying was fast becoming institutionalised, this was a bold but also a potentially risky strategy.

It then became a matter of public record that many senior political figures were wealthy men, particularly through the ownership of real estate — a delicate matter in Korea, given the shortage of land and the many housing and property scandals that had come to light during the previous administration. Following these disclosures, the ruling party found it necessary to effect a purge of senior members. Eleven Assembly members, including the speaker, were urged to give up their seats or leave the party.

Though a move to counter corruption, this development was also part of a political strategy. When in 1990 Kim Young-sam brought his political movement into coalition with the then ruling party, he was forced to share power with the political machine of former President Chun Doo-hwan and President Roh Tae-woo, a political machine dominated by former military figures, most of whom were from the common hometown of Chun and Roh. Kim had long been one of their chief opponents and critics, but had come to realise that his own political movement was not sufficiently strong to gain him the presidency when Roh stepped down.

While Kim acknowledged Roh's contribution to the process of democratisation, his alliance with Roh's machine was chiefly one of convenience. This can be seen from the fact that, of the eleven senior politicians censured by the party, only one was not a member of Roh's faction. This is not to say that Kim Young-sam's supporters altogether escaped the effects of the new climate in Korean politics. Two of Kim's original cabinet, his appointee as Mayor of Seoul and his party secretary-general were all forced to resign as a result of misdemeanours (real estate speculation and gaining backdoor admission to university for their children) which in the past would not have been publicised.

In a political system long dominated by former military elites, Kim's approach to the military was without precedent. In asserting his dominance, Kim underlined the fact that the military and security establishments no longer possessed even the power of veto in Korean politics.

The military were unlucky in being caught in the simultaneous pursuit by the president of three reforming objectives. Since 1961, all of the president's political career had been spent under governments of military origin, and Kim Young-sam was determined to assert the principle of civilian supremacy. He was also dedicated to the task of destroying the *Hanahoe*, the society of senior officers who formed the core of the preceding Chun and Roh administrations. And he was very much concerned to eradicate the growing practice of official corruption from which the military were not exempt.

Thus, in an unscheduled reshuffle of senior commanders, the army chief of staff and head of the Army Defense Security Command (its intelligence arm) were replaced. Both were well-known members of *Hanahoe*, which has now been declared dissolved. By the end of his first four months in office, President Kim had replaced or reshuffled eleven of the fourteen most senior Army positions; he also had a similar impact on the senior posts in the Ministry of National Defence. Further, in his first 100 days in office, five Air Force generals were arrested in a corruption scandal which exposed alleged cases of bribe-taking by senior officers in exchange for accelerated promotion. A former Air Force Chief of Staff was also implicated in this case. An official inquiry into the *Yulgok* force modernisation program then recommended the prosecution of a number of senior civilian and military figures in the defence establishment on charges of corruption.

Kim's initial policies apparently reaped him public support. In April 1993 his party won three by-elections, all occasioned by resignations from the Assembly as a result of these scandals. But, in the longer term, Kim will more likely be judged by his attention to Korea's economic difficulties. Here his achievements have been less remarkable.

In 1992 the Korean economy grew by 4.7 per cent, a healthy figure by many standards, but the lowest seen in Korea in a decade. In March 1993 a 100-day economic reform package was announced, providing measures to stimulate economic activity including a reduction in regulated interest rates, and assistance to manufacturing industry to expand investment. There was also a freeze on public-sector wages, and a government austerity drive which has seen senior government officials forsake golf courses and expensive restaurants for less conspicuous consumption practices.

The reform package was followed in June by a lengthy statement on economic reform. In this statement, the government embraced the need for deregulation of the still very considerable controls the government holds over economic activity. However the statement included no concrete timetable for reforms in such crucial issues as government requirements for banks to issue 'policy loans' at low interest to the big conglomerates, or regarding the lifting of exchange controls to make the Korean currency internationally convertible. Though the days of bureaucratic direction of the economy were over, and accordingly many Korean economists were agreed on the need for deregulation, the government was still to show wholehearted commitment to that cause.

Meanwhile, Kim's biggest challenge remained North Korea's failure to observe its obligations under the Nuclear Non-Proliferation Treaty, and the concomitant threat posed by Pyongyang's development of nuclear weapons. The fact that his administration was quite free of military influence gave the president great flexibility in dealing with North Korea. This flexibility, though it prevented an earlier collision between the two Koreas, has (at the time of writing) still to provide a lasting improvement in inter-Korean relations.

In dealing with North Korea, Kim Young-sam was fortunate to inherit an external situation which had been utterly transformed by the administration of Roh Tae-woo. South Korea's 'Northern Policy' had long since borne fruit, in the form of full diplomatic relations with Russia and China. By 1993 most vestiges of Russian nuclear and military co-operation with North Korea had disappeared. On a visit to Seoul in November 1992, President Yeltsin had announced that all Russian assistance for North Korea's nuclear activities would cease. Subsequently, in February 1993, a presidential envoy conveyed the news to Pyongyang that Russia would no longer honour the military alliance which had tied the two countries since 1961. The Russian role in 1994 raised queries regarding the status of this undertaking. At any rate, it was reported in 1993 that the Russian government had prevented a party of missile engineers from travelling to North Korea to take up lucrative employment contracts offered by Pyongyang.

The position taken by China has been more complex, even while South Korea–China trade has grown to rival China–Taiwan trade in importance. While Beijing has always urged caution in the treatment of North Korea, stories have emerged that the Chinese leadership has grown impatient with North Korean intransigence and has been offended by claims that members of the North Korean inner circle have criticised China for practising 'revisionism'. The co-operation of Beijing would be essential for the functioning of any international sanctions regime imposed on North Korea. Although the leadership in Beijing appeared reluctant to abandon one of the last of its socialist allies, the Korean question raised acute difficulties for China. Beijing's economic stake in its burgeoning relationship with South Korea was considerable, and refusal to co-operate in bringing pressure to bear on Pyongyang induced Washington to review trade and human rights matters of dispute with China. Having recently joined the Nuclear Non-Proliferation Treaty, and having no interest in nuclear proliferation in North-east Asia, the North Korean problem provided the best indicator of China's approach to the post-Cold War order.

But though the security concerns generated by North Korea are a matter of concern to all Koreans, in the longer term the Kim Young-sam era will probably be judged more for the extent of its contribution to the creation of a new style of politics in the Republic of Korea. However, Kim Young-sam's status as the first effective non-military president since 1961 is already assured.

2

An Analysis of South Korea's Political Process and Party Politics

Sung Chul Yang

Introduction

The South Korean political system is making headway in transforming itself from one featuring prolonged authoritarianism to a more democratic and pluralistic political system. A number of concrete signs of democratisation are evident. Twice the presidential power has been transferred peacefully, though not *between* the parties but *within* the ruling party. In February 1988, President Chun Doo-hwan of the Fifth Republic handed the power over to Roh Tae-woo. During the Roh regime, liberalisation in the press, civil liberties and civil rights has taken root, though temporary setbacks have not been infrequent. In 1992 South Korea has achieved another democratic milestone. For the second time in its modern political history, there was a peaceful transfer of power from one president to another.

The presidential transition from Roh Tae-woo to Kim Young-sam, though once again within the ruling party, is significant in four important respects. First, Kim Young-sam is the first civilian president in 32 years. From 1961, when Major General Park Chung-hee staged a military coup, up to now, all presidents have been army generals excluding Choi Kyu-ha, who was a brief interim president during the 1979–80 military putsch period.

Second, Kim is the first president who has had a long legislative career. He holds the record for being elected nine times to the South Korean National Assembly. His long legislative political career will indeed be a great plus in dealing with the National Assembly. Moreover, most of his legislative career has been with the opposition party. Thus, unlike his predecessors who were anti-parliamentarian in political orientation and treated the legislature either as the executive handmaiden or as a sheer nuisance, President Kim is more sympathetic and empathic toward the National Assembly, especially in dealing with the legitimate role of the opposition.

Third, his political strongholds are Pusan–South Kyongsang province (PK division), which is contiguous to but different from the so-called Taegu–North Kyongsang province (i.e. TK division), the regional power house since 1961. His presidency may thus signal a lasting shift in the ruling elites' power base from the so-called TK division to the PK division, a new acronym for Pusan–South Kyongsang region. Initially, his political ascendancy was based on the fusion or collusion of the TK and the PK divisions, but many of his closest associates are now from the PK rather than the TK division.

Fourth, Kim Young-sam faces no major or serious challenges from the opposition for the time being. The Democratic Party (DP), the major opposition party has been embroiled in internecine leadership struggle since Kim Dae-Jung, its party boss, retired from politics. The third minor party, the United National Party (UNP), has now also become defunct since Chung Ju-yung ended his short and unsuccessful political stint and withdrew his support for the party he singlehandedly created. Hence, in theory at least, with the majority party (the Democratic Liberal Party) under his control, he can *exercise* power virtually unchecked by the moribund opposition. In reality, however, his presidency is being put to a severe test by the challenges from the almost insurmountable and even intractable problems such as corruption scandals in education, economic downturn and stagflation at home, and the crossfire of protectionist pressures and GATT-propelled open trade demands from abroad. Ironically, then, his power has been moderated and restrained, not by the traditional checks and balances of various countervailing political forces, but by the pressures generated by internal and external problems.

Theoretically, South Korea's democratic development lies somewhere between an anti-authoritarian ('shouting') stage and a de-authoritarian ('experimental') stage. The first phase of democratisation, which is called here an anti-authoritarian or shouting stage, is manifest in a political condition in which the ruling elites continue to practise authoritarian rule while the opposition groups and the mass public openly resist it and vociferously advocate democracy. Despite advocating democracy, democratic belief systems are not firmly ingrained in the minds and behaviours of the opposition and the mass public alike.

The second phase of democratisation — the de-authoritarian or experimental stage — starts when both the ruling elites and the opposition, as well as the mass public, begin to question their non-democratic belief systems and to recognise the glaring inconsistency in advocating democracy and yet clinging to undemocratic behaviour and belief systems. In this phase of democratisation, virtually everyone advocates democracy. Both the government in power and the opposition, including the extreme left and the extreme right, clamour for democratisation, although each uses the term 'democracy' to mean quite different things. More often than not, both the extreme leftists and rightists are self-contradictory in their advocacy and action. While demanding democracy, the radical left often resorts to physical violence and/or subversive tactics. Contrarily, the radical right frequently displays intolerance under the pretext of defending democracy.

Specifically, from 1988, the Roh Tae-woo government set the process of democratisation in motion. Even before he assumed the presidency, Roh unleashed the so-called eight-point declaration of 29 June 1987, as a response to a massive anti-government popular upsurge. These points were:

1 assuring the peaceful transfer of power and allowing a direct popular election through the constitutional revision;
2 revising the presidential election laws and guaranteeing fair election management;
3 releasing and pardoning of political prisoners and restoring of their civil rights;
4 upholding human dignity and guaranteeing the people's basic civil rights;
5 guaranteeing the freedom of the press;
6 guaranteeing self-government and autonomy in all aspects of social life;
7 promoting sound political activities on the part of political parties and cultivating the political practice of dialogue and compromise; and
8 eradicating those criminals who are threatening the safety and security of citizens and correcting instances of chronic social corruption and irregularity.[1]

After Roh assumed the presidency, he tried, by and large, to fulfil these pledges, notwithstanding occasional setbacks and retractions. The government and the opposition had been at loggerheads only over their differences regarding the speed, scope and method of democratisation. But issues on the political agenda no longer centred on the non-recognition of the opposition or the demand for democratisation *per se*. The controversy between the ruling Democratic Liberal Party (DLP) and the opposition parties surrounding the implementation of mayoral and provincial gubernatorial elections, as required by law, was a prime example. President Roh's surprise announcement in October 1992 that he was quitting his ruling DLP membership and forming a 'neutral cabinet' for the presidential election in December, not to mention his undertaking to terminate domestic political surveillance activities (including the so-called 'strategy meeting of relevant public offices' by the Agency for National Security and Planning) were the cases in point.[2]

The final stage of democratisation, or South Korea's attainment of full-fledged democracy, will be realised only when democratic advocacy and action, and democratic belief systems, become the prevailing political norms and behaviour of the politicians and the people. But a full-fledged democracy is, as Arend Lijphart correctly pointed out, 'a rare and recent phenomenon'.[3] Higley and Burton, too, arrived at a similar finding: 'despite dramatic changes in mass conditions and orientations during the modern historical period, the modal pattern of Western politics was one of persistent elite disunity and resulting regime instability'.[4] Lijphart noted that not a single democratic government existed until the first decade of the twentieth century when two countries, Australia and New Zealand, established fully democratic regimes with governmental institutions and universal suffrage fully under popular control. According to Lijphart, only 22 countries have been continuously democratic since about World War II, and among them only Japan is non-Western.[5]

Meanwhile, Field, Higley and Burton contend that a key feature of stable democracies is substantial consensus and accommodation among elites on rules of the political game and the worth of political institutions. They identify three historical routes to elites' consensual unity: special colonial legacies where consensus is achieved prior to national independence; elite settlements, where elites negotiate a deliberate compromise; and two-step elite transformations, where first a consensually oriented bloc gains stable majority electoral support, and at a later stage a radical minority abandons its distinctive ideological position, adhering to the consensus achieved by its adversaries.[6]

Interestingly enough, Higley, Burton and Field notice, though cursorily, that 'South Korean elites are apparently moving at present' in that direction.[7] They call this process 'elite convergence', in which some of the powerful but previously warring factions in a disunited elite form a winning electoral coalition and, through repeated electoral victories, eventually leave dissident elites no alternative but to compete for government executive power under the same rules of the game and other tacit understanding as the winning coalition. In his recent study, James Cotton, too, is 'hopeful', albeit uncertain, about South Korea's liberalisation and democratisation: '. . . the opening of the political system to pressures from interests formerly marginalised is a hopeful development for the course of Korean democracy, but is not to be regarded as sufficient to guarantee a comprehensive and irreversible liberalisation'.[8]

In the final analysis, only the passage of time will indicate whether or not South Korea is presently undergoing some kind of elite settlement or elite convergence. The December 1992 presidential election was the second major test to have proven the viability and resilience of South Korea's democratisation efforts.

In this chapter, the current state of democratisation in South Korea will be examined from two different perspectives. First, it will attempt to explain the persisting incongruity between democratic intent and undemocratic 'habits of the heart', between democratic advocacy and authoritarian behaviour and between democratic form and undemocratic process. Second, it will probe the current state of South Korea's democratisation on the basis of available quantifiable indices.

Persisting undemocratic values and behaviours

South Korea has been one of the fastest growing economies in the world. Whether the nation is called 'the miracle of the Han River' or one of the four dragons or tigers, South Korean economic development has been phenomenal, at least since the mid-1960s. Higher living standards, improved housing, roads, transportation and communication networks and other life amenities are some visible signs. In 1949, for example, South Korea's per capita national income was $35, in 1962 it was $110, but in 1990 it was $5569. As of 1990, South Korea was 77.8 per cent urban; 72.1 per cent of its housing demand was met; 71.5 per cent of its roads were paved; 79 per cent of its pipe water demand was supplied; and 31 per cent of its sewerage system was in operation. By the year 2001, when the current third development plan (1992–2001) is due to be completed, the government is projecting that South Korea will be 86.2 per cent urban; and its housing supply and paved roads will reach 92.8 per cent and 100 per cent respectively. By then, the pipe water supply rate and the sewerage system will increase to 90 per cent and 70 per cent respectively.[9]

Few nations can, in fact, match South Korea's rapid economic growth during the same period. Before 1948, Korea was a typical agrarian society. Now it is regarded as one of the fastest growing newly industrialising countries (NICs). The *World Development Report 1991* places South Korea in an 'upper-middle-income' nation category.[10] The agricultural sector's contribution to South Korea's gross domestic product (GDP) declined from 38 per cent in 1965 to 10 per cent in 1989, while industrial, manufacturing and service sectors all increased during the same period from 25 per cent to 44 per cent, 18 to 26 per cent, and 37 to 46 per cent respectively.[11]

During this rapid economic structural metamorphosis, South Korea has also become, outwardly at least, an urban society. In 1965, South Korea's urban population constituted 32 per cent of its total population, but in 1989 it jumped to 71 per cent. In 1960, only three cities in South Korea had a population over 500 000, but in 1990, six cities had a population over 1 million. Again in 1990, the population of the capital city area and its environs was 18 million, which represented 42.7 per cent of the entire South Korean population.[12]

Negatively, however, South Korea's fast economic transformation and urbanisation have also created a series of concomitant problems, such as urban overcrowding and squalor, traffic congestion, air, water and soil pollution, crimes, labour–management disputes, regional and sectoral disparities, generational conflicts and student radicalism.

The rapidly transforming socio-economic and demographic landscapes of South Korea notwithstanding, the people's traditional mores — what Tocqueville called 'habits of the heart' — persist. By 'habits of the heart', Tocqueville meant notions, opinions and ideas that 'shape mental habits' and 'the sum of moral and intellectual dispositions of men in society'.[13] As Bellah and his associates aptly pointed out, the habits of the heart are closer to the concept of mores, which involve not only ideas and opinions but habitual practices with respect to such things as religion, political participation and economic life.[14]

A reciprocal giving and receiving common in a traditional setting, for example, may lose its original virtue and become the root cause of corrupt practices in urban and industrial life. Corruption, which permeates contemporary Korean society, may also have originated from some transplantation of rural and traditional values and behaviours to urban and industrial living. Like cancer, it has now spread through the entire community — schools and academe, business, commercial and labour establishments, civil services, mass media and political parties. Few individuals or organisations are, in fact, free of, or immune from, such a nexus of corruption and bribery. Two scandals of the Roh administration, the

Suso real estate development project irregularities and the Ministry of Defense land scam, which led to the imprisonment of several National Assemblymen, real estate developers and high government officials, are only conspicuous symptoms of a much deeper socio-political disease rooted in agrarian belief systems and traditional behaviour transplanted into a rapidly urbanising milieu. South Korea's newly achieved urban life and industrial economy demand commensurate urban behaviour and non-traditional codes of conduct, but traditional and rural folkways are deeply rooted.

The more industrialised and urbanised South Korea becomes, the more glaring and outmoded its traditional and rural modes of behaviour and transaction appear. Attitudinal and behavioural impediments to South Korean democratisation are political corruption and ritualism, unpredictability and political parochialism, deficient representation, party bossism and ultimate power cultism (*daekwon*).

Before these anti- or undemocratic belief systems and behaviours are probed in some detail, five caveats are spelled out. First, these behavioral and belief systems are by no means uniquely and peculiarly Korean. Rather they are — by and large, if not universally — common among people leading agrarian and rural lifestyles.

Second, these behaviours and beliefs, with their rural roots, are on the decline. The public outrage at the Suso scandal and the Defense Ministry land scam dramatically illustrates the public's intolerance for political corruption. The practice of political corruption, long believed to be the political norm, is now perceived increasingly by the mass public as a political aberration, if not an outright illegality. To put it another way, this shift seems to pinpoint the development of legal norms in South Korea. Figuratively speaking, a new seed for the rule of law is being planted in a crack of the deep-seated tradition of 'the rule of man'.

Maine explains that the rise of contract has contributed to the declining role of kinship as the exclusive basis of social organisation; Durkheim saw restitutive sanctions replacing repressive ones as a result of the growth of the division of labour and the corresponding shift from mechanical to organic solidarity; Dicey observed the growth of statutory lawmaking from the increased articulateness and power of public opinion; and, most notably, Weber viewed the development of formal legal rationality as an expression of, and precondition for, the growth of modern capitalism.[15]

To use Weber's typology, South Korea may be in the process of moving from traditional to charismatic and thence to rational–legal authority.[16] Korea is, however, still far from becoming the society of rational–legal authority. Examining the number of lawyers in Korea may illuminate this point. According to the Korean Lawyers Association, out of 43 million people, 2754 were lawyers as of February 1991, and of that number, 2009 were practising law while 745 remained professionally inactive. By contrast, according to *The United States Statistical Almanac* (1990), out of 239 million people, 655 191 were lawyers in the United States in 1985. This translates into one lawyer per 21 403 people in South Korea and one lawyer per 360 people in the United States. To put it another way, South Korea has a long way to go in becoming a rational–legal society, even if the United States has perhaps become *too* legalistic.

Korea's non-legal and authoritarian traditions have had much deeper roots. The law was not developed to protect either the individual's political rights or economic positions. Rather, as Hahm pointed out, it was perceived as an 'instrument of chastising the vicious and the depraved' in the Korean political tradition. The law always signified 'a norm with physical force as a sanction behind it. It was therefore synonymous with punishment, no more no less.'[17] From this standpoint, the current rational–legal orientation of the South Korean political scene is certainly laudable, but it also signifies a long and arduous journey ahead.

Third, as stated at the outset, democratic *format* is easy to establish, but democratic *performance* is more difficult to realise, for the latter requires the interaction of attitude, advocacy and action.

Fourth, what is rational and ideal in one context may be irrational and undesirable in another. For example, *mip'ung yangsok* (venerable behavior and cherished mores), based on Korea's rural and agricultural life, may easily become burdensome and outmoded in the contemporary urban and industrial environments.

Finally, in a broader context, the debate on whether cultural factors such as Confucianism or Confucian ethics have a causal relationship with economic development can be extended to political development or democracy as well. In postulating a causal relationship between cultural values and economic development, Confucian-derived cultural values such as the work ethic, habits of thrift and diligence, respect for educational achievement, avoidance of overt conflict in social relations, loyalty to hierarchy and authority, and emphasis on order and harmony are often identified. A broad consensus exists in fact that Confucianism has been a factor, if not the dominant variable, in explaining the economic dynamics of Japan and the so-called Asian NICs.[18] However, the same case cannot be made for the postulation of a positive connection between Confucianism and political democracy. On the contrary, Confucianism and/or other traditional value systems, such as Buddhism and Shamanism, have been more of an impediment than a contributing factor to democratisation in Korea. Confucianism (and also Buddhism and Shamanism, for that matter) was associated with the millennia-old Korean autocratic and authoritarian monarchical system. Even for the positive causal relationship between Confucianism and economic development, the following questions must be answered satisfactorily before the debate can be settled.

1 As Max Weber identified the spirit of capitalism with the Protestant ethic, not Christianity *in toto*, what branch of the Confucian ethic has been conducive to economic development of Japan and of the Asian NICs? Confucian values contain elements both facilitative and detrimental to economic growth. The rigid social hierarchy and lack of social mobility, the low status of the merchant and commercial classes, wasteful ceremonial and ritual functions such as wedding, funeral and burial rites and ancestor worship are cases in point. What is more, Confucianism has been changing over the years and its practices vary considerably among the Asian nations.

2 Similarities exist between aspects of the Protestant ethic, such as the Calvinistic notion of 'calling', and the emphasis upon diligence, thrift, sobriety and prudence[19] and the aforesaid Confucian ethic. Does this mean, then, that the scholars have been merely searching retrospectively for the cultural values which are conducive to economic growth *after* a country has developed? If a phenomenon can be explained through an *ex post facto* analysis, then an Islamic ethic may be used to explain the fast economic growth of the Arab nations in the future, should they develop rapidly. Weber contends that capitalism is 'at least a rational tempering of the irrational impulse — the impulse to acquisition, pursuit of gain, of money, of the greatest possible amount of money'. Further, he argues that the 'state itself, in the sense of a political association with a rational, written constitution, rationally ordained law, and an administration bound to rational rules or laws, administered by trained officials, is known, in this combination of characteristics, only in the Occident, despite all other approaches to it'. [20] In this connection, it is interesting to note that Kim Kyong-dong, for one, attributes Korea's rapid economic growth to what he called 'adaptability', combined with a motivational force called *han* — a mixture of feelings and emotional states, including a sense of rancour, regret, grief, remorse, revenge or grievance. These feelings have to do with an accumulated sense of frustration, repeated deprivation of need gratification, or constant suppression of one's own desires. He argues further that if rationality is a requisite for capitalist development, the future of South Korea's capitalist development will largely depend on how successfully Korean people can utilise their capacity to acquire such rationality.[21]

Setting Weber's rationality argument aside for the moment, if the Protestant ethic and the Confucian ethic (or the Islamic ethic, for that matter) are merely *ex post facto* explanatory variables, the postulation of a causal relation between religious ethic and economic development seems untenable.

Bearing the abovementioned caveats and limitations in mind, a few key features of political underdevelopment in South Korean politics and the political process will be examined in some detail in the following section.

Political corruption and ritualism

It is posited here that incidences of political corruption such as the Suso scandal and the Defense Ministry land scam which so outraged the public originated from deep-seated traditional and rural practices of *reciprocity*, or the trading of favours or services. It is further assumed that reciprocity in a rural and agricultural community represents a typical *mip'ung yangsok*, which is common in any rural or farming community.

In Korea today, such practices of reciprocity and mutual help are not uncommon in the rural areas. Seeding, planting and harvesting of rice as well as other crops are labour-intensive tasks. Hence, everyone works together until the tasks of the entire farming village are completed. All the food, drinks and snacks are provided by the family whose farm is being ploughed on a given day. Rapid urbanisation and shrinking farming population, the introduction of mechanisation in farming and of cash payments in farm work have considerably dampened the deep-rooted non-cash reciprocity of mutual assistance. Under accelerated urbanisation and industrialisation, one can now seldom see typical traditional and rural lifestyles or, for that matter, the prototype of an urban and civic culture. In Moore's phraseology, the Koreans are now witnessing 'departures from traditional norms and canons of behavior and the process whereby adults . . . become involved in and perhaps emotionally committed to novel social situations'. He is also correct to stress that pre-industrial structural and cultural differences may persist because the economic system does not wholly determine other components of the social system.[22] As Halpern pointed out, we can no longer speak of a rural-to-urban transition or a rural–urban continuum, but can talk only in terms of changing rural and urban contexts. He further writes:

The dynamics of the situation . . . are not simply the extension of urban influences into the countryside but the impact of rural migrants and their values upon the city — the peasantisation of the town — and the simultaneous evolution of both types of communities within the larger society.[23]

Three conspicuous examples of what Halpern called 'the peasantisation of the town' in contemporary urban Korean life may be the practices of one person paying the bill for the group, extravagant wedding ceremonies, prohibitively expensive funeral services and other celebrations such as the 60th birthday, retirement and graduation parties. Non-contractual and unwritten reciprocity (*p'umasi*), which works in a farming village, cannot work in an urban setting. Worse still, unlike the farmers, the urbanites' wages and salaries are fixed while their nightly drinking, eating and other entertainment costs are largely unpredictable. Yet the practice of one person paying for the group continues. This is the urbanite's dilemma of adhering to rural habits. It epitomises a behavioural theorem — what is rational and desirable in one spatial and temporal setting may be irrational and undesirable in another context.

The city-dwellers in Seoul or any other city in Korea today have few options available to overcome or escape this dilemma. One way is simply to stop this practice at the cost of becoming a loner and suffering ostracism from fellow workers or other acquaintances as being unsociable, selfish or *yamch'ae* (a cad, or an egomaniac). The next option is to avoid such social ostracism by throwing lavish drinking and entertainment parties for friends and business associates, thereby incurring a huge debt. A Korean name for such a person is *bong* (a wastrel).

Despite the incongruence of peasant behaviour in an urban setting, one who indulges in lavish drinking and entertainment parties is still admired for being a *sanae daechangbu* (a big man, or a macho man). Also, typical Seoulites are stereotyped as being *yaksakpparuda* (shrewd, or tactful), and the new arrivals from the countryside as being *huhada* (generous, or unselfish). It should be kept in mind that real Seoulites, often pejoratively called *kkakjangi* (a shrewd, stingy person) — by which is meant two generations of people: parents and their children, who were born and raised in Seoul — only constitute a minority of today's Seoul population. The majority of residents in Seoul today came from the countryside. Thus peasant behaviour still prevails in Seoul. The fact that, during holidays such as *Ch'usok* (Autumn Harvest Moon Festival) or *Sol* (Lunar New Year), nearly half of the residents of Seoul visit their hometown to meet family members and relatives illustrates this point. Generally speaking, people over 40 still prefer, on the whole, the practice of one person paying for the group. Interestingly enough, however, a majority of the younger generation today shares expenses for a group party or recreation. A Dutch treat is becoming the social norm of group behaviour among the youngsters. From this standpoint, traditional behaviour is vanishing from Korean urban life, and will soon be replaced by more sensible behaviour in tune with an urban lifestyle.

Other ramifications of traditional or peasant ritualism in urban life today are found at the scenes of wedding ceremonies, funeral services and other functions. Traditional wedding rituals are now seldom performed either in the city or in the countryside. Two kinds of wedding scenes are typical today. If the bride or the groom hails from a rich and/or powerful family, the lavishness of the wedding ceremony is beyond description. Row after row of expensive floral wreaths and a long line of people delivering envelopes containing money as their wedding present are the usual scenes. The parking lots are full of cars of the guests who came to pay tribute. Similar scenes are repeated at the funeral services of rich or powerful family members. The wedding of a member of a poor family contrasts dramatically: instead of lavishness, there is an almost market-like atmosphere; the ceremony is run like a factory shift; and the ceremony must be completed within half an hour since several sets of bridal parties are waiting in line to go through the same ritual in the same room within the given time limit. The wedding hall, usually a four- or five-storey building, has two dozen rooms which are run along commercial lines. Only a few weddings are performed in the churches and temples by the clergy. Most wedding ceremonies are conducted by a celebrity at the commercial wedding halls. Unlike the hustle and bustle of the guests at the funeral services of the rich and powerful, stillness reigns at the poor man's funeral service, where only the closest family members and relatives sit and mourn for the dead. Today the wedding and funeral services of the rich or the poor have virtually lost their solemness and sacredness. In fact, it is not infrequent for a rich or powerful family to receive a large sum of money from the guests at such a funeral, wedding or other ceremonial occasion. These scenes represent behaviour which is a socially dysfunctional adaptation of the traditional wedding, funeral and other rituals. When *p'umasi* was transplanted from rural to urban life, it became wasteful and excessive, and above all, it has contributed to widespread corruption in virtually every aspect of the society.

The National Assemblyman's routine activities serve to strengthen this argument. As Table 2.1 illustrates, the Assemblyman attends far less National Assembly (NA) sessions than those required by the law. Except for the 1st National Assembly session, all the rest usually occupy less than half of the required session days. When the NA is not in session, the Assemblyman's day usually begins with a breakfast meeting at a hotel or at a restaurant with his business or political friends. Then, between lunch and dinner, he may have to attend a wedding or two on top of visiting one or more funeral services. After dinner or an evening reception, he usually goes to a drinking party with political or business associates at one to three bars. Hence, by the time he returns home, it is well past midnight, and this hectic and unproductive pace

Table 2.1 *The regular sessions of the ROK's National Assembly*

Assembly	Term	Session days	Session days held (%)
1st	2 yrs	640	399 (62.3)
2nd	4 yrs	1307	631 (48.3)
3rd	4 yrs	1270	609 (48.0)
4th	2 yrs 2 mnths	686	212 (30.9)
5th	10 mnths	25	142 (55.0)
6th	3 yrs 6 mnths	798	345 (43.2)
7th	4 yrs	806	261 (32.4)
8th	1 yr 4 mnths	402	81 (20.1)
9th	6 mnths	615	167 (27.2)
10th	1 yr 7 mnths	118	28 (23.7)
11th	4 yrs	482	144 (29.9)
12th	3 yrs 1 mnth	414	120 (28.9)
13th	4 yrs		
14th	4 yrs		

Source: Kukjong Shinmun (Government News), 12 March 1992. Also, Lee Soo-hoon, Hankuk kwa Chesamsaekye ui Minju Byonhyok (Democratic Reforms in Korea and the Third World), Seoul: Kyungnam University Press, 1989, p. 134, quoted in Ro Sang-hyun, A Comparative Analysis of South Korea's National Assembly and North Korea's Supreme People's Assembly: Structure, Functions, and Process (Master's thesis, the Graduate Institute of Peace Studies, Kyunghee University, Seoul, Korea, 1990, p. 63.)

of life is repeated the next day. During the weekends, he is often requested by a constituent to preside at a wedding ceremony. During the wedding season, an Assemblyman receives a handful of wedding invitation notices from his constituents in a day. These invitations are like a debt which has to be repaid, as are the funeral notices. The Assemblyman needs up to ten times his regular salary to meet such expenses alone. How and from where can he obtain the extra money or funds for such expenses? Most of all, when and how can he function as a legislator when he has to act like a political clown at these wasteful and unwholesome traditional rituals?

Unpredictability and political parochialism

Destruction of proper authority in social and political life is a significant feature of authoritarianism. Conversely, therefore, restoration of proper authority to all aspects of social and political life marks the termination of authoritarian politics. An authoritarian regime ignores, undermines and even destroys proper authority at home, at school, in business and in other social and political organisations. Only the authoritarian leader matters, and all the other leaders or authorities are subjected to the former. Under such circumstances, multiple authorities of complex social and political organisations are quickly replaced by the ultimate authority of a dictator. In the process, predictability is sacrificed to the ultimate authority's personal whims.

Political unpredictability is most evident in recruitment and promotion practices. If predictability prevails in a democratic polity, unpredictability — especially in elite recruitment — dominates in an authoritarian polity. For example, if a headmaster's job becomes vacant, one should be able to predict with a reasonable amount of certainty who would be next in line to assume the post by taking into account seniority and other necessary qualifications. If an expected person is not appointed or promoted, and a totally unexpected person fills the position, the rules of the game are no longer valid. The mark of political development, then, is to minimise such unexpectedness and maximise rationality. Unpredictability in political recruitment is closely related to nepotistic and other traditional practices. It may be true that what is being regarded as a surprise or an unpredictability from a legal–rational point of view may not be necessarily so from a traditional perspective. For example, a man with a traditional turn of mind may not be surprised at seeing someone catapulted to a high position overnight because he and the man in power are connected to each other through the same region (*chiyon*), the same school (*hakyon*) or the same family (*hyolyon*). But to a man with a rational–legal turn of mind, the same incident may be perceived as being not only unexpected but even improper, if not illegal.

Without going too much into detail, it is posited here that South Korean politics are still plagued by surprises, unpredictability and nepotistic practices. As an example of the practice of recruiting top political elites and establishing a political–business–military elite nexus from a particular region or a school, the TK division (Taegu-Kyongbuk High School graduates) of the Chun and Roh periods comes to mind. The persistence of the TK division reveals not only undemocratic behaviour patterns in the present South Korean political arena, but is also the representative example par excellence of Korean regional parochialism and ascriptive elite recruitment practices.[24]

Deficient representation and party bossism

The third feature of political underdevelopment or unrepresentativeness is party bossism. Party bossism is characterised by at least two undemocratic political practices. One of the central characteristics of party bossism is manifested in what is called the 'politics of reverse order', in contrast to the 'politics of democratic order'. The logic for the politics of democratic order runs as follows: contemporary democracy necessitates a representative procedure in which a legislature plays the key role; an election is necessary to create such a legislative body; and hence political parties are organised to find the candidates to run for legislative office. Differently put, today's democracy is representational, requiring a legislative body which, in turn, necessitates periodic elections through open competition among political parties.

By contrast, the logic for the politics of reverse order operates in the opposite direction: the party boss almost single-handedly creates (or dissolves) a political party at will, which in turn manages the election by controlling almost exclusively the power of nominating the party candidates of each and every electoral district, and the successfully elected representatives arrive at the National Assembly (NA) and function like robots under the strict guidance and leadership of the party boss.[25] The practices of voting strictly according to the party line, and of censuring or 'disciplining' members who defy party voting at the NA, are major manifestations of this situation. Hence, unlike the legislature in a working democracy, where a party's electoral function virtually ceases after the election, and the legislature, be it the United States Congress or the British Parliament, becomes the centre of the political and policy process, in South Korean politics today, not only is the NA not in session most of the time, but even when it is in session, control by the party boss of his representatives in the NA continues unabated.

If the politics of democratic order are that of a bottom-up organisational and operational structure based firmly on the politics of the grassroots, the politics of reverse order are that of a top-down command and control hierarchy guided often single-handedly by the party boss. Hence cronyism thrives in the political arena.

From a citizen's point of view, the true meaning of representation is undermined by the politics of reverse order and party bossism. It may be much more accurate or realistic to say that the general public's lack of a clear understanding of the concept of representation and of representative democracy has given rise to such undemocratic practices as the politics of reverse order and party bossism. Both the citizens and the politicians are at fault in misunderstanding and even abusing political representation. Still, a large number of people believe that the political candidates, if elected, will amass a large sum of money. Hence these voters think that they, too, should have a share of their representatives' amassed wealth, real or imagined. Consequently, they often demand money or other support from their representatives for their private entertainment expenses. (One of my politician friends informed me that some voters had the nerve to ask for a round-trip airplane ticket to Cheju Island for their son's and daughter's honeymoon, not to mention their constant requests for floral wreaths and contributions to wedding ceremonies and funeral services.)

The politicians, on the other hand, willingly or unwillingly, respond to the absurd demands of their constituents in the hope of winning their support for the next election. So the vicious circle created by the politicians responding to the voters' demands continues, as do corruption and bribery of all sorts. Under such political circumstances, little or no room exists for either the proper meaning of representation or of the legitimate roles of representatives to survive. To repeat, this vicious circle will not end in Korea until and unless the general public and the voters realise that they are electing their representatives to protect and promote their interests and the welfare of their district and the nation. Thus they must stop portraying their representatives as extortioners or embezzlers of public money or funds.

In addition, the party boss acts like a father, who provides security and sustenance to the family members. When the father is gone, the family experiences hardship. Likewise, when the party boss is gone, or is out of power, the party too will go out of existence. If the South Korean party is likened to a house on the sand, the party members are the sand and its boss the house. When President Syngman Rhee, head of the Liberal Party, was removed from power in April 1960, the Liberal Party collapsed; when Prime Minister Chang Myon was ousted by the military coup leaders in May 1961, his Democratic Party quickly became defunct; when President Park Chung-hee was assassinated in October 1979 by Kim Chae-kyu, then the Korean CIA Director, his ruling party, the Democratic Republican Party, was dissolved too. When President Chun Doo-hwan gave up his power to President Roh Tae-woo, his erstwhile ruling party, the Democratic Justice Party, disappeared. Roh even abandoned his ruling party membership before his departure from the presidency, which is unprecedented in Korea or elsewhere. Unlike the fate of previous ruling parties, however, the present Democratic Liberal Party may survive, given that its presidential candidate Kim Young-sam won the 1992 presidential elections.

Politics dominated by the party boss has a number of salient characteristics. First, as noted above, South Korean party politics has yet to set the precedent of separating the death or exit of the ruling party leader from the dissolution of the party. The political tradition of the ruling party's survival, irrespective of the exit or demise of its party head, is still absent in South Korean party politics. The ruling DLP may yet be the first uncertain exception to this rule.

Second, the dissolution of the ruling party often means not its permanent extinction, but its re-emergence under a new name with the old members.

Only the party *name* disappears, while its members continue to survive politically under different party labels.

Third, the opposition party members frequently resort to organisational shuffling and reshuffling among themselves, usually just before or immediately after the election. This behaviour demonstrates that the party members are more interested in receiving the party nomination and being a successful candidate than in upholding the ideological tenets and political banners of their party.[26]

Fourth, the South Korean political party system cannot be characterised as a two-party system, a multi-party system, or a dominant party system. There has always been a dominant ruling party and a handful of weak and fragmented but vociferous opposition parties. But, unlike Japan's ruling Liberal Party, South Korea's ruling parties — be they Rhee's Liberal Party, Park's Democratic Republican Party, Chun's Democratic Justice Party or Roh's and now Kim's Democratic Liberal Party — have not formally and officially permitted intra-party political competition. To repeat, if Japan's Liberal Democratic Party (LDP) could be seen, before the realignment of 1994, as a typical dominant party under a parliamentary system which allowed intra-party competition in the absence of a serious inter-party competition, South Korea's ruling parties have been part of a dominant party arrangement under a presidential system run virtually single-handedly by the incumbent president in the absence of intra-party competition. If Japan's LDP was a multi-headed dominant party, South Korea's ruling parties have been single-headed dominant parties. Noteworthy is the fact that the current ruling party, the DLP, which was created by the merger of three parties (the Democratic Justice Party, the Reunification Democratic Party and the New Democratic Republican Party), has shown incipient signs of intra-party rivalry, especially in President Kim's purge in 1993 of parliamentarians associated with the Chun era.

Several corollaries of such party politics come to mind. The first is the blurring of ideological distinctiveness. That is, party members in power and in opposition are conservative or anti-communist. As long as the party members profess anti-communism, no other ideological, political or policy differences really matter. What is more, due to the existence of two regimes in the Korean Peninsula, leftist or strong reformist party organisations and activities in the political arena are restricted or prohibited by legal or institutional sanctions such as the National Security Law, and they are under the close scrutiny and surveillance of the intelligence apparatus like the Agency for National Security and Planning.[27]

For example, in the Fourteenth National Assembly election held on 24 March 1992, no candidate from the socialist or the so-called *minmin wun* (national-democracy movement) won a seat, and the two groups barely generated 2.13 per cent of the total national vote. From this standpoint, legal and institutional restrictions and prohibitions also undermine the proper meaning of representation and representative democracy.

The ephemeral nature of the party life is another political corollary. Few parties — or, more accurately, few party *names* — have in fact survived beyond one republic; no party or party *names* have lasted more than two Korean republics thus far.

The third corollary is that a loyalty to, and an identification with, a specific party, its label or organisation are absent. Members cannot be loyal to the party because the party names change frequently and also because party organisation consists usually of a group of key politicians at the central and national level and virtually none at the local or the grassroots level. Hence, unlike in the democratic countries in the West and Japan, where the party *names* have survived for decades and even centuries, in understanding South Korean politics another distinction is shown in the nature of the citizen's so-called party identification and party support. Namely, because of the frequent changes in party *name*, people have no sense of attachment to and identification with the name of any party. Regardless of the party *name*, they are, thus, prone to identify either with the ruling party of the moment or with the opposition party (or parties) when they vote at an election. Although party *names* change frequently, at any given moment there are always the governing party and the opposition party. Besides, the old ruling party politicians are usually co-opted into the new ruling party. Similarly, the opposition politicians remain in opposition even after the old opposition party is reshuffled and renamed.

A study on the March 1992 National Assembly election by Park Chan-wook and Cho Jung-bin examined the South Korean voters' identification with the ruling party and the opposition parties, without weighing the political significance of the party's name or label itself. Park seemed to dismiss the importance of the party *name* by calling the Democratic Party *chont'ong yadang* (the long-standing opposition party).[28]

Cho discovered that, among the opposition-leaning voters who decided on a candidate two weeks before the actual election, the majority tended to support the major opposition party, the Democratic Party (DP) (77 per cent), while for those who decided to vote for a candidate on the day of the election, only 47.5 per cent voted for the DP and the rest voted for the newly created Unification National Party (15.9 per cent) and for the independents (27.3 per cent).[29] This indicates that, unlike, for example, in the United States, where party *labels* such as the Democratic Party or the Republican Party have a significant bearing on the voters' party identification, the South Korean voters are primarily divided into the pro-government or the pro-opposition groups, regardless of the party names or labels. Cho Ki-sook confirmed this point rather persuasively. Her research found that the higher rate of Koreans voting for a party rather than for the candidate stemmed from their categorical perceptual bifurcation of the parties — the democratic party versus the anti-democratic party or the anti-dictatorship party versus the dictatorial party.[30]

From a somewhat different perspective, Lee Nam-young discovered in an analysis conducted in 1992 that 28.9 per cent of the voters would vote for a candidate based on party affiliation. Still, he did not clearly differentiate the party *name* and its political status (i.e. the ruling party or the opposition). In any case, he learned that the majority of the non-voters are pro-opposition party rather than pro-ruling party. Specifically, among the non-voters, 36 per cent leant towards the Democratic Party, 19.5 per cent to the Unification National Party, 8.5 per cent to the New Political Party and 4.3 per cent to the People's Party (*Minjung-tang*), while those favouring the ruling party accounted for 31.7 per cent. Hence, the lower the level of voter turnout, the more advantageous it is for the ruling party.[31]

In brief, the various immature aspects of the Korean party system and its activities graphically testify to the extent of South Korean political underdevelopment. The vanishing of party bossism and the emergence of a viable and enduring party system may not occur overnight. Until this happens, South Korea's representative democracy will continue to be in an embryonic stage.

Ultimate power (*daekwon*) cultism

The concept of the ultimate power (*daekwon*) denotes the power of the highest office in the South Korean political system: the presidential power or the presidency. This concept, implicitly or explicitly, assumes that political power is ultimately concentrated in one person: the president; hence little or no room exists for the concept of power diffusion or power sharing. It is a concept which is used frequently in public by the South Korean mass media and by politicians and citizens to refer to the presidential power. Perhaps the prolonged authoritarian politics of the past are responsible for the popular notion that the president *can* do or be anything. This view may be unreal or even exaggerated, but nevertheless, it is not utterly groundless or false. There is no question that the presidential powers are truly extraordinary (the presidential powers are specified in the 1987 Constitution, especially in articles 66 to 100). The general public and the politicians, however, tend to perceive presidential powers and authority as unlimited and unrestricted. In so doing, they tend to overlook the enormous responsibilities and obligations underlying such power. For example, the expressions *daetongryong*, an official Korean term for the highest political office and *daekwon*, an unofficial term for the office, dramatise this one-sided portrayal of the presidency with its uniqueness and concentration of power and authority. *Daetongryong* refers exclusively to the office-holder of the South Korean presidency. This term can only be applied to the incumbent president. But the term 'president' in the United States may signify many different persons and positions, ranging from the head of an elementary school student body to corporate officers and to the highest political office, the American presidency. The word *daetongryong* generates special awe in Korean people, unlike the terms 'president' or 'prime minister'. Additional images, meanings and dimensions accompany the term *daekwon*, which literally means a 'great power'. In other countries, the term 'great power' is rarely used by the public, the press or politicians to depict the power of the highest political office, president or prime minister. Only in international politics are the terms 'great powers' or 'superpowers', used to describe economically and/or militarily powerful nations such as the United States and the former Soviet Union. Unlike in the internal politics of a nation, the international political arena is often characterised as being in a state of near-anarchy or having a very high degree of lawlessness, and thus there is room for the role of the so-called superpowers. The question, then, is why and how did the term *daekwon* become a favorite topic of the South Korean mass media, the general public and the politicians? Does the usage of this word reflect a relatively high level of lawlessness and near anarchy in South Korean internal politics? One thing seems to be self-evident: the indiscriminate use of the term may stem from the habits of mind which developed in the prolonged period of authoritarian politics. From this standpoint, identifying the presidential power as a 'great power' without understanding its accompanying 'great responsibility' is not only a linguistic vestige of authoritarianism but another undemocratic habit of mind.

Some observable evidence of democratisation

The Social Science Research Center at Seoul National University conducted a political survey of 2007 people who were interviewed from 20 October to 2 November 1988. The survey revealed a number of interesting trends. As Table 2.2 indicates, 64.4 per cent and 27.5 per cent of the respondents said that the South Korean regime five years ago (in 1983 under President Chun Doo-hwan) was a dictatorship or a dictatorial authoritarianism respectively.

Table 2.2 South Korean regime types and regime changes

Regime type	Five years ago (%)	Now (1988) (%)	Five years later (%)
A. Non-democratic			
Dictatorial	64.4	17.4	3.3
Dictatorial-Authoritarian	27.5	36.9	11.6
B. Democratic			
Democratic-Authoritarian	6.6	34.9	32.0
Democratic	1.1	10.6	52.5

Source: Adapted from Shin Doh-chull et al., *Hankuk Minjujuiei Mirae* (The Future of Korean Democracy), Seoul: Seoul National University, 1990, p. 21.

That is, 91.9 per cent of the respondents believed that the regime five years ago was not democratic, while 17.4 per cent and 36.9 per cent of the same respondents revealed that the South Korean regime at the time of the survey was dictatorial or dictatorial–authoritarian, respectively. And only 14.9 per cent of the respondents predicted that the regime would still be undemocratic five years after the survey.[32]

On the nature of possible regime changes in five years, the respondents were also cautiously optimistic, and only a little more than a quarter of them (26.6 per cent) believed in a gradual democratic transformation (for details, see Table 2.3). Shin and his colleagues also found, in another study, that nearly one in three (31.7 per cent) respondents were shown to adhere to authoritarian values while only one in seven (13.7 per cent) respondents were oriented toward libertarian values.[33] Lee's earlier survey also revealed that Koreans who were consistent both in democratic attitudes and behaviour constituted less than 10 per cent of the survey respondents.[34] He noted elsewhere that less than one-half of the adult population exhibited some commitment to fundamental democratic values and beliefs — that is, attitudes toward competition, majority rule and minority rights and self-role perception (political efficacy), while a majority still remained predominantly under the old influence of authoritarian Confucian values.[35]

Meanwhile, Pae undertook a comparative analysis of democratisation among 129 countries in 1989 using a longitudinal, dynamic approach and presented a rather upbeat assessment of South Korea's democratisation. He stated that South Korea, though one of the latest starters in the process of democratisation, 'has been progressing most rapidly and dynamically'. Further, he pointed out that when Gastil's eleven political rights and fourteen

Table 2.3 The nature of the regime change in five year

Nature of regime change	Responses (%)
1 Will deteriorate further	(1.7)
2 Will be the same	(23.7)
a Will continue to be dictatorial	2.4
b Will continue to be dictatorial-authoritarian	3.8
c Will continue to be democratic-authoritarian	7.4
d Will continue to be democratic	10.1
3 Will change gradually	(53.0)
a from dictatorship to dictatorial-authoritarianism	7.2
b from dictatorial-authoritarianism to democratic-authoritarianism	19.2
c from democratic-authoritarianism to democracy	26.6
4 will change radically	(20.8)
a from dictatorship to democratic-authoritarianism	5.0
b from democratic-authoritarianism to democracy	13.2
c from dictatorship to democracy	2.6

Source: Adapted from Shin Doh-chull et al., *Hankuk Minjujuiei Mirae* (The Future of Korean Democracy), Seoul National University, Seoul, 1990, p. 28.

civil liberties variables were applied to South Korea for 1987 and 1988, there was no doubt that 'South Korea had entered [the] threshold of near-full and complete democracy'.[36]

On the basis of survey results which utilised a three-dimensional model of value conflict to estimate the breadth and magnitude of Left–Right conflicts among the South Korean people over political, economic and cultural values, Shin and his associates concluded somewhat cautiously that:

> . . . the people in Korea today are deeply divided over the basic values which they hold for themselves and their country. They are divided over 'bread and butter' and other economic issues of the Old Politics. They are even more divided over freedom and other non-economic issues of the New Politics. More so than over the issues of the Old and New Politics, Koreans are divided over the question of whether or not their indigenous cultures should be accommodated to those of foreign origin. Korea is no longer a country of homogeneous people; it is a country where a sizeable portion of the mass public is in intense conflict over one or more types of basic values . . . [and] over the proper roles to be played in the process of democratisation. While an

overwhelming majority feels that more democracy is needed for their country, only a small minority offers unqualified support for the democratic transformation of authoritarian rule. There is little doubt that the lack of full support among large segments of the mass public for the democratic transformation makes it difficult for Korea to become a state of full and stable democracy within a short span of time.[37]

As noted above, only 20.8 per cent responded in Shin's survey that future regime change would be radical while 1.7 per cent anticipated the regime's further deterioration five years later (Table 2.3). This survey also revealed that more people identified with the presidential system (55.5 per cent) than with a cabinet-responsible system (16.0 per cent). But more people preferred the cabinet-responsible system (34.8 per cent) to the presidential system (28.3 per cent).[38]

An interesting finding of this survey is that the people's support for any political party is extremely low. No party, whether it is in power or in opposition, received more than 22.5 per cent of support.[39] Another notable piece of data in this study concerns the tolerance level of people. For example, while people are very tolerant relating to issues concerning North Korea (88.6 per cent), sexual equality (86.4 per cent) and support for the labour union movement (85.3 per cent), they are extremely intolerant of issues dealing with the communist movement (92.2 per cent), the withdrawal of United States forces (68.4 per cent), the confiscation of private property (60.1 per cent) and demonstrations (52.7 per cent).[40]

Finally, a recent survey by the Seoul National University's Social Science Research Center presented some noteworthy results. Regarding South Korea's current state of democratisation, less than half of the participants (46.7 per cent) replied positively, while 37.2 per cent responded that little or no progress has been made in that direction and 16 per cent even indicated

Table 2.4   The degree of democratisation since the Sixth Republic

Responses	Per cent
Greatly democratised	5.0
Somewhat democratised	41.7
Little change	37.2
Further deteriorated	16.0
No answer	0.2
Total	100.0

Source: Seoul National University Social Science Research Center, *A Survey Report of the Korean People's Belief System in Reference to the Coming 21st Century,* Seoul National University Social Science Research Center, Seoul, 1990, p. 28.

deterioration in South Korea's democratisation efforts (see Table 2.4). The same survey cited corruption of politicians (40.7 per cent), the government's lack of will to democratise (29.4 per cent) and the radicalism of students and opposition groups (14.2 per cent) as the three major obstacles to democratisation (see Table 2.5). It also revealed that the politicians were the group considered to be most corrupt (70.1 per cent), businessmen were next (10.9 per cent), and government officials were rated third (9.3 per cent) (see Table 2.6). Despite the persistent corrupt practices and imperfect democratisation efforts in South Korea, one index in the survey showed a

Table 2.5 *Obstacles to democratisation*

Responses	Per cent
The government's insufficient will to democratise	29.4
Radicalism of students and some opposition forces	14.2
Excess demands of workers and farmers	7.1
Politicians' corruption	40.7
Military's political intervention	5.6
Others	2.0
Find no obstacles	0.3
No answer	0.7
Total	100.0

Source: Seoul National University Social Science Research Center, *A Survey Report of the Korean People's Belief System in Reference to the Coming 21st Century*, Seoul: Seoul National University Social Science Research Center, 1990, p. 30.

Table 2.6 *Corruption in South Korea by group or profession*

Responses	No. of responses	Percent
Politicians	1071	70.1
Businessmen	167	10.9
Government officials	141	9.3
Journalists	50	3.3
Military	38	2.5
Educators	31	2.1
Others	20	1.3
No answer	85	5.6
Total	1526	100.0

Source: Seoul National University Social Science Research Center, *A Survey Report of the Korean People's Belief System in Reference to the Coming 21st Century*, Seoul: Seoul National University Social Science Research Center, 1990, p. 73.

Table 2.7 Important factors for success ten years later

Factors	No. of responses	Per cent
Personal efforts and ability	1192	78.0
Education	204	13.4
Family and parents	86	5.7
Regional or local ties	2	2.1
Others	8	0.5
No answer	5	0.3
Total	1497	100.0

Source: Seoul National University Social Science Research Center, *A Survey Report of the Korean People's Belief System in Reference to the Coming 21st Century*, Seoul: Seoul National University Social Science Research Center, 1990, p. 76.

bright spot. On the question dealing with the factor most crucial to personal success and advancement ten years later, the overwhelming majority (78 per cent) cited individual effort and ability as the most important ingredient. The same respondents considered factors such as family background and ties, school connections and localism, which are still considered very crucial in personal career advancement and success, insignificant or nearly negligible in the future (Table 2.7).

To summarise, a broad consensus exists that democratisation in South Korea is on course, although opinions differ on its speed and the precise nature of the changes which are underway. Most importantly, the future prospect for the South Korean polity is by and large positive and optimistic. From this perspective, the present political situation, which appears transitional and even traumatic, is only a birth pang of a more democratic and more mature Korean polity.

Concluding remarks

It is evident from the above that South Korea is undergoing a rapid transformation resulting from accelerated urbanisation and industrialisation and from conscious efforts to democratise. Interfacing of the traditional and/ or agrarian values and belief systems amid a predominantly urban and industrial life setting, of the ascriptive elite recruitment practices in an increasingly meritorious society and of traditional and charismatic authority patterns in a newly emerging rational and legal system continues.

South Korea's current problem is not simply the by-product of a traditional society in transition. Nor is it merely the after-effects of an old tradition being rapidly replaced by new belief systems. Rather, it is the case of the old habits of the heart being misplaced, misconstrued and misapplied. Development towards a desirable polity does not necessarily entail a wholesale removal of the old political tradition. Rather, it will occur when the people, elites and the mass public reach a level of sophistication sufficient to distinguish what is or is not viable old tradition in a swiftly transforming urban industrial context. Ideally, a good polity requires the harmonious coexistence of both viable and vital political traditions and modernity. South Korea, a textbook case of a rapidly transforming society and polity of the old tradition and habit, is no exception in this regard.

Notes

1 The English translation is the present author's. Roh's eight-point proposal in Korean is found in *Chugan Kukjong News* [Weekly Government News], 29 June 1991.
2 *The Korea Times*, 26 September 1992.
3 Arend Lijphart, *Democracies: Patterns of Majoritarian and Consensus Government in Twenty-One Countries* , Yale University Press, New Haven, 1984), p. 37.
4 H. Higley and M.G. Burton, 'The Elite Variable in Democratic Transitions and Breakdowns', *American Sociological Review*, vol. 54, 1989, pp. 22, 25.
5 Lijphart, *Democracies*, pp. 37–38.
6 Higley and Burton, 'The Elite Variable'. Also, J. Higley, M.G. Burton and G.L. Field, 'In Defense of Elite Theory: A Reply to Cammack', *American Sociological Review*, vol. 55, 1990, pp. 421–26.
7 Higley and Burton, 'The Elite Variable' , p. 423.
8 For details, see James Cotton, 'Understanding the State in South Korea: Bureaucratic-Authoritarianism or State Autonomy Theory?', *Comparative Political Studies*, vol. 24, 1991–92, p. 529; and 'The Limits to Liberalization in Industrializing Asia: Three Views of the State', *Pacific Affairs*, vol. 64, 1991, pp. 311–27.
9 *World Development Report, 1991*, Oxford University Press, Oxford, 1991, p. 209. The 1949 and 1962 data are quoted in Karl Deutsch, *Nationalism and Social Communication,* MIT Press, Cambridge, 1966, appendix. Other data and statistics are from *Chugan Kukjong News* (Weekly Government News), 9 September 1991.
10 *World Development Report, 1991*, p. 205.
11 *World Development Report, 1991*, p. 209.
12 *Chugan Kukjong News.*
13 Quoted in R.N. Bellah et al., *Habits of the Heart: Individualism and Commitment in American Life,* Perennial Library, New York, 1985, pp. 37, 287.

14 Bellah, *Habits of the Heart*, p. 37.
15 Quoted in Y.A. Cohen (ed.), *Man in Adaptation: The Cultural Present*, Aldine Atherton, Chicago, 1968.
16 Max Weber, *The Theory of Social and Economic Organization*, trans. A.M. Henderson and Talcott Parsons, The Free Press, New York, 1947, pp. 56–77.
17 P.C. Hahm, *The Korean Political Tradition and Law*, Hollym Corp., Seoul, 1967, pp. 19, 210. Yoon, too, wrote that, in the Yi dynasty, law as 'an instrument for preserving a social order under Confucian ethics . . . assumes the form of penal and public law, designed to regulate personal conduct as prescribed by government regulation . . . individuals represent merely targets of government action, not persons capable of asserting their rights vis-a-vis [the] state.' See also Yoon Dae-kyu, *Law and Political Authority in South Korea*, Westview Press and Kyungnam University Press, Boulder and Seoul, 1990, p. 17.
18 See, for instance, Keith B. Richburg, 'Why is Black Africa Overwhelmed while East Asia Overcomes?' *International Herald Tribune*, 14 July 1992.
19 Max Weber, *The Protestant Ethic and the Spirit of Capitalism*, trans. Talcott Parsons, Charles Scribner's Sons, New York, 1958, p. 3.
20 Weber, *The Protestant Ethic*, pp. 16, 17.
21 K.D. Kim, 'The Distinctive Features of South Korea's Development', in P.L. Berger and H.H.M. Hsiao (eds), *In Search of An East Asian Development Model*, Transactions Books, Oxford, 1988, pp. 206–7, 217.
22 W.E. Moore, *The Impact of Industry*, Prentice-Hall, Englewood Cliffs, N.J., 1965, pp. 18, 38.
23 J.M. Halpern, *The Changing Village Community*, Prentice-Hall, Englewood Cliffs, 1967, pp. 43, 125.
24 For a comprehensive study of South Korea's ascription-oriented elite recruitment practices, see Yang Sung-chul and Ahn Byong-man, 'A Study of North and South Korean Political Elite Recruitment, 1948–1988' (in Korean), a Korean Research Council Project, 1990.
25 In this connection, Weber's description of an (American) party boss at the turn of the twentieth century is pertinent: 'The boss is indispensable to the organisation of the party and the organisation is centralised in his hands. He substantially provides the financial means . . . The boss, with his judicious discretion in financial matters, is the natural man for those capitalist circles who finance the election . . . He seeks power alone, power as a source of money, but also power for power's sake. In contrast to the English leader, the American boss works in the dark . . . The boss has no firm political "principles"; he is completely unprincipled in attitude and asks merely: what will capture votes? Frequently he is a rather poorly educated man. But as a rule he leads an inoffensive and correct private life.' For details, see Max Weber, 'Politics as a Vocation', in *From Max Weber* trans., ed. and with an introduction by H.H. Gerth and C. Wright Mills, Galaxy, New York, 1958, pp. 109–10.

26 Lee Kyae-hee, for instance, posits that, ideologically, the South Korean opposition parties have metamorphosed from being the party of conservative coalition in the 1940s and the 1950s to being the party of anti-dictatorship and democratic struggle in the 1950s through the 1980s and to being the catchall party in the 1980s and beyond. For details, see his 'The Prototype of South Korean Opposition Politics' (in Korean), in *Sahoekwahak yonku* (Social Science Studies), Sowon University Social Science Research Center, 1991, pp. 103–29.

27 You Kwang-jin, for instance, listed a number of reasons for the moribund status of the socialist and/or reformist parties in South Korean political arenas, besides the government's legal restrictions. They are: (1) the leaders of these parties were often politically naive and sentimental without having a firm ideological stance; (2) they had internecine leadership struggles within or between the reformist parties; (3) under the edgy ideological and political atmosphere surrounding the North–South confrontational settings, the mass publics were often suspicious of these reformist parties being pro-communistic; (4) from the launching of the Republic the South Korean government tried to emulate the American-style two-party system and, as a result, the people, too, prefer the one powerful opposition party instead of numerous splinter parties; (5) their political slogans and platforms have often been too radical, anti-systemic and extra-parliament-oriented. For details, see his 'An Analysis of South Korean Socialist Parties' Platforms and Policies' (in Korean), *Social Science Studies*, Sowon University Social Science Research Center, 1991, pp. 131–62.

28 Park Chan-wook, 'An Analysis of Party Support in the 14th National Assembly Election', paper delivered at the Korean Political Science Association Summer Seminar, Kyongju, Korea, 2–4 July 1992.

29 Cho Jung-bin, 'Pro-government or Opposition-leaning Voters and Their Party Support in Relation to Their Vote Decision Time' (in Korean), paper delivered at the Korean Political Science Association Summer Conference, Kyongju, Korea, 2–4 July 1992.

30 See Cho Ki-sook, 'The Voters' Rational Choice Model and An Analysis of the Korean Election' (in Korean), paper delivered at the Korean Political Science Association Summer Seminar, Kyongju, Korea, 2–4 July 1992.

31 For details, see Lee Nam-young, 'Voter Participation and Non-voting', paper delivered at the Korean Political Science Association Summer Seminar, Kyongju, Korea, 2–4 July 1992.

32 Shin Doh-chull et al., *Hankuk Minjujuiei Mirae* (The Future of Korean Democracy), Seoul National University, Seoul, 1990, pp. 20–26.

33 D.C. Shin et al., 'Left–Right Polarization and Support for Democratization among the Mass Public in Korea', in *Korean National Community and State Development*, vol. 1, 1989, pp. 109–54.

34 N.Y. Lee, 'The Cultural Basis of Democracy: A Case Study of Public Attitudes and Belief Consistency in Korea' (Master's thesis, University of Iowa, Iowa City, Iowa, 1982).

35 N.Y. Lee, 'The Democratic Belief System: A Study of the Political Culture in South Korea', *Korean Social Science Journal*, vol. 12, 1985, pp. 46-89.

36 S.M. Pae, 'Korea Leading the Third World in Democratization', in *The Korean National Community and State Development*, vol. 1, pp. 167–90.

37 D.C. Shin, 'Left–Right Polarization and Support for Democratization among the Mass Public in Korea', p. 12.

38 ibid., p. 60.

39 ibid., p. 92.

40 ibid., p.169.

3

South Korea's Politics of Succession and the December 1992 Presidential Election

Manwoo Lee

Introduction

For the first time since 1961, a civilian was elected President of Korea in December 1992, symbolising the termination of military rule and the legitimacy controversy. It seems that the tradition of the losers accepting their defeat was also established in this historic election. Both Kim Dae-jung and Chung Ju-yung gracefully conceded their defeat and congratulated Kim Young-sam, who won with 42 per cent of the vote. When Kim Dae-jung announced his retirement from politics, even people who had demonstrated hostility towards him in those regions such as Yongnam where he had never enjoyed much support felt sad and praised him. His popularity has since shot up exponentially.

Unlike the presidential election of 1987, there were no significant crowd-gathering contests among the major presidential candidates in this presidential election. Pressuring soldiers to vote for the ruling party, deliberately fostering violence to divide the opposition forces, and mobilising public officials for the ruling party candidate — all of which happened in previous elections — were absent this time, though widespread distribution of money and gifts, particularly by Chung Ju-yung's Unification National Party and Kim Young-sam's Democratic Liberal Party, somewhat tarnished the electoral process. In general, this was the cleanest and fairest election since the founding of the Republic in 1948. After the election, there were neither complaints from the opposition parties nor student demonstrations.

Between May and December 1992, Korean 'politics as usual' was volatile and unpredictable. The division within the ruling Democratic Liberal Party (DLP), compounded by the threat of defection by some DLP members, the uneasy relationship between President Roh Tae-woo and Kim Young-sam, the confrontational politics of the two Kims — Kim Young-sam and Kim Dae-jung — symbolising the severe regional antagonism of the Honam (south-west) and Yongnam (south-east) regions, the emergence of Chung Ju-yung as a possible spoiler for Kim Young-sam's candidacy, an attempt by the opponents of the two Kims to enlist a national candidate to end the era of the two Kims — all these added to the drama of Korean presidential politics.

In the end, eight candidates were in the race to succeed Roh. During a campaign no longer dominated by the issue of democracy or military rule but by apprehension about Korea's sagging economy and social disorder, the fight was mainly between Kim Young-sam, 65, and Kim Dae-jung, 67, the final showdown being between the two Kims — men who had been both collaborators and rivals since the early 1970s.

This chapter examines in detail South Korea's politics of succession and the serious political disorder in the ruling party, focusing on Kim Young-sam's quest for the presidency. The main thesis of this chapter is that the division, power struggle and instability within the ruling party — a rare phenomenon in the past — did not result in the disintegration of the party and its leadership. Rather, the DLP's political disorder was transformed into an instrument for electoral reforms for Kim Young-sam. During the 1987 presidential election, the opposition was so divided that the election victory went to the ruling party. This time the ruling party was so divided that some people really believed that a genuine change of government was possible. But that did not happen. The ruling party, despite its instability and disunity, managed to win. The main purpose of this chapter is to explain why this was so. This chapter also assesses Kim Dae-jung's third, and perhaps last, bid for the presidency, and places Chung Ju-yung's candidacy in perspective. This election was determined not by policies but by the images, personalities and aura of leadership projected by each candidate. Minor presidential candidates, such as Park Chan-jong and others, will not be discussed here.

Daekwon, the essence of Korean politics

At the risk of over-generalisation, one can say that the essence of Korean politics is *daekwon,* a term meaning 'great governing power'. Though the word is an anachronism, it encapsulates the central reality of power politics in South Korean political life. South Korean journalists, pundits and scholars use the word, thereby elevating the concept in Korean politics. The game of *daekwon* attracts thousands of people seeking power, status and fortune. It is an expensive game. In the previous presidential election in 1987, the ruling Democratic Justice Party reportedly spent several billion (US) dollars. The amount spent by various parties for this election is not available, but many suspect it to be very large.

The politics of d*aekwon* is full of drama and excitement. One commentator noted that though the pro-baseball season lasts only one year, the *daekwon* game lasts for five.[1] Ever since the dramatic merger of three parties into the Democratic Liberal Party in 1990, the Korean people had been obsessed with the question of who would succeed President Roh Tae-woo. In offices, coffee shops and hotel lounges, *daekwon* was the favorite topic of conversation.

Daekwon aspirants are like actors in a dramatic television series, the conclusion of which the people are anxiously watching for. Kim Young-sam, a long-time opposition leader, shocked the nation by joining the ruling establishment, and for two years he was a kind of Hamlet: to quit or not to quit was the question. The aging Kim Dae-jung tried his best to project a new, more moderate image. Chung Ju-yung, a newcomer in the *daekwon* game, behaved like a street peddler selling potent medicines promising a cure for everything.[2]

Though the pursuit of *daekwon* is couched in the rhetoric of democracy, social justice and economic progress, it involves an endless series of acts of manipulation, conspiracy, manoeuvring, rationalisation and deception. The *daekwon* game can seriously affect the fate of the nation. In the 1945–48 period, *daekwon* aspirations among politicians in both the South and North helped create the division of the peninsula. The two Kims in South Korea claimed to be fighters for democracy, but their real motive, many suspect, was simply to acquire *daekwon.* A politician obsessed with *daekwon* is said to be infected with '*daetongryong byung*' — that is, 'presidential disease', or aspiration for the highest office and lust for power and glory, but without a clear vision. Many Koreans were disenchanted with the behaviour of sufferers of presidential disease. The merger of the three parties in 1990 was carried out in the name of saving the nation, but most people believed the real motive was to prolong the ruling party's hold on power.

The dynamics of Korean politics can be summed up in one sentence: they are about acquiring *daekwon*, maintaining *daekwon* and challenging *daekwon*. The history of South Korean politics since the founding of the Republic in 1948 has been a series of transitions in *daekwon*. Ultimately, all *daekwon* holders since 1948 — both usurpers and non-usurpers alike — ended up more or less in disgrace. Even Roh's future is uncertain at best.

One of the outstanding characteristics of these *daekwon* holders is that none of them, including Roh, enjoyed the solid support of the people. There has always been a serious conflict between leaders and the people. Post-1948 regimes, with the possible exception of the Roh regime, were called 'hoodlum' or 'fascist' as much by ordinary citizens as by radical groups.

The chronic clash between authoritarian regimes and popular forces should be understood in terms of the asymmetrical relations between the state and civil society in Korea. The state possesses a near monopoly of power and authority and the mechanisms of the state have rarely been subordinated to popular forces.[3] Korean political development has manifested a continuing conflict between state autonomy and civil society. The June 29 Declaration in 1987, which brought about the demise of the authoritarian Chun Doo-hwan regime, was an important milestone in Korean politics that symbolised the victory of civil society over state autonomy. But the state's capacity for arbitrary authority was only partially diminished as a result.

Conflict between the state and civil society

Broadly speaking, one can distinguish two types of leadership in Korean politics. The first type is typified by soldiers such as Park Chung-hee, Chun and Roh, who were recruited from state institutions. The second is rooted in society, and includes civilians like the two Kims and Chung. Korean leaders of the first type acquired *daekwon* through the mechanisms of state — the police, the Agency for National Security Planning (ANSP, formerly the Korean Central Intelligence Agency or KCIA), the Military Security Command and the government bureaucracy. These powerful institutions effectively controlled and dominated civil society by subordinating the business community, weakening labour organisations and manipulating civic or voluntary groups. As a result, none of the state-oriented regimes was able to establish legitimacy and enjoy the diffuse, social and political support of the people. Close examination of South Korea's political turmoil shows that, since the early 1950s, all serious political controversies were about the perceived illegitimate acquisition and maintenance of *daekwon*.[4]

However, Korean politics have undergone a remarkable democratisation since the late 1980s. Barrington Moore Jr suggests that the development of pluralistic democracy has been a long and incomplete struggle to accomplish three related things: 'to check arbitrary rules; to replace arbitrary rules with just and rational ones; to obtain a share for the underlying population in the making of rules'.[5] Students, dissidents, intellectuals and journalists, as well as the two Kims, played decisive roles in Korea's democratic odyssey. Roh's June 29 Declaration of 1987, actually dictated by Chun himself, was a surrender to the demands of the people for political reforms. Roh saw this as the Korean equivalent of the British Glorious Revolution of 1688.

In 1992, for the first time since 1961, presidential candidates were not recruited from military institutions of the state. For nearly four decades, citizens complained about government-manipulated elections, especially about the 'premiums' controlled by the ruling party. These were the ruling party's ability to utilise financial resources and organisational strength — nearly 800 000 national and local officials — to determine the outcome of elections. This kind of election, controlled by national and local officials, is called a *hengjungsunkuh* or administrative election. Free competition in South Korean elections was not really allowed until 1992. No opposition leader has come to power except very briefly in 1960–61 during the government of Chang Myon. Since the 1992 March general elections, the clash between the two Kims has revolved around the very politicised issue of holding local elections to choose governors, mayors, county chiefs and other local officials. The ruling party was firmly against holding elections, while opposition parties were determined to push them in order to prevent administrative elections. This hot political issue, however, lost much of its steam when, in September, Roh suddenly announced the formation of a neutral cabinet to oversee a fair presidential election.

Consequently, the efficacy of the ruling party's premiums was greatly diluted. Even during the March 1992 general elections, the involvement of secret agents in an attempt to unseat some opposition candidates backfired and the ruling party lost many seats. The weakening of the ruling party's premiums has been made possible by the rapid social and economic changes that have revitalised South Korean society. During the March general elections in 1992, some 281 civic election watch groups emerged demanding 'clean' politics. Compared to the 1988 general elections, the number of cases involving illegal campaigning was sharply reduced.[6]

Symbolically, at least, Korea's civil society has gained the upper hand and retains veto power over meddling by the state in election processes. In 1987, the military chief of staff openly warned against Kim Dae-jung's election.[7] However, in 1992, key military figures vowed to remain neutral regardless of the election outcome.[8]

Since Roh's inauguration in 1988, the number of periodicals often critical of the president's performance has tripled. A wide variety of civic interest groups has emerged, including labour organisations, farmers, consumers, students, economic justice groups, the print media, religious groups, Bar associations, women's groups and environmentalists. Though their influence on the outcome of the recent elections has been negligible, their participation in politics is strengthening pluralism.[9]

Korea's past rulers, such as Park Chung-hee and Chun Doo-hwan, who acquired their *daekwon* through means other than fair elections, were mainly responsible to the state apparatus, not to the people. Today, the situation has been reversed, and this time around the presidential candidates had no choice but to appeal to the voters. Realising that it could no longer rely on the military and the government bureaucracy to win elections, Roh's Democratic Justice Party (1980–90) had to invite Kim Young-sam's Reunification Democratic Party (1987–90) to merge with it in order to prolong the ruling group's political life. The merger meant that the ruling party could only survive by politically grafting part of the democratic forces on to itself.[10]

The saga of Kim Young-Sam's quest for the presidency

Since 1980, South Korea's ruling parties have demonstrated the ability to partially reform themselves. Chun Doo-hwan's Democratic Justice Party terminated the tradition of protracted, one-person rule and the June 29 Declaration of 1987 allowed the first direct election of a president in sixteen years. Squabbles and power games within the ruling Democratic Liberal Party (1990–) resulted in a series of political reforms such as introducing a presidential nomination contest, instituting a neutral cabinet to manage a fair election, and making it illegal for government bureaucrats to influence elections. Below is a detailed account of the saga of Kim Young-sam's quest for the presidency, which reveals how he promoted his candidacy by taking advantage of the shortcomings within the ruling party.

Motives behind the mega-party

To understand political succession within the ruling party, one must go back to January 1990 when Roh and Kim Young-sam, together with Kim Jong-pil (at one time Park Chung-hee's prime minister and inheritor of part of his political machine) created a grand, conservative, majority party in the name of a new political order, democracy, prosperity and unification. The three leaders supposedly agreed to introduce a parliamentary cabinet system, promising Kim Young-sam the first chance to head the cabinet, and to share power among the three major factions made up of the former Democratic Justice Party (DJP), former Reunification Democratic Party (RDP), and former New Democratic Republican Party (NDRP). But the real motive for the merger is to be found in the regional reality of Korean politics. The April 1988 general elections produced four regionally oriented minority parties. The ruling DJP had 127 seats, the RDP 59, the NDRP 35 and the Party for Peace and Democracy (PPD) 71.

However, the merger of the three parties failed to produce political stability. Rather, the new mega-party itself dissolved into intra-party squabbles over who would succeed Roh after he stepped down in 1993. The DJP, a minority ruling party, was badly split between the followers of Chun and Roh and between the 'TK group' and 'non-TK group' factions. TK refers to powerful politicians and bureaucrats from Taegu and North Kyongsang province, the home province of Roh, Park and Chun.

None of the factional leaders possessed political credentials impressive enough to challenge the two Kims in the 1992 presidential election. Thus the DJP faced two serious problems: who would lead the party after Roh stepped down; and what should be done to end its status as a minority ruling party. The DJP chose alliance with one or more of the opposition parties.

It was natural for Kim Jong-pil's NDRP to join the DJP and give it a parliamentary majority, indistinguishable as it was from the DJP in terms of policy and political colour. But this kind of merger of parties on the right would tarnish the image of both, since it would be viewed as a resurrection of the discredited parties of Park and Chun.

For his part, Kim Young-sam was shocked and humiliated in 1987 and 1988. He came in second in the 1987 presidential election, and the 1988 general elections reduced his party to number two opposition status. His efforts to improve his own and his party's image were futile. So he decided to join with Roh and Kim Jong-pil, and justified his political gamble in the name of new thinking.

Kim Young-sam's strategy

It took Kim Young-sam two and a half years to become the ruling party's presidential nominee. He pursued a winning strategy throughout. First, he held the future of the ruling party hostage. He and his followers continually threatened to play their trump card of breaking up the party unless Kim was assured of the succession to Roh, and this threat proved decisive in the end.

Second, Kim always took the offensive when challenged by his opponents and wasted no time dividing DJP factions, thereby eliminating any potential challenger. Third, he cultivated a close friendship with Kim Yoon-hwan, a key figure within the DJP faction of the DLP, who felt that Kim Young-sam should succeed Roh. Fourth, he always emphasised that he maintained solidarity and friendship with Roh, even though this was not true. Fifth, he did not hesitate to work with Kim Dae-jung, his arch rival, whenever there was a movement to end the era of the two Kims. The two Kims maintained their status as the prime movers of Korean politics.

The two Kims' *kyongryon* and their power base

The two Kims dominated the Korean *daekwon* game for several reasons. First, people remember that they were unjustly treated by successive dictatorial regimes and deserved their last chance to become president in an environment of fair competition. Second, both still remained heroes to many people because they were credited with slaying the political 'monsters', Park and Chun.

No other *daekwon* aspirants possessed such heroic political credentials. In Korean, this kind of political vitae is called *kyongryon*. Park Tae-joon, Lee Jong-chan and Park Chul-un, all of whom challenged Kim Young-sam's leadership, all had one thing in common: they lacked *kyongryon*. They worked for the discredited regimes of the past. Park Tae-joon's career was closely identified with military rule, since he worked for both Park and Chun. Even granted his legendary performance as builder of the Pohang Steel Company, he was no match for Kim Young-sam. Lee Jong-chan, who tried desperately to stop Kim Young-sam from becoming the ruling party's presidential nominee, began his career as a military man and intelligence officer. Though known as a moderate reformist who had often been at odds with both Chun and Roh, it was difficult for him to escape his past. Park Chul-un, who challenged Kim's leadership of the DLP, grew up under the shadow of Chun and Roh; the fact that he was a member of the Roh family clan discredited him in the eyes of some voters.

Another thing these challengers had in common was the absence of a popular power base. Kim Dae-jung, for example, was dominant in two provinces: South and North Cholla. Kim Young-sam had a solid base in Pusan and the large South Kyongsang province, and was able to use it to political advantage. For example, Ro Jae-bong, a close confidant of Roh who served five months as prime minister in the first half of 1991, could not save himself when Kim Young-sam demanded his resignation and made him a scapegoat for the death of a student at the hands of the riot police in May 1991. Unlike the two Kims, Ro had no popular power base. Thus the phenomenon of the two Kims in contemporary Korean politics manifested the reality of Korea's regional power politics.

Division within the ruling establishment

Elites of the Fifth Republic (1981–87) were divided between followers of Chun and Roh. After becoming president, Roh gaoled or excluded many of Chun's henchmen in order to distance himself from the latter's abusive rule. Clearly, major cracks developed within the TK power structure with Roh's ascension.[11] Though Kim Young-sam's faction was much smaller than the DJP faction under Roh, it was able to emerge as the most viable force because of the cracks within the DJP faction. There was no visible TK leader to succeed Roh, and TK groups were divided into old and new groups. The old TK, represented by Kim Yoon-hwan, believed that the TK could continue to wield power only by making Kim Young-sam the next president. The new TK, represented by Park Chul-un, feared that Kim Young-sam's presidency could mean the end of their privileged position. Other TK leaders acted independently. Kim Bok-dong, ex-general and Roh's brother-in-law, tried to emerge as a new leader. Chung Ho-young, another ex-general who helped in Roh's rise to power but who, in 1990, was made a scapegoat for the 1980 oppression of Kwangju, openly defied Roh by winning a legislative seat as an independent candidate. Division within the TK establishment was welcome news for both Kim Young-sam and Kim Dae-jung. The TK group's protracted rule was attacked by other regions, and was warmly endorsed by Kim Dae-jung and his party.[12]

Cracks within the ruling party were also encouraged by the 'SK' group (from Seoul and Kyonggi province), who sought to end the TK domination and prevent either of the two Kims from becoming president. They promoted Lee Jong-chan, who was deeply involved in Chun's rise to power and served as floor leader of the DJP and party secretary and who proclaimed himself as leader of a new generation. He had been against the merger of the three parties in 1990 and constantly attacked Kim Young-sam after the merger occurred.

The cabinet system controversy

A constitutional amendment controversy flared up off and on throughout 1990 and 1991, and this issue further divided the DJP faction. In October 1990 it developed into a crisis. The merger of the three parties in 1990 was engineered to obtain an absolute majority in the National Assembly in order to amend the constitution to prolong the DLP's power. When this secret deal was deliberately revealed by the DJP faction to discredit Kim, he decided to distance himself permanently from the constitutional amendment deal. Anti-Kim Young-sam forces within the ruling party then began to attack him. In September 1990, some anti-Kim Young-sam people openly accused Kim Young-sam of pursuing 'hegemonic politics' and questioned Kim Young-sam's ability to run the country.[13] On 29 October 1991, President Roh, attending the 40th anniversary celebration of the *Hankuk Ilbo* newspaper, reaffirmed his desire to amend the constitution.[14]

Kim Young-sam took this as an open attack on his leadership and complained that Roh and his faction within the ruling party were conspiring against him. He left for Masan seriously considering leaving the party. He refused to carry out his duties as the executive chairman of the DLP for ten days, and so the DLP nearly collapsed. Some of his supporters strongly urged Kim Young-sam to bolt the party. Kim Yoon-hwan, then DLP secretary, rushed to Masan and pleaded with Kim to return to work. This controversy over the constitutional amendment lingered on well into 1991.

Anti-Kim Young-sam forces versus *daesaeron*

Kim Young-sam and his followers insisted that the only leader entitled to lead the DLP and succeed Roh was Kim Young-sam. This view was known in Korean as *daesaeron* or *soonri*, and it gave Kim the upper hand in his moral claim to succeed Roh. *Daesaeron* includes the notion of the inevitableness of succession determined by history, while *soonri* refers to the 'proper course of history'. Kim Yoon-hwan accepted the idea and publicly promoted it. According to him, the TK group and the military had ruled Korea since 1961, while Kim Young-sam and Kim Dae-jung, representing the progressive democratic forces, were victims of this repressive rule. The long conflict between the two ended when the former elite decided to change by putting forth the 29 June Declaration, known as the 'great political compromise'. Kim Yoon-hwan argued that if the TK and the military continued to rule without regard for changes that had occurred during recent years, tremendous resistance from popular forces could be expected. Therefore, Kim Young-sam, a civilian and non-TK politician, should succeed Roh if the TK groups and the military wanted to maintain power.[15]

As the *daesaeron* idea gained momentum, the anti-Kim Young-sam forces reaffirmed the need to adopt a cabinet system and convened a series of gatherings to demonstrate the solidarity of the DJP faction. Roh himself gave the impression that the ambition of Kim Young-sam must be checked. Roh met Park Tae-joon in mid-July 1991, and asked him to maintain solidarity with the DJP faction. Also, they tried to debunk the myth of Kim Young-sam's *daesaeron*.[16] Park Tae-joon led the anti-*daesaeron* movement as co-chairman and caretaker leader of the DJP faction. Park promoted the notion that he was the natural leader of the largest DJP faction and expressed his desire to succeed Roh.[17] Also, rumours were floated that if Park Tae-joon failed to succeed Roh, other prominent figures such as former prime ministers Kang Young-hoon or Ro Jae-bong would be drafted. Kim Young-sam and his faction were sufficiently irritated to again seriously consider quitting the party.

The DJP faction's fair competition rule

The feud between the Kim Young-sam faction and his foes resulted in introducing the fair competition rule regarding presidential nomination, the first in Korean political history. Initially, Kim Young-sam and his followers shunned the idea of a free and fair competition for the nomination of the presidential candidate simply because they were outnumbered by the DJP faction. In July 1991, a presidential aide, Choi Young-choel, said that Roh had no intention of hand-picking his successor.[18] This made Kim and his followers furious, and Kim Young-sam went to Cheju island, ostensively for a vacation, from 27 July to 5 August 1991. Many suspected that Kim would make an 'important decision' (i.e. to leave the party). The prospect of a fair and free competition pleased the DJP faction because it had sufficient numbers to defeat Kim Young-sam. Again, Kim Yoon-hwan, siding with Kim Young-sam, asserted that 'a fair and free contest . . . is unthinkable' and emphasised arbitration among factions.[19] Kim Yoon-hwan's argument did not persuade party members and Kim Young-sam eventually half-heartedly accepted the principle of fair competition.

Controversy over the timing of nomination

The Kim Young-sam faction undermined its foes by persistently demanding that the DLP presidential candidate be chosen before the National Assembly elections set for March 1992. Though Kim Young-sam had never said that he would bolt the party if not nominated before January 1992, his followers always used that threat to break up the party.

After Kim returned from his Cheju Island trip, Roh urged an immediate halt to the dispute. Kim and Roh agreed not to raise the issue until the end of 1991. However, in December 1991 the controversy resurfaced. In a meeting with visiting United States Congressman Stephen Solarz, Kim said he would force a showdown with Roh on early nomination. Park Tae-joon immediately retaliated by saying that 'it is wrong (for him) to have a showdown with his superior'.[20] However, at a party executive council meeting at the Blue House in January 1992, Roh said, 'Kim Young-sam will lead the party as the center force', and called on the party members to help Kim win the general elections in March 1992.[21] At this time, there was much attention to Roh's choice of successor. Kim strongly hinted that Roh supported him and emphasised the 'strong mutual trust' between the two.[22] The anti-Kim forces downplayed Kim's assertion. In the March elections, Kim Young-sam sounded and acted like a presidential candidate during a barnstorming tour of his home region of Pusan and South Kyongsang province. This drew angry criticism from Park Tae-joon.[23]

Controversy over the March election defeat

Kim Young-sam demonstrated his political acumen by transforming the setback created by his party's poor showing in the March general elections into a major political offensive against his enemies. Strife among rival factions flared as to who should be blamed for the shocking setbacks in the March elections in which the ruling mega-party lost (by one seat) its majority status. Kim Young-sam immediately assigned responsibility to the incompetence of the Blue House and Roh, the interference of secret agents in the election process, and the party's failure to designate the ruling party's presidential candidate for the December election. The anti-Kim forces were angry, and Kim Jong-pil, co-chairman of the DLP, turned in his resignation. Lee Jong-chan and others blamed Kim Young-sam for the defeat.[24]

On 28 March 1992, without consulting Roh, Kim Young-sam unilaterally declared his presidential candidacy, and claimed that he and Roh had become 'one in mind', meaning that Roh supported him.[25] Though Roh was clearly leaning toward Kim to prevent the breakup of the party, Kim's unilateral action angered Roh. By these actions, Kim shifted the focus from who should be blamed for the defeat to the candidacy issue and caught his enemies such as Park Tae-joon off guard.

The failure of the first experiment in fair contest

Roh was in a dilemma, since it was virtually impossible to satisfy both pro-Kim and anti-Kim forces within the ruling party. In reality, the only way for Kim Young-sam to get the nomination safely was to dilute the principle of a fair contest. Roh had to endorse Kim directly or indirectly to assure enough votes from party delegates for him to win. The principle of fair competition combined with Roh's neutrality would guarantee the defeat of Kim Young-sam because he simply would not have enough votes in an open contest.

Maintaining the rule that the presidential nominee should be named through democratic procedures was interpreted as Roh's opposition to Kim Young-sam's call for his nomination. Kim Young-sam insisted that Roh would not strictly adhere to that principle. 'Roh never said he would stay neutral,' Kim insisted. 'I only think about victory and have never thought about other possibilities.'[26] These remarks were attacked as undemocratic and interpreted by the anti-Kim Young-sam forces as his determination not to abide by the results of a fair contest if defeated.

Kim Young-sam, however, kept up the heat by demanding that Park Tae-joon should not run and Roh's relatives, such as Park Chul-un and Kim Bok-dong, should not get involved in the nomination process. He also demanded that the DJP faction not put forth a single candidate to challenge him.[27] Supporting these demands, nine prominent pro-Kim Young-sam supporters in the DJP faction led by Kim Yoon-hwan declared support for Kim Young-sam in early April 1992.

Expecting Roh to adhere to the principle of fair competition, the anti-Kim Young-sam groups searched for a single candidate in April, and a seven-man committee was established to select that candidate, key members of which were Park Tae-joon, Lee Jong-chan, and Park Chul-un. The seven-man committee decided to make public its single candidate by 15 April. The pro-Kim Young-sam forces were concerned that Park Tae-joon, whom Kim Young-sam feared most, might be named as the single candidate. Park Tae-joon, for his part, was quite serious about his candidacy. Roh met the anti-Kim Young-sam people and assured them there would be a fair competition. Park Tae-joon always stated publicly that Roh would never pick Kim Young-sam and claimed that Kim had 'no character, no knowledge, and no vision'.[28]

By this time, however, Roh had decided to support Kim Young-sam, but Park remained in the dark. On 8 April, Kim Jong-pil met Roh and immediately after met with Kim Young-sam. Kim Jong-pil told reporters that he had decided whom he would endorse, and Kim Young-sam said, 'I am satisfied'.[29] On 27 April, Kim Jong-pil endorsed Kim Young-sam in exchange for the latter's promise, once elected, to make him executive chairman of the DLP.

It is a well-known secret that Park Tae-joon was pressured to quit the presidential race by the Blue House and the Agency for National Security Planning. With Park out of the way, the only thing required for Kim Young-sam's nomination was a political show. The promised free competition was thus breached when Park was pressured to quit. Roh's catch-22 was that a fair competition would break up the party, and thus to save the party he had to dilute the principle of fair competition.

Lee Jong-chan versus Kim Young-sam

By the time Lee Jong-chan was picked as the candidate of the anti-Kim Young-sam forces, the pro-Kim forces contended that everything was 'set between their (our) boss and Roh'.[30] However, Lee Jong-chan and his followers maintained that Roh would never leave the political interests of the ruling establishment in the hands of a stranger, Kim Young-sam, and therefore Roh's secret choice would be Lee Jong-chan. Some polls showed Lee in good standing and people talked about the possibility of his leadership role in the post-Kim era.[31] The grandson of a well-known independence fighter, Lee called for the termination of the confrontational era of the two Kims and argued that chronic regional antagonism would only end if the two Kims retired.[32]

Lee threatened that if fair competition was not guaranteed, he would make a 'grave decision'.[33] He began to sound and behave much like Kim Young-sam, urging Kim Young-sam to leave his post until the party convention and to stop having weekly meetings with Roh, and he repeatedly asked for joint campaign appearances with Kim Young-sam. But Kim denied these requests, causing Lee to become increasingly frustrated as he began to realise that the race was over. Lee attacked Kim Young-sam's support groups for engaging in backroom dealings, payoffs and coercion, and called for punishment of those officials for spreading deliberately 'distorted' impressions of Roh's opinion on the race.[34] On 9 May, Lee accused the Blue House of engaging in 'a free competition in disguise',[35] and, in mid-May, even attacked Roh for guiding the nomination race by secretly supporting Kim Young-sam. On 18 May 1992, Lee, wearing a solemn face, declared that the nomination race was 'null and void'. 'It is unavoidable for me to commit a historic sin by participating in a fake nomination race,' said Lee.[36]

The DLP's nomination convention was held on 19 May, with Kim Young-sam unopposed. Kim got 66 per cent of the delegate votes, but Lee obtained 33 per cent, even though he was not running. Roh called for the party to take 'stern' steps to punish Lee, because Lee's boycott of the party convention had jolted the DLP and severely damaged Roh's leadership.

Despite Roh's anger, Lee could not be punished for fear of affecting Kim Young-sam's chance to win the December presidential election. It was reported that supporters of Kim Young-sam had coerced politicians to stay away from Lee's New Political Forum group and blocked financial support channels to the group, thus crippling Lee's ability to form a new party.[37] Meanwhile, Daewoo chairman Kim Woo-choong, a high-school classmate of Lee's, stepped in to arbitrate the Kim–Lee conflict. Towards the end of June 1992, Kim Young-sam and Lee met, and Lee decided to remain in the party for the time being, but insisted that Park Tae-joon, not Kim Jong-pil, should be the party's future executive chairman. Thus the question of who should succeed Kim Young-sam rocked the party. Lee finally left the DLP on 17 August to create a new party with the supposed goal of ending the era of the two Kims. The exit of Lee somewhat weakened the ruling DLP, and its ability to promote a united front campaign for Kim Young-sam's march to *daekwon* was questioned. The continuing inter-factional disputes in the DLP gave a ray of hope to the opposition camp. Kim Young-sam kept himself busy trying to mend fences to prevent lawmakers from crossing over to join the new party promoted by Lee Jong-chan. Lee began contacting some prominent figures like Chung Ho-young and others and he launched the People's Alliance for New Politics on 3 September 1993. He tried in vain to recruit former prime minister Kang Young-hoon and Kim Joon-yop, former president of Korea University, to head the new party and run against Kim Young-sam in the December presidential election.

Roh versus Kim Young-sam

On 28 August, Kim Young-sam succeeded Roh to head the DLP, but the relationship between Roh and Kim soon became strained, dramatically transforming the nature of the ruling party. In August, the selection of a consortium led by the Sunkyong Business Group for the second mobile telephone project touched off a major controversy that was to haunt the Roh government. Awarding the multi-billion-*won* business venture to a firm owned by a relative of Roh created severe friction between Roh and Kim Young-sam. Kim Young-sam warned that the issue would cause a serious setback in the presidential election. Opposition parties waged an advertisement war in the media to draw voter attention to this matter, accusing the government of using large-scale public projects like the mobile phone business, the consortium of an international airport and a high-speed railway project to collect political funds. Consequently, the government rescinded its decision, resulting in a souring of relations between Kim Young-sam and Roh Tae-woo.

Another case that estranged the relation between Kim Young-sam and Roh was the declaration of conscience by Han Jun-su, ex-county chief of Yongi county in South Chungchong province, that he received money and instruction from the Home Minister and Governor to help the ruling party candidate win in the March general elections. Opposition parties saw the scandal as the tip of the iceberg and raised suspicion about a large-scale government scheme to rig the March elections nationwide, causing one of the worst confrontations between the government and the opposition parties. Kim Young-sam, affected by this scandal, held a press conference on 16 September 1992, during which he demanded a sweeping cabinet reshuffle that included replacing the prime minister, who was having high-level talks in Pyongyang at that time. This move angered Roh.

On 18 September 1993, Roh dropped a bombshell by announcing his decision to quit the party. He later announced that he intended to form a neutral cabinet capable of holding a clean and fair presidential election. Roh's move, many observers argued, was motivated by Kim Young-sam's irritating attitude. Kim was the champion in the struggle to force the government to cancel the contract on the mobile phone project. The event severely damaged Roh's reputation.[38] Also, Roh felt that Kim Young-sam crossed the line and encroached upon his exclusive domain with regard to the cabinet change. It was believed that Roh's decision was in retaliation against Kim Young-sam rather than a move to ensure a fair presidential election. Kim Dae-jung hailed Roh's move by calling it 'a Copernican turning point in politics'.[39] He ended the boycott of the National Assembly that began after the March elections on account of Roh's refusal to hold local elections.

Suddenly, in theory, the ruling party was no more; there was just the majority party. Those anti-Kim Young-sam people within the DLP saw this as an opportunity to undermine Kim, and others, shaken by Roh's decision, began preparations to bolt the party. Once again, Kim Young-sam faced the possibility of mass defection by DLP members. With the inauguration of a neutral cabinet headed by Hyun Soong-jong in early October, a half dozen DLP Assembly men bolted the party to launch the anti-Kim Young-sam front. They tried to recruit Park Tae-joon as their leader. Kim Young-sam was desperate, trying to keep DLP members from bolting in the wake of Park's decision to leave the party. His departure created serious unrest within the DLP. Kim and Park met on 10 October for three and a half hours, but they decided to go their separate ways.

On 23 October, the New Korea Party was launched without a head. There was talk of recruiting Daewoo Business Group chairman Kim Woo-choong to head the party and run against the two Kims, but the New Korea Party was soon thrown into disarray over finding a proper flagbearer. Nevertheless, the DLP was very tense. On 3 November, Lee Jong-chan himself was promoted as its presidential candidate. By this time, Lee's political clout, if he had any, had evaporated. His candidacy posed no threat to Kim Young-sam. Also, other anti-Kim people such as Park Chul-un, Kim Bok-dong and others joined Chung's UNP. More interestingly, Lee Jong-chan also eventually dropped out of the race just one week before the election on 11 December and joined Chung's UNP.[40] This is how the movement of the anti-Kim forces within the DLP ended.

The victory of Kim Young-sam

Having eliminated or substantially weakened the anti-Kim Young-sam forces within the DLP, Kim kicked off his presidential campaign by promising to cure the 'Korean disease' — rampant corruption, lawlessness and the lack of authority — and create a new Korea. He promised to bring about reforms in politics and society with stability. If Korea's presidential candidates could be compared to sales products, Kim Young-sam's product attracted more customers than others. Also, if Korea's election laws had allowed accurate opinion polls, voters would have known the outcome of this election beforehand. Opinion polls were not released until after the election. Those who had access to the polls knew all along that Kim Young-sam would be the winner. Kim Young-sam consistently maintained his lead in the major polls: 39.9 per cent (17 November), 36.3 per cent (27 November), 36.2 per cent (2 December), 37.7 per cent (7 December) and 39.5 per cent (17 December). Kim Dae-jung always trailed behind him throughout the campaigning period: 25.3 per cent (17 November), 26.4 per cent (27 November), 27.5 per cent (2 December), 29.5 per cent (7 December) and 31.1 per cent (17 December). Chung Ju-yung's popularity, despite his boom during the first part of December, never went beyond 17 per cent.[41]

Table 3.1 *The 1992 presidential election results (major candidates)*

	Votes	Kim YS	Kim DJ	Chung JY
Seoul	6 021 311	2 167 298	2 246 636	1 070 629
Pusan	2 135 546	1 551 473	265 055	133 907
Taegu	1 172 636	690 245	90 641	224 642
Inchon	1 081 011	397 361	338 538	228 505
Kwangju	685 797	14 504	652 337	8 085
Taejon	582 613	202 137	165 067	133 646
Kyonggi	3 502 774	1 254 025	1 103 498	798 356
Kangwon	834 891	340 528	127 265	279 610
N. Chungchong	750 483	281 678	191 743	175 767
S. Chungchong	973 070	351 789	271 921	240 400
N. Cholla	1 126 597	63 175	991 483	35 923
S. Cholla	1 285 110	53 360	1 170 398	26 686
N. Kyongsang	1 559 478	991 424	147 440	240 646
S. Kyongsang	2 118 601	1 514 043	193 373	241 135
Cheju	265 252	104 292	85 889	42 130
Total	24 095 170	9 977 332	8 041 284	3 880 067
Per cent	100	41	33.8	16.3

Source: The Central Election Management Committee, *Hankuk Ilbo*, 22 December 1992.

Note: Figures for minor candidates not included here.

The election returns showed that Kim Young-sam won everywhere except in Seoul and the Cholla provinces. He received 60 to 70 per cent of the votes in the Yongnam region — the two Kyongsang provinces and the two major southern cities of Pusan and Taegu. Voters in their twenties were more or less evenly split between Kim Young-sam and Kim Dae-jung, contrary to the expectation that the latter would do better among them. Voters in their thirties gave a slight edge to Kim Young-sam. However, among the voters in their forties, five out of ten voted for Kim Young-sam and three out of ten for Kim Dae-jung. Among voters in their fifties, six out of ten voted for Kim Young-sam and two for Kim Dae-jung. Among voters in their sixties and seventies, seven out of ten voted for Kim Young-sam. Voters in their twenties and thirties accounted for 57 per cent of the total votes in this election. Those voters over 40, who constituted 43 per cent, overwhelmingly voted for Kim Young-sam.[42] Housewives, small- and medium-sized business owners, and even blue-collar workers favoured Kim Young-sam over Kim Dae-jung.[43] Kim Dae-jung won overwhelmingly in his Cholla provinces, receiving 90 per cent of the votes, and maintained a slight edge in Seoul. Kim Dae-jung failed to overcome his image as a regional candidate. Chung, who counted on the mid-regions such as Kyonggi province, North and South Chungchong provinces and Kangwon province, did very poorly. Though there was an initial boom for his candidacy in North Kyongsang province and Taegu, he ended up receiving only 10 to 20 per cent of the votes there. The credible explanation for this phenomenon is that Korean voters did not vote for policies. They were motivated by emotion rather than rational calculation. The whole contest was highly personalised in that voters' affection or attachment (in Korean, known as *chung*) toward Kim Young-sam was decisive in his victory.

To be more precise, the crucial element in this election was the image factor. Of the three major candidates, Kim Young-sam's image was most acceptable to the bulk of the voters. Despite the criticism that he had crossed over to the ruling party in 1990 to satisfy his political ambition and the never-ending feud within the DLP, Kim Young-sam maintained his image as a clean, honest, virtuous, sincere and decisive man. It is to his credit that he was able to separate himself from the unpopularity of the DLP and Roh by portraying himself as a reformist candidate. Kim's image was not made overnight. His political *kyongryon* included his 30-year battle against dictatorship and his colourful political career as the youngest legislator ever elected to the National Assembly at the age of 25. He served as floor leader of his party five times, headed opposition political parties three times, and emerged as the head of the ruling party most recently. By joining the ruling party in 1990, he was instrumental in pressuring Roh to implement reforms in the electoral process, culminating in the formation of a neutral cabinet in the weeks before the election.

Images of other candidates were not as positive as that of Kim Young-sam. As for Kim Dae-jung's image, voters recognised his brilliance and knowledge, but basically they distrusted him, except in his own regions. In Korea the image of rich people such as Chung is viewed negatively because of the corrupt way (speculation, exploitation, symbiosis between government and business, and tax evasion) by which they are perceived to have made their fortunes.

Second, as in the 1987 presidential election, regionalism played a decisive role in this election. Though all candidates did their best not to engage in exploiting regional antipathy, voters in the Honam and Yongnam regions overwhelmingly voted for their native sons. Kim Young-sam had the advantage of more voters in his power base. Lee Ki-taek, current head of the opposition Democratic Party, told the author that when the Yongnam people saw on television that 50 per cent of the Honam voters had voted by noon on the polling day, compared with only 35 per cent in the Yongnam region, the Yongnam voters rushed to the polling stations to defeat Kim Dae-jung.[44]

Third, that Kim Young-sam won everywhere except in the Cholla provinces and Seoul showed the conservative nature of Korean voters in general. Voters have traditionally preferred stability over radical reforms. In particular, voters were disturbed when they heard that North Korea had allegedly endorsed Kim Dae-jung.

Fourth, even though the government went out of its way to guarantee a fair election and stay neutral, Kim Young-sam's candidacy was closely identified with the government. Naturally, government officials — both national and local — generally identified with and favoured Kim Young-sam. Furthermore, Kim Young-sam had the advantage of the largest party organisation, both as the ruling and majority party, the organisational strength of which played a decisive role in this campaign. It made a difference whether the candidate travelled as the ruling party candidate or an opposition candidate.

Fifth, there was talk of Chung receiving more than 20 per cent of the votes, thus handing the victory over to Kim Dae-jung. In fact, Kim Dae-jung counted on this possibility. Had Chung received 20–25 per cent of the votes, Kim Young-sam might have been defeated or have won with a slim margin. This did not happen. Chung's unreasonable campaign promises, such as reducing the price of apartments by half, his involvement in vote-buying and mobilising Hyundai workers for campaigning, and the electronic bugging of a political meeting attended by supporters of Kim Young-sam all contributed to the demise of his short-lived political boom.

Politics of *daekwon* in the opposition camp

Kim Dae-jung's last bid for the presidency

Kim Dae-jung, 67, is one of the most controversial political figures South Korea has ever produced. He lost his first bid for the presidency to President Park Chung-hee in 1971, with the election widely viewed in opposition circles as rigged in favour of Park. The election was so close that Park felt compelled to proclaim the repressive *Yushin* constitution under which he ruled the country by decree until assassinated in 1979. Kim Dae-jung was gaoled repeatedly for his political views and nearly lost his life when he was kidnapped by KCIA agents in Tokyo in 1973. He was sentenced to death by a military court in 1980. Released in 1982, he went into exile in the United States and returned to Korea in 1985.

The rivalry between Kim Dae-jung and Kim Young-sam goes back to the early 1970s. During the 1971 presidential election, the young Kim Young-sam nearly became the chief opposition candidate, but Kim Dae-jung snatched the prize from him. Kim Young-sam showed no enthusiasm for Kim Dae-jung's candidacy and did not campaign for him. In 1980, their rivalry contributed to Chun's rise to power. In 1987, they ran against each other and the beneficiary was Roh.

The two Kims maintained a unique relationship. They worked together against their common enemies — Park and Chun — but when it came to who should get *daekwon,* they went their separate ways. When one of them was in trouble, the other was also in trouble. Since neither could exist without the other, both needed to prolong the era of the two Kims. It meant that only *they* could challenge each other. During the Roh presidency, they were strangely able to work together on certain issues and shared similar views on political reforms whenever they were in trouble. For example, in April 1991, they met in Taegu and agreed on the need to hold local elections, change the national security laws, eliminate repressive national security politics and resist the ruling party's attempt to introduce a cabinet system.

Despite his impressive assets as a charismatic leader whose appeals often received the widest acceptance among a people who felt oppressed by and alienated from the existing political system, Kim Dae-jung faced two major liabilities that were not easily overcome. First, due to propaganda efforts by past repressive regimes, Kim Dae-jung acquired a reputation for being radical and even dangerous. Second, his main political support was concentrated in one of the smaller regions in southern Korea, the Cholla provinces, and in parts of Seoul. These two factors helped ensure his loss in the 1987 presidential election. These liabilities were again decisive in determining the outcome of the contest between the two Kims. Though Kim Dae-jung's image underwent enormous changes during the past five years, he was unable to take advantage of the serious disunity in the ruling party.

The new Kim Dae-jung

When the merger of the three parties occurred in 1990, Kim Dae-jung emerged as the sole opposition leader and inherited the mantle of the traditional opposition forces. He had no outstanding rivals since Kim Young-sam had joined the establishment. Kim Dae-jung realised that he could not become president unless he changed his image and the conservative middle-class elements accepted him as a viable leader. Since 1988, this was exactly what he had been trying to accomplish. First, he began to bury his image as a radical politician. His attempt to gain the image of moderation began in 1989 when he reversed his position on the issue of an interim appraisal for Roh. He advised Roh not to hold a no-confidence referendum, suggesting that it would undermine political stability. His action alienated the *chaeya* (hard-line dissident) forces, who continually demanded the ousting of the Roh regime. Curiously, Kim Young-sam sided with the hard-liners during the referendum controversy.

Kim Dae-jung often said that 'his image was shaped by Park and Chun for 20 years. It cannot be changed overnight. The most important task is to shed the 20-year old image.'[45] He wanted to show what he believed was his real self — a charismatic and compassionate politician.[46] Kim Dae-jung smiled and used humour, realising its importance as a tactic to make people like him. The new Kim Dae-jung plan also included deemphasising regionalism. Kim Dae-jung linked his policies to interest groups and talked less about the need to end military rule and human rights violations. Instead, he concentrated on boosting the nation's sagging economy. He presented a detailed plan for solving the nation's economic problems entitled 'How to Overcome the National Economic Crisis' to the Korea Newspaper Editors' Association in April 1992.[47] In it, he turned his attention to price stability, regaining a competitive edge in foreign trade, promoting small and medium-sized firms, fostering peaceful relations between labour and management and the strengthening of domestic technological levels. He was shown learning how to operate a computer on television. While Kim Young-sam was bogged down in factional feuding within his party, Kim Dae-jung was seen attending seminars and frequently giving talks, proving that he was presidential timber, knowledgeable about politics, diplomacy, economics and Korean unification. He even contributed a statesman-like article to the American journal, *Foreign Policy*.[48]

To set himself apart from Kim Young-sam, Kim Dae-jung emphasised his four supposed qualities: honesty, morality, leadership and economic knowledge.[49] Of course, this implied that Kim Young-sam lacked morality and was ignorant of economic problems. Kim Dae-jung also stressed character differences between himself and Kim Young-sam. He emphasised his devotion to democracy and painted Kim Young-sam as a lackey of the military who gave up the crusade for democracy and broke his promise to the people to pursue his own ambition for power.[50]

To woo the military and the conservative elements, Kim Dae-jung nominated four ex-generals and ten businessmen — traditionally the sort of people who would oppose him — to run in the March elections, and did not press charges on the vote-rigging reported in some army units. His appeasement policy worked. Even Chun Doo-hwan gave Kim Dae-jung a rare positive appraisal for his moderate political stance.[51]

In order to shed the image that he only represented the Honam region, he made major concessions to Lee Ki-taek, who broke away from Kim Young-sam at the time of the DLP merger. In 1991, Lee's minor party, known as the Democratic Party, merged with Kim Dae-jung's Party for Peace and Democracy (PPD). Kim Dae-jung accepted Lee's suggestion that the merged party be named the Democratic Party. Lee and his followers were from Pusan and the Yongnam region and were disenchanted with Kim Young-sam and the ruling party. To lure Lee's followers into his party, Kim Dae-jung made Lee co-chairman of the merged party. In June 1992, Kim Dae-jung promised that he would hand over party leadership to Lee as his political successor, regardless of what happened in the December presidential election,[52] a promise he kept in 1993. Kim Dae-jung also succeeded in bringing into his party some former dissidents representing *chaeya* forces, including such prominent leaders as Lee Boo-young, one of the few dissidents who is widely respected for his views on clean politics.

Kim Dae-jung believed that a number of factors favoured his election to the presidency. First, the military changed: political generals were a thing of the past. Kim even gave credit to Chun for stepping down after seven years in office. Second, the TK group failed to come up with its own leader, and so the ruling establishment was badly split. Third, business groups turned against the government. The tension between the Hyundai Group and the government was a case in point. Moreover, the *chaebol* groups did not necessarily oppose Kim Dae-jung's election. Fourth, regionalism was weakened because of Kim's successful merger with Lee Ki-taek's party. Fifth, Roh's domestic policies failed and the creation of the ruling mega-party in 1990 failed to confront economic stagnation, rising crime, rampant corruption, political instability and social disorder.[53] He believed that he had a better chance of winning this time than in his previous attempts, insisting that he could defeat Kim Young-sam if a 'fair election is guaranteed'.[54]

Also, Kim Dae-jung was encouraged by the fact that his party increased the number of seats it held in the National Assembly from 71 to 97 in the March elections, whereas the DLP's seats declined from 213 to 149.[55] Though the Democratic Party did not gain a single seat in the Yongnam area, its overall vote total increased. For example, during the April 1988 elections, Kim Dae-jung's party gained only 1.9 per cent of the vote there, but in 1992 it received 19.4 per cent there. Also, in North Chungchong in 1988, the PPD gained only 0.4 per cent, but this time it netted 23.8 per cent.

Despite these impressive changes and gains, Kim Dae-jung faced powerful opposition in the Yongnam region, as well as from former refugees from North Korea and from the middle and upper classes. There was a strong undercurrent of anti-Kim Dae-jung sentiment left over from the past era.

Kim Dae-jung's campaign theme was 'change of government' and 'grand national reconciliation'. Intellectuals and the young voters believed that he was the best candidate. Kim Dae-jung was the favourite candidate among foreign correspondents and received a good press coverage abroad. During the campaign, Kim Dae-jung sought an alliance with dissident groups — the National Council of Student Representatives, the National Farmers' Council, the National Teachers' Union and the National Federation of Trade Unions. To discredit his moves, the government revealed a massive North Korean spy network operating in South Korea and implicated one of Kim Dae-jung's aides. Though Kim Dae-jung apologised for the incident, the DLP charged that Kim Dae-jung, in alliance with pro-north Korean dissidents, threatened the very foundation of the nation.[56] This debate over Kim Dae-jung's political colour resulted in ideological and ethical charges being levelled between the two Kims. About 4.2 million copies of a booklet by the DLP slandering opposition candidates — Kim Dae-jung and Chung Ju-yung — depicted Kim Dae-jung riding on two horses — one bearing the sign of the new Kim Dae-jung and the National Federation of Juche Thought Factions and the second horse carrying the North Korean flag.[57] At the same time, he promised that he would form an advisory panel with ex-presidents Choi Kyu-ha, Chun Doo-hwan and Roh Tae-woo, to achieve a grand national reconciliation if elected.[58] Kim Dae-jung thus tried desperately to be accepted by all elements in society. He even resigned from his party post, promising to end his political career if defeated. He used this as his final card during the campaign.

Chung Ju-Yung and *daekwon*

Some Korean voters were tired of the protracted *daekwon* game in the ruling and the opposition parties as well as the corruption in political campaigns. They were tired of the continuing Kyongsang and Cholla provincial antagonism symbolised by the protracted dominance of the two Kims. They were also disappointed with high inflation and sluggish exports, frightened of increasing crime, and uneasy about labor unrest. Thus many people yearned for viable, alternative presidential candidates.

A number of factors were responsible for the emergence of Hyundai founder Chung Ju-yung as a *daekwon* challenger. First, many felt that Korea's *chaebol* (giant, family-owned business conglomerates) had grown too big for the government to control, and two decades of symbiotic ties had failed to provide a secure basis for economic growth. In exchange for contracts and credit, the *chaebol* made large cash donations to the ruling party. Chung, for instance, admitted he paid $40 million to Roh. At the same time, the *chaebol* have become increasingly critical of the government's heavy-handed control, from production to prices and loans. Tension between the government and the *chaebol* sector reached its climax in November 1991, when Chung publicly defied the government by refusing to pay penalty taxes levied on him and several of Hyundai's subsidiaries.[59]

Second, many in Korea did not take Roh very seriously. He was portrayed in the news media as incompetent, in sharp contrast to his positive image abroad. He was often criticised more harshly than his predecessors were because people were able to voice their opinions more freely than under the Park and Chun regimes.

Third, the DLP merger in 1990 and the consolidation of the opposition parties in 1991 left many politicians with nowhere to go. They needed a third party to join. Chung Ju-yung's political debut was welcomed by those disenchanted with current politics. Several million people nationwide are dependent on Hyundai for their livelihood. Chung quickly transformed them into his political cadres. Using the best and most efficient staff of the Hyundai company, Chung created a boom in less than two months after the establishment of his Unification National Party (UNP). In the March elections, the UNP obtained 32 seats in the National Assembly, receiving 17.4 per cent of the total votes. Chung, likened to Ross Perot in the United States, promised to 'get the job done' quickly. For instance, he would provide apartments at half the current prices, turn the $10 billion trade deficit into a $30 billion surplus within a couple of years, and boost the per capita income from the present $6000 to $20 000 in five years.[60]

Chung often demonstrated a predilection to reduce complex realities to simple statements. When asked about how he would run the country with only 32 seats in the legislative branch, he said he would dissolve the National Assembly.[61] Asked what he would do to achieve unification, he snapped 'absorption'. [62] Asked how he would win the presidency in December facing the formidable two Kims, he said, 'Voters in 1987 thought Roh would make a better president than the two Kims. Roh has plunged the nation into misery. Why should people vote for the two Kims who are less than Roh?'[63] His message was very simple: give me *daekwon* and I will fix the economy, get rid of corruption and inefficient government and politics, revitalise national education, and unify the country. His performance in debates, press conferences and seminars, some believed, was better than that of the two Kims. His positive spirit, down-to-earth statements and accomplishments (a rags-to-riches story from labourer to Korea's richest business tycoon) appealed to many voters who were tired of stalemated politics.

During the March elections, the Roh government feared Chung's infant party more than the opposition DP. The government constantly attacked Hyundai in an attempt to cut off its financial channels to Chung and thereby cripple the UNP. The police arrested his son and a half-dozen Hyundai executives on charges of tax evasion. However, the government's crackdown on the UNP only helped Chung to be perceived as an underdog. Chung warned that the government's 'politically' motivated suppression of his business groups would ruin the nation's economy. The government treated the UNP the same way during the December presidential election.

Despite his simple appeal, Chung was a novice in the complex world of politics, a ground more familiar to the two Kims. Some believed that Chung was an 'embodiment of contradictions: an uncommonly informal and unpretentious guy but also an authoritarian boss called the King chairman'.[64] Because of his authoritarian tendency, the UNP's top officials — Chough Yoon-hyung and Kim Kwang-il — left the party. After the presidential election, the UNP's number two man, Kim Dong-kil, also decided to leave, precipitating its dissolution.

Chung's inexperience in politics cost him dearly. His remark that the government should tolerate a communist party and his insistence that the national security laws breached freedom of thought shocked the nation. His statement that South Korea should leave the North Korean nuclear issue to the International Atomic Energy Agency was widely ridiculed.[65] The furore over these remarks was a severe blow to his presidential aspirations. Though he was encouraged by the polls indicating that people wanted the next president to solve Korea's economic problems, simple, arithmetic realities prevented his election to the presidency. Both Kims had fixed regional blocs, and Kim Young-sam had a larger bloc because his region was more populous.

For Chung to have any chance, he had to garner more than 20 per cent of the vote in all provinces and corral at least 60 per cent of the vote in Seoul. This proved impossible.

Chung made tremendous efforts to recruit some of the prominent DLP legislators to join his party in order to stop Kim Young-sam from becoming president. He tried to recruit Park Tae-joon, but failed. Chung's attempt to recruit Kim Bok-dong, a relative of Roh, touched off a political fury for several days in the middle of November when Kim was pressured by the Blue House to remain in the DLP. Roh's neutrality was tarnished, but eventually Kim joined the UNP.

In early December, there was an upsurge in support of Chung's candidacy threatening Kim Young-sam's chance to become president. Many thought that he could absorb 20–25 per cent of the total votes, and some 50 per cent of the undecided voters. In fact, Chung began to draw more crowds during his stumping rallies in various parts of the country than the two Kims. The Kim Young-sam camp, dismayed and even bewildered by the growth in Chung's support, decided to attack Chung rather than Kim Dae-jung. Although the government was supposed to stay neutral, it collided head-on with the UNP on 4 December. On 5 December 1992, a female accounting clerk working for Hyundai Heavy Industries revealed to the press that Hyundai had a secret fund for the UNP. By this time, the Hyundai probe had emerged as the key election issue. The extensive investigation conducted into the massive involvement of Hyundai Business Groups in electioneering on behalf of Chung provoked a severe controversy about the impartiality of the Roh government. Prosecution and tax authorities embarked on a full-scale probe of Hyundai subsidiaries. A few executives were arrested for forcing their employees to campaign for Chung. Kim Young-sam and the government believed that it was better to stop Chung's clandestine vote-buying activities than worry about the neutrality of the government in this election. In fact, Chung's ability to carry on his campaign was severely limited due to the government's massive intervention. Both the UNP and DP joined hands in countering offensives against the government for its 'biased' investigation of the Hyundai Group. Also, the public in general was sympathetic to Chung at this stage of the game. Chung responded by staging a massive outdoor rally at Yoido Plaza in Seoul on 12 December to denounce the government and nearly a half to one million supporters (mostly mobilised) of Chung braved the snow and rain to attend.

Furthermore, the UNP revealed just a few days before the election that the mayor of Pusan, together with the chief of police, the head of intelligence and other pro-government agency heads in Pusan, secretly gathered on 11 December to discuss how to help Kim Young-sam win. This meeting was presided over by former Minister of Justice Kim Ki-chun, who stressed the need to capitalise on regionalism, urging the local heads to exert efforts to help Kim Young-sam.[66] This jolted Kim Young-sam's campaign. But it turned out that an official of the Agency for National Security and several Hyundai officials were involved in making an illegal tape recording of the Pusan secret meeting in exchange for money. As a result, Chung's UNP was completely discredited, and his attempt to purchase the presidency with money was further demonstrated. In fact, during the presidential campaign, which was officially kicked off on 21 November, front pages of the vernacular dailies were flooded with articles on corrupt practices aimed at buying votes. All three major parties were accused of doling out wrist watches and other gifts. The UNP was hit hardest, followed by the DLP and the DP in that order.

Conclusion

The December 1992 presidential election was unique in that the verdict showed that political grafting *did* work. The election was also unique in that it took place at a time when the ruling party was as badly split as the opposition parties had been in the past. The political stakes were much higher for Kim Young-sam than for Kim Dae-jung. Kim Young-sam's failure in December could have resulted in the breakdown of the ruling party but it also could have undermined his place in history. Kim Young-sam won and emerged as the most successful politician in modern Korean history.

The December election took place in the context of significant changes in the relationship between the Korean state and civil society. There was no Park, Chun or Roh with a power base in the state apparatus seeking *daekwon*, and the military's veto power over civilian politics had been eliminated. *Daekwon* aspirants had to persuade the voters. The revitalisation of Korean society has been in the making for the past 30 years as Korea's export-oriented economic development has accelerated the growth of a private sector and pluralised society. The state is no longer completely insulated from civil society, as it was under Park or Chun. Many Koreans today believe that the private sector and interest groups can make better decisions than can the state.[67] The phenomenon of Chung Ju-yung was not abnormal in this sense. His attack on the effects of state interference in business management commenced with the inauguration of Roh in 1988.

The ruling party came close to defeat in 1971, 1978, 1985 and 1987. To prevent future defeats, the ruling party grafted part of the democratic forces on to itself by merging with Kim Young-sam's party and nominating him as its presidential candidate. Kim Young-sam's nomination was made possible because of the ruling party's inability to continue the pre-1987 style politics. Kim took advantage of the ruling party's fatal weakness — the cracks in the ruling TK establishment and its inability to come up with its own leader — by holding the future of the party hostage.

Clearly, Kim Young-sam was not Roh's preference for a successor, but in the end Roh accepted Kim. If he had picked Park Tae-joon, the caretaker of the DLP faction, it might have destroyed the party and the DLP would have been a sure loser in the December election. For Roh, the most important consideration was to avoid the break-up of the DLP and prolong the life of the ruling party beyond 1993.

The significance of the 18 December election is that it ended the 32-year legitimacy controversy: student demonstrations, self-immolation and tear-gas almost vanished. It also meant the end of the drama of the two Kims who had dominated Korean politics since the early 1970s.

A number of factors determined the outcome of the December presidential election. Kim Young-sam had five advantages. First, he was strongly supported in the Yongnam region, which includes two of Korea's major cities — Pusan and Taegu. This region has roughly 8.5 million voters compared with the 3.5 million in the Honam region, the power base of Kim Dae-jung. Thus Kim Young-sam started out with many more potential votes than Kim Dae-jung. Second, Kim Young-sam was also strong in small towns. Third, Korean voters over 40 years of age have always favoured the ruling party. Fourth, lower class people, farmers and fishing communities generally favoured the ruling party. Fifth, Kim was favoured by those people who believe that Roh succeeded in democratisation and by those who supported the merger of the three parties in 1990.[68]

However, Kim also had serious weaknesses. First, he was running on the negative record of Roh. Second, there was the widely-held perception that he lacked a clear vision of how he would govern the country if elected, and that he was a poor speaker unable to articulate his views clearly. Third, he faced enemies, such as the diehard anti-Kim forces within the ruling establishment who were determined to undermine his aspirations for *daekwon*. Finally, there was the perception that Kim Young-sam's ability to effectively bring about reforms was limited because he was politically indebted to too many establishment politicians.

Kim Dae-jung enjoyed the absolute support of the Honam region and maintained a slight edge in Seoul. He also had the support of students, people in their twenties and thirties, and those with a higher education. He was also supported by those who believed that Roh failed to democratise Korea and by those who were unhappy with the merger of the three parties.[69]

Once in office, President Kim Young-sam has had to face enormous political, social, and economic problems, including sagging exports, high interest rates and land prices, Seoul's traffic and pollution problems, the need to restructure Korea's industry and distribution systems, volatile party politics and parliamentary instability, and the unresolved problem of inter-Korean relations and North Korean nuclear proliferation. All these have tested his abilities. South Korea's politics of *daekwon* was a limited preparation for these tasks, since it was not about which candidate, if elected, could best handle them. It was a highly emotional and ultimately personalised contest.

Notes

1 See Kim Hyun-chong, 'Daekwon Game Ei Shin Gamsang Bup [New Way of Looking at the Presidential Election Game]', *Wolgan Chungang*, May 1992, pp. 239–42.
2 Kim Hyun-chong, 'Daekwon Game', p. 242.
3 James Cotton, 'Understanding the State in South Korea: Bureaucratic–Authoritarian or State Autonomy Theory?', *Comparative Political Studies*, vol. 24, January 1992, pp. 527–29.
4 Manwoo Lee, *The Odyssey of Korean Democracy: Korean Politics, 1987–1990*, New York: Praeger Publishers, p. 5.
5 Barrington Moore Jr, *Social Origins of Dictatorship and Democracy*, Boston: Beacon Press, 1966, p. 414.
6 See Son Bong-sook, '14dae Kookhoewewon Sunkuh Wa Siminwundong [The 14th National Assembly Elections and the Civil Movement]', paper presented at the Korean Political Science Association conference, Kyongju, Korea, 3 July 1992; *Korea Herald*, 14 January 1992, p. 12.
7 *New York Times*, 19 July 1987.
8 *Korea Times*, 17 June 1992.
9 See Lee Chung-hee, 'Hankuk, Eeikjipdan Ei Sunkuh Julryak Yeunku [A Study of the Election Strategy of Korean Interest Groups]', paper presented at the Korean Political Science Association Conference, Kyongju, Korea, 3 July 1992.
10 See Young-ki Kwon, 'Kunbu Saeryuk kwa Minjusaeryuk Ei Hwahakjuk Kyulhap [A Chemical Fusion between the Military and the Democratic Camp]', *Wolgan Choson*, June 1992, pp. 172–91.
11 *Korea Times*, 18 February 1992.
12 *Korea Times*, 28 December 1991.
13 *Hankuk Ilbo*, 28 September 1990.
14 *Hankuk Ilbo*, 1 November 1990.
15 Kim Doo-woo, 'Kim Young-sam Bijang Ei Mukinun [Kim Young-sam's Secret Weapons]', *Wolgan Chungang*, June 1992, p. 164. See also Young-ki Kwon, 'Kunbu Saeryuk', p. 185.

16 *Hankuk Ilbo*, 15 July 1991.
17 *Hangyore Shinmun*, 31 October 1991; *Chosen Ilbo*, 18 October 1991.
18 *Korea Herald*, 5 August 1991.
19 *Korea Times*, 31 July 1991.
20 *Korea Herald*, 24 December 1991.
21 *Korea Herald*, 12 January 1992.
22 *Korea Herald*, 16 January 1992.
23 *Korea Times*, 19 March 1992.
24 *Korea Times*, 27 March 1992.
25 *Korea Herald*, 29 March 1992. An official at the Blue House and a confidant of Kim Young-sam told the author that Roh's decision to make Kim his successor was finalised around the end of 1991.
26 *Korea Herald*, 4 April 1992.
27 See Huh Nam-jin, 'Roh Tae-woo Ei Y.S. Daekwon Mandulki [The Making of President YS by Roh Tae-woo]', *Wolgan Chungang*, May, 1992, p. 141.
28 Huh Nam-jin, 'Roh Tae-woo', p. 142.
29 *Korea Times,* 10 April 1992.
30 *Korea Newsreview*, 25 April 1992.
31 A poll conducted by Korea Research and the *Illyo Shinmun* showed that Lee got 36.9 per cent and Kim Young-sam 31.2 per cent when the respondents were asked whom they liked as candidates. The respondents, however, also answered that Kim would be nominated. See Kim Hyun-chong, 'Roh Tae-woo Eh Banki Dun Lee Chong-chan Ei Guesan [The Calculations of Lee Chong-jan, who Raised a Flag of Revolt against Roh Tae-woo]', *Wolgan Chungang*, June 1992, p. 242.
32 *Korea Times*, 26 April 1992.
33 *Korea Herald*, 22 April 1992.
34 *Korea Herald*, 2 May 1992.
35 *Korea Herald*, 15 May 1992.
36 *Korea Herald*, 19 May 1992.
37 *Korea Herald*, 28 June 1992.
38 *Korea Times*, 19 September 1992.
39 *Korea Times*, 22 September 1992.
40 After the December presidential election, Chung Ju-yung refused to endorse the merger between Lee's party and his.
41 See *Choson Ilbo*, 20 December 1992. Korea's major opinion survey centres such as Korea Gallup, Korea Research and Media Research all showed a similar trend.
42 Conversation with Professor Park Chan Wook, Political Science Professor at Seoul National University, who is a leading expert in election analysis, 6 January 1992.
43 Conversation with Professor Park Chan Wook, 6 January 1992.
44 Conversation with Lee Ki-taek, 17 December 1992.
45 Kim Dong-chul et al., 'Kim Young-sam Kim Dae-jung Chung Ju-yung Ei

Jakum Jojik Dunoe [Money, Organisation and Brains of Kim Young-sam, Kim Dae-jung and Chung Ju-yung]', *Shin Dong-A*, June 1992, p. 173.

46 Kim Dong-chul et al., 'Kim Young-sam'.

47 *Korea Times,* 11 April 1992.

48 See his article entitled 'The Once and Future Korea', *Foreign Policy*, Spring 1992, pp. 40-55.

49 Kim Dong-chul et al., 'Kim Young-sam', p. 175.

50 Kim Dae-jung's speech at the Korean Political Science Association meeting, Kyongju, Korea, 3 July 1992; *Korean Herald*, 5 July 1992.

51 *Korea Times,* 14 June 1992.

52 *Korea Times,* 6 June 1992.

53 See Kwon Young-ki, 'Interview with Kim Dae-jung', *Wolgan Choson*, June 1992, pp. 227–43.

54 Conversation with Kim Dae-jung, 3 July 1992, Kyongju, South Korea.

55 The DLP has more than 149 now because some independent lawmakers joined the DLP.

56 *Korea Times*, 15 December 1992.

57 *Korea Times*, 13 December 1992.

58 *Korea Times,* November 28, 1992.

59 *Korea Herald*, 31 December 1991. Hyundai was ordered to pay 131.1 billion *won* in back taxes on stock trading.

60 Chung's speech at the Korean Political Science Association meeting, Kyongju, Choson Hotel, 4 July 1992.

61 Conversation with Chung Ju-yung, Ramada Olympia Hotel, 2 May 1992. Under the current Constitution the president does not have the authority to dissolve the National Assembly.

62 Chung's speech at the KPSA meeting, Kyongju, 4 July 1992.

63 Chung's speech at the KPSA meeting, Kyongju, 4 July 1992.

64 Choe Sang-hun, 'Chung J.Y. Sets Out to be Savior of Economy', *Korea Herald*, 5 July 1992.

65 *Korea Herald*, 17 June 1992.

66 *Hankuk Ilbo*, 16 December1992.

67 Carter J. Eckert, 'The South Korean Bourgeoisie: A Class in Search of Hegemony', *The Journal of Korean Studies*, vol. 7, 1990, p. 126.

68 See Park Chan Wook, 'Jae 14Dae Kukhoeiwon Chongsunkuehsuhei Jungdangjiji Bunsuk [An Analysis of Party Support in the 14th National Assembly]', paper presented at the Korean Political Science Association meeting, 2 July 1992, Kyongju, Korea, pp. 24–27.

69 Park Chan Wook, 'Jae 14Dae Kukhoeiwon'.

4

Continuity or Change: The Voter's Choice in the 1992 Presidential Election

Bae Sun-kwang

Introduction

In the fourteenth presidential election held on 18 December 1992, the ruling Democratic Liberal Party (DLP) candidate, Kim Young-sam, won a five-year single-term presidency in a contest with his long-time arch-rival, Kim Dae-jung, the Democratic Party (DP) candidate. The election was, one way or another, to result in a civilian government, ending nearly three decades of rule by presidents from a military background. On this occasion, none of the candidates, including the ruling party candidate, were military figures. The election campaign was also fairly managed without significant evidence of government interference or election rigging.[1] It was the second presidential election since the direct election system had been restored in 1987 (along with other democratic measures), and perhaps it was the first time in Korean electoral history that the election outcome was readily accepted by the people as well as by the defeated candidates.

The electoral victory of Kim Young-sam was a resounding one. Kim Young-sam won almost 10 million of a total about 24 million votes (about 42.0 per cent), while Kim Dae-jung won about 8 million votes (33.8 per cent).[2] The election was in general expected to be a closer contest, given that the ruling DLP, which was formed in early 1990 by the merger of three parties — the Democratic Justice Party led by Roh Tae-woo, the Reunification Democratic Party led by Kim Young-sam, and the New Democratic Republican Party led by Kim Jong-pil — polled merely 38.5 per cent of the votes in the fourteenth National Assembly election on 24 March 1992.[3] The DLP, which had commanded more than 70 per cent of the Assembly members before that election, scarcely secured a majority of the seats (149 out of a total 299), partly because of the successful emergence of the Unification National Party (UNP) led by a big businessman, Chung Ju-yung, which commanded 31 seats, and partly due to the winning of 21 seats by independents, who altogether polled 11.5 per cent of the votes. The main opposition, the DP, regained its strength by securing about one-third of the seats from its prior share of one-fourth. Contrary to expectations, however, Kim Young-sam further improved the electoral performance of the DLP, and took a sound lead with a margin of nearly 2 million votes over Kim Dae-jung in the presidential election.

The Korean voters, who had delivered what was apparently a protest vote against the arbitrary party realignment of the ruling DLP several months previously, this time approved (at least tacitly, if not resolutely) that party's presidential candidate. Who, then, supported Kim Young-sam, and who voted for the other party candidates? In other words, what are the main characteristics of their respective supporters? More fundamentally, are there changes or continuities in the pattern of party preferences compared with the past? These are questions asked in this chapter, which is framed to explore the nature of Kim Young-sam's electoral victory by utilising empirical data provided by a nationwide sample survey.[4] Apart from the voting choice variables, the variables of education and residential region are selected as explanatory variables in this paper, because these variables are the most effective indicators of long-observed patterns of voter alignment in Korea — that is, the urban–rural dimension of voter alignment, and the regional proclivity in voting choice. Detailed discussions regarding the selection of those variables will be included in the respective sections.

The party preferences of the voters: Continuity or change?

Since the last presidential and assembly elections, Korean political parties had gone through party realignment.[5] On 22 January 1990, Roh Tae-woo, Kim Young-sam and Kim Jong-pil jointly announced the merger of their party machines and the creation of the ruling DLP, thus leaving only Kim Dae-jung's Party for Peace and Democracy (PPD) in opposition. Although party realignment or changes in the party affiliation of politicians had not been uncommon in Korean political history, the wholesale merger of the ruling and the opposition parties was an unprecedented step. Indeed, party realignments were rather common among the opposition parties whose intention was to strengthen their electoral fortunes for upcoming elections, while cross-changes of party affiliations among the ruling and the main opposition party politicians were rather exceptional and usually the result of personal factors.

In retrospect, the DLP merger was somewhat successful. The party secured (albeit tenuously) a majority of the Assembly seats, and managed to have its presidential candidate elected. Thus the DLP was able to continue its hold on power for a further five years. However, in terms of vote distribution, its success was a limited one. That is, the DLP's overall share of the votes deteriorated remarkably in the 1992 elections, compared with the performance of the party's components before the merger — for example, the (former) constituents of the DLP altogether had polled about 73 per cent of the votes both in the 1987 and 1988 elections, but its share of the votes was reduced to far less than two-thirds of the former share of its constituents in the 1992 elections. It is necessary to determine, therefore, who remained with the party and who deserted. Table 4.1 shows how voting choices in 1987 were distributed in the elections of 1992.[6]

Panel 1 of Table 4.1 shows how the voting choices in 1987 were distributed in the 1992 National Assembly election, and Panel 2 shows the distribution in the 1992 presidential elections. First of all, the support for Kim Dae-jung was quite consistent: most of those who had supported Kim Dae-jung in 1987 stayed in the 1992 elections — about 83 per cent in the Assembly election and about 90 per cent in the presidential election. Further, his DP gained some support from the former Kim Young-sam voters in the Assembly election (22.7 per cent), and in the presidential election he attained about 10 per cent of net gains from the former Kim Young-sam votes.

Contrary to this situation, Kim Young-sam suffered a severe loss among his supporters of 1987.[7] More than half of his 1987 voters deserted in the 1992 Assembly election (44.5 per cent of his former voters stayed with the DLP), and nearly half of them behaved likewise in the presidential election of 1992 (about 57 per cent continued to support him). Interestingly enough, the main beneficiaries of those switching support were the DP in the Assembly election, and Chung Ju-yung in the presidential election. The Roh Tae-woo votes of 1987 largely stayed with the DLP (59.9 per cent) and its candidate, Kim Young-sam (65.6 per cent). The main beneficiaries of the

Table 4.1 *Changes in voting choice between the 1987 presidential election and the 1992 national assembly and presidential elections*

	Roh87	YS87	DJ87	JP87	Non-voters	Mean (N)
[1]						
DLP92	59.9%(286)	44.5%(101)	6.0%(19)	39.3%(20)	24.0%(51)	37.0%(478)
DP92	9.8%(47)	22.7%(51)	82.6%(267)	8.5%(4)	27.9% (59)	33.2% (429)
UNP92	13.0%(62)	18.2%(41)	3.8%(12)	20.4%(10)	7.6%(16)	11.0%(142)
Others	7.2%(35)	6.8%(16)	1.2%(4)	9.5%(5)	7.4%(16)	5.8%(75)
Non-voters	10.1%(48)	7.7%(18)	6.5%(21)	22.3%(11)	33.1%(70)	13.1%(169)
[2]						
YS92	65.6%(314)	56.9%(129)	2.6%(8)	43.4%(22)	32.8%(70)	42.0%(543)
DJ92	8.5%(41)	12.5%(28)	89.7%(290)	12.0%(6)	33.8%(72)	33.8%(437)
JY92	20.3%(97)	20.6%(47)	5.6%(18)	28.4%(15)	16.3%(35)	16.3%(211)
Others	5.6%(27)	10.1%(23)	2.2%(7)	16.2%(8)	17.1%(36)	7.9%(101)
Mean (N)	37.0%(479)	17.5%(227)	25.0%(323)	4.0%(51)	16.5%(213)	100%(1292)

Note. Roh – RohTae-woo; YS – Kim Young-sam; DJ – Kim Dae-jung; JP – Kim Jong-pil; JY – Chung Ju-yung

switchers were the UNP and Chung Ju-yung. Far less than half of the former Kim Jong-pil votes stayed with the DLP and its presidential candidate (39.3 per cent and 43.4 per cent respectively). The main beneficiaries of those switchers were again the UNP and its presidential candidate.

In examining this table, there are a number of points to be emphasised, in terms of changes to or continuities in voter preferences. First, there is a singular continuity in Kim Dae-jung votes — Kim Dae-jung and Kim Young-sam ran in both presidential elections of 1987 and 1992. That is, there were few flow-out votes, and also minimal flow-in votes, in Kim Dae-jung's personal or party votes. The only substantial flow-in of votes came from the non-voters, a majority of whom were new voters. Thus it can be said that Kim Dae-jung was successful on the one hand in maintaining his support, but at the same time failed in broadening his basis of support.

Second, there is also continuity in the votes of Roh Tae-woo. Nearly two-thirds of his supporters in 1987 stayed with the new DLP and its presidential candidate. This is quite remarkable, considering the fact that Roh had withdrawn from his membership of the DLP before the presidential election. These are, perhaps, core governing-party supporters, who may have voted for the DLP irrespective of the candidate nominated by the party.

Third, by joining the ruling DLP, Kim Young-sam alienated a significant proportion of his former supporters. Indeed, in the 1992 presidential election, he won a greater following from among those who had formerly been Roh supporters than from his own former supporters. Even though it may not have been possible for the DLP to stay in power without the additional support of former Kim Young-sam followers (and, to a lesser degree, from the former Kim Jong-pil voters), it is apparent that Kim Young-sam was more successful in wooing the Roh supporters of 1987 (these perhaps traditional governing-party supporters), than in maintaining his former supporters or in attracting new voters. The non-voters in 1987, of whom a large portion consisted of new voters, voted for him far less than the national average.

Finally, the newcomer, Chung Ju-yung and his UNP, attracted a majority of the defectors from the DLP — indeed, in this respect they were much more successful than Kim Dae-jung and his party. In a sense, the general expectation that Chung Ju-yung and his party would erode the basis of the governing party was correct insofar as Chung and his party were the main beneficiaries of the defection. However, it may also have been the case that Chung and his party denied the opposition party the chance of victory. That is, although there was little defection from Kim Dae-jung voters to Chung and his party, the switchers among the former Kim Young-sam and Kim Jong-pil supporters — perhaps those whose orientations were closest to the opposition — would otherwise have gone to Kim Dae-jung if Chung had not been a candidate. Indeed, Chung and his UNP attracted more switchers from among the Kim Young-sam and Kim Jong-pil supporters than from the supporters of Roh Tae-woo. Thus the electoral victory of Kim Young-sam can be attributed to the fact that, as Darcy et al. once rightly observed, 'the opposition tendency in the electorate, being more negative against the government rather than positive toward a particular party, will be more fragmented and unstable from election to election'.[8]

In short, there has been continuity as much as change. The DLP merger resulted in some changes in the electoral behaviour of the supporters of its former constituents (i.e., supporters of Kim Young-sam and Kim Jong-pil) on the one hand, but, on the other, had little effect on the supporters of Roh Tae-woo. The switchers, their behaviour resulting from the DLP merger, largely went to the newcomer, Chung Ju-yung and his party, rather than to the main opposition, Kim Dae-jung and his DP. Kim Dae-jung obviously failed to attract the defectors among the former Kim Young-sam (and Kim Jong-pil) supporters. He succeeded, however, in maintaining his strong, but limited, basis of support. In the following sections, the nature of the change in the voting choice will be discussed by closely examining some characteristics of the voters.

Regional strongholds of electoral support

From the presidential election of 1987 onwards, Korean voters have exhibited profound regional differences in the pattern of their support.[9] During the election campaign of 1987, all of the four main presidential candidates exploited regionalism by emphasising their own regional attachment or denouncing the other candidates' regional attachments. Indeed, the four candidates performed exclusively well in their home provinces: Roh Tae-woo in North Kyongsang (Kyongbuk), Kim Young-sam in South Kyongsang (Kyongnam), Kim Dae-jung in Cholla, and Kim Jong-pil in Chungchong. This pattern was replicated in the following National Assembly election of 1988.

In the 1992 National Assembly election, which was held after the DLP merger and the subsequent merger of the opposition DP, this pattern of regional voting was again manifest. Although the change of leadership to Kim Young-sam within the DLP resulted in some defections, especially in North Kyongsang and Chungchong, such defections only favoured the UNP or independents whose orientations were close to that of the ruling DLP. The regional distribution of the DP votes was almost the same as that of 1987 and 1988.

Table 4.2 Voting choices between the 1987 and 1992 presidential elections by region.

		[1] YS92	[2] DJ92	[3] JY92	[4] Mean (N)
[1] Roh87		65.5% (314)	8.5% (41)	20.3% (97)	37.0% (478)
	Seoul	67.0%(51)	8.9%(7)	18.0%(14)	23.2%(76)
	Kyonggi	53.0%(61)	9.0%(10)	32.5%(38)	46.6%(116)
	Kangwon	69.1%(16)	6.8%(2)	15.5%(4)	55.8%(24)
	Chungchong	62.1%(41)	9.7%(6)	20.4%(14)	52.0%(66)
	Cholla	32.3%(4)	67.7%(9)	0.0%(0)	7.3%(13)
	Kyongbuk	70.3%(65)	3.9%(4)	19.7%(18)	63.4%(92)
	Kyongnam	81.8%(75)	3.5%(3)	11.3%(10)	41.4%(92)
[2] YS87		56.9% (129)	12.5% (28)	20.6% (47)	17.5% (226)
	Seoul	47.4%(32)	8.2%(6)	30.7%(21)	20.8%(68)
	Kyonggi	49.4%(18)	17.5%(6)	25.1%(9)	14.5%(37)
	Kangwon	36.2%(4)	7.8%(1)	56.0%(6)	25.6%(11)
	Chungchong	39.3%(7)	21.6%(4)	24.2%(4)	13.4%(17)
	Cholla	33.4%(1)	66.6%(2)	0.0%(0)	1.7%(3)
	Kyongbuk	46.1%(13)	23.8%(7)	17.4%(5)	19.3%(28)
	Kyongnam	84.8%(54)	5.4%(3)	2.6%(2)	28.8%(64)
[3] DJ87		2.6% (8)	89.7% (290)	5.6% (18)	25.0% (324)
	Seoul	4.3%(4)	84.6%(86)	7.1%(7)	30.9%(101)
	Kyonggi	1.7%(1)	81.3%(34)	17.0%(7)	16.9%(42)
	Kangwon	0.0%(0)	30.4%(1)	49.7%(2)	7.0%(3)
	Chungchong	0.0%(0)	84.8%(11)	15.2%(2)	10.2%(13)
	Cholla	0.5%(1)	99.5%(146)	0.0%(0)	82.1%(147)
	Kyongbuk	48.0%(1)	52.0%(1)	0.0%(0)	1.4%(2)
	Kyongnam	10.8%(2)	73.5%(11)	0.0%(0)	6.8%(15)

[4] JP87		43.4% (22)	12.0% (6)	28.4% (15)	4.0% (51)
	Seoul	44.9%(7)	6.3%(1)	26.4%(4)	4.9%(16)
	Kyonggi	22.6%(3)	17.6%(2)	34.5%(4)	4.4%(11)
	Kangwon	0.0%(0)	0.0%(0)	0.0%(0)	0.0%(0)
	Chungchong	46.0%(10)	14.6%(3)	30.4%(7)	17.3%(22)
	Cholla	0.0%(0)	0.0%(0)	0.0%(0)	0.0%(0)
	Kyongbuk	0.0%(0)	0.0%(0)	0.0%(0)	0.0%(0)
	Kyongnam	100%(3)	0.0%(0)	0.0%(0)	1.4%(3)
[5] Non- Voters		32.8% (70)	33.8% (72)	16.3% (35)	16.5% (213)
	Seoul	27.4%(18)	41.8%(28)	16.9%(11)	20.2%(66)
	Kyonggi	14.5%(6)	35.2%(15)	37.2%(16)	17.3%(43)
	Kangwon	21.1%(1)	0.0%(0)	0.0%(0)	11.6%(5)
	Chungchong	66.0%(6)	19.4%(2)	0.0%(0)	7.1%(9)
	Cholla	0.0%(0)	94.2%(16)	0.0%(0)	9.5%(17)
	Kyongbuk	36.1%(9)	22.6%(5)	8.3%(0)	16.6%(24)
	Kyongnam	61.0%(30)	12.7%(6)	11.4%(6)	22.1%(49)
[6] Mean (N)		42.0% (543)	33.8% (437)	16.3% (211)	100% (1293)
	Seoul	34.4%(113)	38.8%(127)	17.4%(57)	25.3%(327)
	Kyonggi	35.8%(89)	27.3%(68)	29.7%(74)	19.3%(249)
	Kangwon	49.5%(21)	8.0%(3)	26.3%(11)	3.3%(43)
	Chungchong	50.3%(64)	20.5%(26)	20.6%(26)	9.8%(127)
	Cholla	3.2%(6)	96.3%(172)	0.0%(0)	13.9%(179)
	Kyongbuk	59.8%(87)	11.4%(17)	17.2%(25)	11.3%(145)
	Kyongnam	73.5%(164)	10.8%(24)	7.9%(18)	17.2%(222)

*Data excludes non-voters; table excludes minor parties and candidates.

As Line 6 of Table 4.2 indicates, virtually the same pattern of regional voting again appeared in the 1992 presidential election.[10] That is, Kim Dae-jung was strongly favoured only in Cholla, and in Seoul to a modest degree, whereas Kim Young-sam was strongly favoured in North and South Kyongsang, had minimal support from Cholla, and fared relatively well in the other regions. Chung Ju-yung fared far better than the national average of his support in the regions of Kyonggi, Kangwon and Chungchong.

As a consequence of the party merger of 1990, the DLP undoubtedly widened its basis of electoral support across regions. Kim Young-sam performed extremely well in his Kyongnam region and in Roh's stronghold, Kyongbuk, and also maintained substantial support in the other regions except in Cholla. The Democratic Party, which was also formed subsequently by a merger of opposition parties aimed at widening its regional basis of electoral support, had only limited success in realising that objective, however. Kim Dae-jung, who had enjoyed only very limited support in the regions other than Cholla, Seoul and Kyonggi in 1987, improved his support somewhat in those regions except in the Kyongsang region, but this improvement was not substantial enough to gain the presidency. He may not have been able to overcome his strong image of being 'a favourite son' of Cholla. This may have resulted in the relatively good performance by Chung Ju-yung in the other regions, except in Kim Dae-jung's Cholla and in Kim Young-sam's Kyongsang.

Table 4.2, which reports the regional distribution of changes in voter preferences between the 1987 and 1992 presidential elections, well illustrates how regionalism shaped the voters' choice. Line 1 shows that there is little regional variation among those Roh Tae-woo supporters of 1987 who stayed with Kim Young-sam in 1992, except that those in Kyongnam and Kyongbuk stayed with him far beyond the average, and that those in Cholla deserted far more than the average (and mostly went to Kim Dae-jung). Roh's Kyonggi supporters were also notable in that they stayed with Kim less than the average, and most of the deserters went to Chung Ju-yung. The main beneficiary of the switchers was Chung Ju-yung rather than Kim Dae-jung, except in Cholla.

Among the Kim Young-sam supporters of 1987, only those in Kyongnam stayed with him beyond the average in 1992, as Line 2 indicates. A majority of deserters again went to Chung Ju-yung, except in Cholla. As Line 3 shows, most of the Kim Dae-jung supporters of 1987 stayed with him in 1992, with the exception of Kangwon voters, a majority of whom voted for Chung Ju-yung. Overall, Kim Dae-jung enjoyed a solid basis of electoral support, especially among those Cholla voters, virtually all of whom stayed with him. Among the Kim Jong-pil voters,[11] most of those in Kyongnam stayed with the

DLP. The main beneficiary of the defections was again Chung Ju-yung. In addition, among the non-voters of 1987, a majority of Kyongnam and Chungchong voters went to Kim Young-sam in 1992, most of Cholla voters went to Kim Dae-jung and Chung Ju-yung enjoyed the support of Kyonggi voters.

In short, the party realignments of 1990 had little impact on the pattern of regional voting. The DLP was largely able to maintain its constituents' regional strongholds, and thus successfully constrained the DP to its former strongholds. The DP, in spite of its efforts to widen its regional basis of support — for example, Kim Dae-jung did not campaign in Cholla during the 1992 presidential election so as not to cause an adverse reaction from voters in the other regions — virtually failed in overcoming its regional image. Indeed, one of the main factors which resulted in the relative success of the UNP and its presidential candidate may have been the failure of the DP to widen its limited regional basis of electoral support. If there has been a change in the parties' regional strongholds because of the leadership change in the ruling DLP, the change has been limited because of the main opposition's inability to accommodate the defectors. The role of accommodating the defectors was played by a third party in the elections of 1992.

Social basis of electoral support

In most of the past Korean elections, the *yochon yado* phenomenon — that the ruling party gets greater support in less urbanised areas, while the opposition receives much more support in more urbanised areas — was the most frequently observed pattern of voter alignment. Most studies in Korean voting behaviour approach this phenomenon in terms of differences in social composition between the urban and the rural areas. Voters in the urban areas tend to be younger, have higher levels of education and enjoy higher incomes. They are thus are less likely to be satisfied with the existing political system than their counterparts.[12] Thus, in modernised urban areas, 'comprehensive voting' — voting with a high degree of political interest and based on one's own opinions and judgment — is practised, whereas in rural areas, 'conformity voting' — to the various kinds of extensive government interference or instruction — is more common.[13]

One of the difficulties of this kind of approach is that the various social characteristics which distinguish urban and rural dwellers are highly correlated. The younger tend to have higher education, have more white-collar jobs, and tend to be concentrated in the urban areas. Among those social characteristics, education and age may be primary variables, which

Table 4.3 Voting choices between the 1987 and 1992 presidential elections by education

	Education level	[1] YS92	[2] DJ92	[3] JY92	[4] Mean (N)
[1] Roh87		65.6% (314)	8.5% (41)	20.3% (97)	37.0% (478)
	Prim	80.1%(115)	5.1%(17)	12.6%(18)	51.6%(143)
	Mid	74.2%(82)	9.1%(10)	13.7%(15)	50.2%(111)
	High	54.7%(96)	8.4%(15)	27.4%(48)	33.1%(176)
	Univ	42.1%(20)	17.6%(8)	32.2%(15)	18.3%(48)
[2] YS87		56.9% (129)	12.5% (28)	20.6% (47)	17.5% (226)
	Prim	78.6%(18)	12.7%(3)	0.0%(0)	8.3%(23)
	Mid	66.2%(23)	12.2%(2)	15.3%(5)	15.8%(35)
	High	54.3%(50)	15.2%(14)	21.8%(20)	17.5%(93)
	Univ	49.3%(38)	9.3%(7)	27.5%(21)	28.9%(76)
[3] DJ87		2.6% (8)	89.7% (290)	5.6% (18)	25.0% (324)
	Prim	0.9%(1)	96.9%(74)	0.0%(0)	27.4%(76)
	Mid	1.2%(1)	92.7%(54)	6.1%(4)	26.7%(59)
	High	3.6%(5)	84.8%(109)	9.6%(12)	24.3%(129)
	Univ	3.8%(2)	88.0%(53)	3.4%(2)	22.8%(60)
[4] JP87		43.4% (22)	12.0% (6)	28.4% (15)	4.0% (51)
	Prim	76.3%(9)	17.8%(2)	0.0%(0)	4.3%(12)
	Mid	39.1%(2)	0.0%(0)	33.7%(2)	2.7%(6)
	High	27.2%(7)	15.2%(4)	39.9%(10)	4.9%(26)
	Univ	52.5%(4)	0.0%(0)	29.4%(2)	2.7%(7)
[5] Non-Voters		32.8% (70)	33.8% (72)	16.3% (35)	16.5% (213)
	Prim	64.9%(15)	24.3%(6)	8.5%(2)	8.3%(23)
	Mid	29.6%(3)	46.2%(5)	15.1%(2)	5.0%(11)
	High	31.9%(34)	31.2%(33)	23.7%(25)	20.2%(107)
	Univ	24.3%(18)	38.8%(28)	7.8%(6)	27.4%(72)
[6] Mean (N)		42.0% (543)	33.8% (437)	16.3% (211)	100% (1293)
	Prim	56.8%(157)	33.1%(92)	7.2%(20)	21.4%(277)
	Mid	50.5%(111)	33.3%(74)	12.6%(28)	17.1%(221)
	High	36.3%(193)	33.1%(176)	22.0%(117)	41.1%(531)
	Univ	30.9%(81)	36.5%(96)	17.6%(46)	20.4%(263)

result in differences in political orientation between urban and rural dwellers and, further, in party preference.[14] For the purpose of this paper, only education will be considered. This is not because education attainment is a better indicator, but because the differences in political orientation which are the consequence of differences in education are almost the same as those which result from age differences. As the main focus of this chapter is on the voter's response to the DLP merger, consideration of one variable, which also represents other aspects of social life, may fulfil the purpose.

Table 4.3 reports the distribution of party preferences in the elections of 1987 and 1992 broken down by education.[15] As Column 4 shows, Roh Tae-woo in 1987 won higher support from the less educated, Kim Young-sam gained higher support from the better educated and Kim Dae-jung showed little educational variation in his support. In 1987, the governing party candidate polled more from the less educated sectors of the population, whereas Kim Young-sam, as an opposition candidate, polled more from the better educated sectors. Since Kim Dae-jung's support was highly concentrated in Cholla, education played no significant role.

In 1992, as Line 6 indicates, the social basis of Kim Young-sam's electoral support is much closer to that of Roh in 1987 rather than to his own. He won more support from the less educated than the more educated. The DLP failed in embracing the well-educated voters, or in shifting the social basis of its support, which may have been one of the purposes behind the party merger of 1990. Kim Dae-jung's support again showed little variation, except for the somewhat better performance among the university graduates, and Chung Ju-yung recorded disproportionately higher support among those who had high school education.

A closer examination of Lines 1 to 5 of Table 4.3 reveals this pattern more thoroughly. Among those Roh supporters in 1987, the more educated were the less likely to stay with Kim Young-sam, and even for his former supporters this pattern was also observed. Of the defectors, Chung Ju-yung had relatively higher support from the better educated. This is highly suggestive, in that Chung Ju-yung eroded the social basis of traditional opposition support, contrary to the general expectation that Chung may have shared a similar social basis of electoral support with the governing party.

In terms of social basis of electoral support, there has been more continuity than change. Although by joining the ruling coalition Kim Young-sam personally experienced a dramatic shift in his social basis of support, the voters exhibited the long-observed pattern of party support — that is, the governing party is less likely to receive support from better educated voters. However (and equally importantly as a determinant of the election result), the main opposition was constrained by its regional image, and was thus not able to project itself as a viable alternative. If an opposition tendency as well as a pro-government tendency still exists in the electorate, the opposition will only achieve electoral success through consolidation of its basis of support.

Conclusion

The presidential election of 1992 represents a watershed event for democracy in Korea, as it brought the first genuinely civilian-controlled government in more than 30 years. The election departed from the contests of the past, in that it was held in a fair manner without government intervention or allegations of election rigging, and in that the contest was, overall, not a choice between 'dictatorship or democracy' of the kind which had characterised past elections. Achieving convincing victory by a sound margin, Kim Young-sam was able to introduce the policy of 'reform while at the same time maintaining stability' for which he had campaigned.

Since the inauguration of his presidency in February 1993, Kim introduced several reforms which have generated great popularity. Various opinion polls were undertaken about his performance, and the support for his performance reached 70 to 90 per cent after one hundred days of his presidency.[16] One of the most important contributing factors for his high popularity was the clean-up campaign involving the disclosure of the personal assets of the president, high-ranking civil servants, ministers and members of parliament, which forced many of them, who had unexplainable assets, to resign. More consequential reform measures, such as adopting the real-name financial transaction system, were later introduced again, generating widespread popular support.

Within this context, the discussions in the preceding sections, which revealed continuity rather than change in the pattern of voter alignment, may be an incomplete discussion of the relevant voting behaviour. That is, even though Kim Young-sam's victory signifies continuity, the new president seems so far to have opted for a policy of refom rather than attempting to combine reforming and stabilising policies. Thus one would expect some changes in the pattern of voter alignment. Further, as a response to the retirement of Kim Dae-jung and Chung Ju-yung from politics after the election (and the serious disarray within Chung's UNP) — with different reasons, to be sure — changes in voter alignment may result. The following are tentative conclusions regarding the changes that may be the longer term consequences of President Kim's reforms.

First, the urban and rural differences in political support, which have characterised Korean electoral politics to the present, will lessen, if not totally disappear. As long as Kim maintains his firm stance on reform, which seems most likely, he may regain to the government side his former educated supporters. On the other hand, he may well maintain some support from the less critical public. For a full test of this proposition, however, a closer examination of the characteristics of the pro-government and the anti-government tendencies in the electorate may be needed. This is because the less sophisticated voters are traditionally supportive of the government, and given that the opposition tendency in the electorate may be receptive to change, his reforms may result in more changes in the traditional pattern of political support.

One would also expect some changes in the regional pattern of electoral support. The National Assembly by-elections, held after the inauguration of Kim Young-sam's presidency, may exemplify this. In three series of by-elections,[17] the DLP was able to secure all but two out of the eight contested seats. Further, the two seats the DLP lost were in its traditionally strong regions — the main opposition DP won one in Kangwon, while the other in Taegu, the biggest city in Kyongbuk, went to the independent. This failure may be contrasted with the overwhelming victory of the DLP in Pusan, the biggest city in Kyongnam. The DLP's loss of two seats in its former regional strongholds, coming about in spite of Kim's high national popularity, signifies a possible change in the pattern of regional support. There may have been changes in the DLP's strongholds. As a result of Kim Young-sam's clean-up campaign, which inevitably mostly affected politicians in Taegu and Kyongbuk, the Taegu and Kyongbuk voters became increasingly critical of Kim Young-sam and the ruling DLP. In Cholla, however, Kim Young-sam and his DLP may now have a far better position than any of his predecessors. The retirement of Kim Dae-jung, who had been strongly identified with Cholla, may not only provide the DP with a new opportunity to overcome its limited regional basis of support,[18] but the DLP may also have more of a chance to improve its position in Cholla given that both the party and its leadership now have a different character. Despite changes in the regional basis of electoral support of the parties, however, the effect of regional voting, which has been one of the dominant factors characterising Korean party politics since 1987, may remain to exert its strong influence. As long as people view electoral contests in terms of regional favouritism, as exemplified by the 1993 by-elections, Korean party politics may remain regionalistic, although the regional distribution of votes may differ.

Notes

1 For fair management of the election, a non-partisan cabinet was formed, following then President Roh Tae-woo's withdrawal from the ruling DLP.

2 See the *Hankuk Daily*, 20 December 1992. Among the minor party candidates, the Unification National Party (UNP) candidate, Chung Ju-yung, polled nearly 4 million votes (16.3 per cent), and the New Politics Party candidate, Park Chan-jong, won about 1.5 million votes (6.4 per cent).

3 See the *Chosôn Daily, Election Results of the 14th National Assembly Election (Che 14 Dae Kukhoiûiwon Sônkô Jaryojip)*, p. 137. In this election, the Democratic Party, formed by the merger of the Party for Peace and Democracy led by Kim Dae-jung and the Democratic Party led by Lee Ki-taek in 1990, polled 29.2 per cent of the votes, and the Unification National Party led by Chung Ju-yung received 17.4 per cent of the votes.

4 The data employed in this paper were collected just after the presidential election by a nationwide sample survey of the voting population of age 20 and over, which resulted in a total sample size of 1500. The fieldwork was carried out by the Korea Gallup Ltd, with a multi-stage probability sampling method. The survey was conducted as part of a research project organised by Dr James Cotton, with the support of the Australian National University, and the Asia Research Centre of Murdoch University, Western Australia. Strictly speaking, this is not a national survey, as Cheju province was excluded from the sample. However, the exclusion of the Cheju voters may not cause serious distortions in the representativeness of the data, as the official returns have not much deviated from the national mean, and as the population of Cheju is small in amount.

5 See, for political processes and implications of the formation of the ruling DLP, Lee Man-woo, *The Odyssey of Korean Democracy*, New York: Praeger, 1990, pp. 127–39. Also see Park Jin, 'Political Change in South Korea: The Challenge of the Conservative Alliance', *Korea under Roh Tae-woo*, ed. James Cotton (Sydney: Allen & Unwin, 1993), pp. 138–52.

6 The voting choice variables of the 1992 presidential election are weighted by the official returns so that they correspondent to the official results. Without weighting, Chung Ju-yung votes were quite under-represented, but measurement errors for the votes of the other candidates were minimal. It should also be noted that Kim Young-sam votes in 1987 were quite under-represented as Table 4.1 showed, and the UNP votes in 1992 were also somewhat under-represented. There were inevitable measurement errors in the survey data, especially for the (recalled) voting choices in 1987; however, such errors will not result in significant misinterpretations as the focus of this analysis is not on predicting the exact direction of a voter's choice.

7 If the gap between the official returns of the Kim Young-sam votes in 1987 and the self-claimed returns of the survey at Table 4.1 resulted from the loss

of his popularity among his supporters, then there may have been even more switchers among the former Kim Young-sam supporters.

8 See R. Darcy, Hyun Chong-min, James Huston and Kim Hyun-woo, 'Political Party Support in the Korean Fifth Republic: An Ecological Analysis 1981-1985', *Australian Journal of Political Science*, vol. 26, 1991, p. 302.

9 For the explanations of the regional nature of voting, i.e. voting for the candidates with the same regional origins, several hypotheses have been developed. For example, Kim Seung-kuk argued that the uneven regional development resulted in the rise of regionalism. That is, as people became increasingly sensitive to regional gaps, a political reaction to regional disparities became manifest as regionalism (see Kim Seung-kuk, 'The Formation of Civil Society and the Rise of Regionalism in Korea', K*orea Journal*, vol. 28, no. 6, 1988, pp. 24-34. For some others, such as Kim Kwang-soo, regionalism resulted from regional disparities in the recruitment of ruling elites, especially for the disproportionate under-representation of Cholla (see '*Hankuk Chongchi e itsoso Chollado* (Cholla-do in Korean Politics), *Hankuk Chongchi Hakhoi Bo*, vol. 20, no. 1, 1986, pp. 85–108). More fundamentally, regional consciousness based on regionality or locality, which may be rather an inevitable condition in every human society, may have been deliberately manipulated by political elites turning it into inter-regional resentments or regional favouritism (see Choi Hyop, 'Regional Development and Regional Consciousness', *Chasangchok Chibang Balchon [Endogenous Local Development]*, Kumi Trading Co. Ltd, 1986). In this paper, however, no attempts are made to assess the relative merits of these hypotheses. The main focus of this paper is rather on whether there has been a significant change in the pattern of regional voting.

10 The official election outcomes, which are distributed by the regions used in this paper, almost exactly correspond to those of the survey, except for a little over-estimation of Kim Young-sam votes in Kangwon and Chungchong. However, the voting figures of 1987, which are reported in Column 4 of Table 4.1, especially for Kim Young-sam votes, deviate considerably from the official outcomes. Thus it is necessary to look at the trends rather than the exact figures for the observations related to the 1987 voting results.

11 The cell size in Line 4 is so small that caution is needed in making an inference.

12 See Ahn Byoung-man, Kil Soong-hoom and Kim Kwang-woong, *Elections in Korea*, Seoul Computer Press, 1988, pp. 231–68.

13 See Yoon Chun-joo, *Tupyo Chamyo wa Chongchi Balchon (Electoral Participation and Political Development)*, Seoul: Seoul National University Press, 1989, p. 44.

14 For the explanation of the opposition's strength in urban areas, Kim Jae-on and B.C. Koh hypothesised that the urban residents, who have better access to mass media and formal education, are more committed to democratic

norms, and thus become more anti-government in their political propensities (see 'Electoral Behavior and Social Development in South Korea: An Aggregate Data Analysis of Presidential Elections', *The Journal of Politics*, vol. 34 no. 3, 1972, pp. 825–59). Regarding age differences, Lee Kap-yun argued that the different experiences of the generations, such as war, disorder or poverty in the past, as well as life-cycle perceptions, result in the younger generation's decreased propensity to support the governing parties (see '*Tupyohaengtae wa Minjuhwa* (Voting Behaviour and Democratisation)', in Kim Kwang-woong, ed., *Hankuk ui Songo Chongchihak (Electoral Politics in Korea)*, Seoul: Nanam, 1990, p. 176.

15   According to the 1990 census, among the population aged 20 and over, 18.8 per cent are now attending, graduated from, or have attended but not yet completed college or university, 36.2 per cent were in high school, 17.2 per cent in middle school, and 27.8 per cent had only primary school education or under. These figures are quite similar to the figures reported in the cell crossing Line 6 and Column 4 of Table 4.3, except for a little over-representation in higher education, and a little under-representation in primary school education.

16   See Ahn Bu-keun, '*San i Nopumyon Gol i Kipta* (The Higher the Mountains, the Deeper the Valley)', *Wolgan Choson*, July 1993, pp. 100–107.

17   In the first series of by-elections held on 23 April 23 1993, the DLP won all the three seats contested — two in Pusan and one in Kyonggi. In the second series on 11 June, the DLP won two of the three seats contested — the DLP won one in Kangwon and one in Kyongbuk, and the DP won in Kangwon. In the third series on 12 August, the DLP won one seat in Kangwon, and lost one seat in Taegu, of the two seats contested.

18   The DP, in the absence of a viable third party because of the UNP's disarray, increased its share of votes dramatically in Kangwon and Kyongbuk — in which the DP showed poorest performance in the precedent elections — in the by-elections, even though it succeeded in winning only one seat in Kangwon.

5

Liberalisation and the Political Role of the Chaebôl in Korea: The Rise and Fall of the Unification National Party (UNP) [1]

Yang Gil-hyun

Introduction: Liberalisation, its meaning and consequences

Korean political history since the coup of 16 May 1961 has been dominated by the role of the military. Since the centre of political power has been dominated by the military elite, the economy has been subordinate to politics. As long as the military dominates politics, it is political reality that business has to provide, in one form or another, political funds. From the Third Republic (1961–72) to the *Yushin* regime and also to the Fifth Republic of Chun Doo-hwan, the state has sought legitimacy through state-initiated industrialisation built on the basis of labour control. Thus business has played the role of handmaiden to the regime. In a country with a low level of industrialisation, as witnessed in some Third World countries, it may be impossible to mobilise capital and technology, and to control labour and the market, without state interference or a certain degree of coercion. [2]

However, as a result — perhaps unintended — of state-initiated industrialisation, some business conglomerates, which had originally been in a subordinate relationship to the state, began to exercise independent power.

Here arises a question of what is the relationship between the direct political participation of business and its newly elevated and apparently independent status. In particular, how is it possible to account for Chung Ju-yung's participation in the Fourteenth National Assembly and the 1992 presidential elections and his degree of success in these elections? In other words, do Chung Ju-yung, his Hyundai business group and the Unification National Party represent a political manifestation of the economic power of the bourgeoisie by which the *Chaebôl* seek direct control over politics based on their economic superiority?[3] Alternatively, was the emergence of the UNP a political attempt of the *Chaebôl* to free itself from the politico-economic connection, which has been a structural weakness of the Korean *Chaebôl*,[4] by taking advantage of the unique political configuration and atmosphere which existed at the end of the Sixth Republic? Or was it an attempt to establish the bourgeoisie's indirect rule during a period of power transition?[5]

The June 1987 democratic upsurge directly resulted from the mass rejection of President Chun Doo-hwan's announcement of 3 April, which prescribed an enforcement in the elections scheduled in 1992 of the indirect presidential election system. The June upsurge — which resulted from the combined contributions of the democratic movement group who stood firmly against the power aspirations of the new military junta, opposition politicians and middle strata citizens who rejected the continuation of authoritarianism — is an historical event that decisively promoted the democratisation of Korean politics. The 29 June announcement[6] which followed the upsurge of June 1987 was, in effect, an official proclamation of surrender by the military ruling group.

The political development witnessed since 1987 demonstrates that the acquisition and legitimisation of political power both have to be achieved by electoral means.[7] The thirteenth presidential election, which was held after the 29 June announcement, ended in a victory for the successor of the military elite, Roh Tae-woo of the Democratic Justice Party. Although this victory was facilitated by the split of the opposition, various political manoeuvrings (including the manipulation of regionalism) and use of monetary inducements, it is hard to deny the importance of this election in the course of democratisation in Korea. Moreover, the Thirteenth National Assembly election clearly revealed the voters' eagerness to end the military rule, by producing the *yôso yadae* (small government, big opposition) phenomenon in the Assembly for the first time since the 16 May coup. The congressional hearing on the misdeeds of the Fifth Republic, held shortly after the Assembly election, eventuated in the prolonged 'banishment' of the former President Chun Doo-hwan from the capital. Thus it became known to the public that political power, which had been exercised almost without restraint during the Park and Chun eras, had become temporary and subject to retrospective impeachment and indictment.

Koreans thus saw the Fourteenth National Assembly elections of March 1992,[8] and the fourteenth presidential elections of December 1992 in a new and positive light. Contrary to the practice of the past, the issue of the Fourteenth National Assembly and presidential elections was not any more that of ending military rule, nor did these elections exhibit the pattern of democratic versus anti-democratic contest. The biggest concern of Korean voters in the presidential election was whether the Democratic Liberal Party (which formed a potentially hegemonic ruling coalition through the merger of three parties in 1990) would regain power or whether it would result in the peaceful transfer of power for the first time in Korean political history. In other words, the issue was which of the two Kims — Kim Young-sam and Kim Dae-jung — would become president. In addition, those who were not willing to accept the dominance of two Kims looked to the Unification National Party, which had been relatively successful in the Fourteenth National Assembly election by the use of money and through the support provided by the Hyundai business group. With its increased political status, it was not clear what kind of impact the Unification National Party would have on the established power configuration.

Put simply, the concern was with who would fill the power vacuum emerging as a result of the withdrawal of the military from the centre of power. In general, in the process of democratisation after military rule, it is a usual trend that political power is handed over to professional politicians, who organise various social forces through political parties. In this process, professional politicians, on the one hand, may well appease the military by guaranteeing its interest as an institution, and on the other hand, try to accommodate social forces within the legal and political boundaries of the social system by employing the representatives of various social forces. To the bourgeoisie — one of the important social forces — opportunities for making money are sufficiently attractive as a recompense for giving up political power. In regard to the intellectuals — professors, journalists, lawyers, students and those in the fields of culture and art — their tacit approval for the fact that political power belongs to professional politicians is being acquired by abolishing the authoritative controls of the past, and by expanding opportunities for material returns. For the working class, by accommodating its demands for improvements to working conditions and wage increases, and by guaranteeing the legal means of labour dispute, the solution of many problems that the working class is now facing can be attributed to the negotiation capability of the working class itself or to the principles of the market. It was reforms or liberalisations of this nature which the Roh Tae-woo government seemed set to pursue at the beginning of the Sixth Republic under the name of democratisation, but was not able to fully implement.

The 29 June announcement confirmed that the influence of the middle strata among the social forces is one of the most important factors which now governs the direction of political power in Korean politics. This is apparent from the fact that, since the announcement, every Korean political party has claimed to speak for the interest or orientation of the middle strata, and has tried to obtain its support.[9] By contrast, organised labour has remained a strong social force, but in potential only, since it has been impossible to form a party based on organised labour due to the labour controls of the Sixth Republic, which banned the politicisation of organised labour. In addition, the *Chaebôl* did not have to adopt an overt political stance since they had virtually become indirect rulers of the society in collusion with the state power. Nonetheless, as Chung Ju-yung and the Hyundai group directly participated in politics in spite of internal objections and concerns,[10] many people took a great interest in the prospects of this participation.

Under the Roh government, the relationship between the state and the *Chaebôl* began to change. Here has arisen a significant point of dispute among Korean scholars as to the reasons for the emergence of tension and conflict between the state and the *Chaebôl*.[11] If Poulantzas is correct[12] in his claim that the capitalist class state 'takes charge, as it were, of the bourgeoisie's political interests and realizes the function of political hegemony which the bourgeoisie is unable to achieve',[13] then for what reason did an important sector of capital try to attain direct political power? To be more specific, what are the motives and economic and political calculations involved, and the socio-economic foundations for the direct political participation of the *Chaebôl*, and what are the implications and effects of such a role? For an attempt to deal with these questions, the following will be considered:

1 the personal motivations of Chung Ju-yung, who chaired the Hyundai group, and the political and economic impact of liberalisation which Hyundai might have estimated;
2 the socio-political background to the direct political participation of the UNP in the National Assembly election in March 1992, the socio-economic impact of the growth of civil society, and the distinctive recruitment practices of the Unification National Party; and
3 the effects on the political system of the UNP's winning of 24 seats in the Assembly, and of Chung Ju-yung's challenge to power.

Political participation of the *Chaebôl*

Personal motivations and socio-economic background

The direct political participation of the Korean *Chaebôl* at this time was unprecedented.[14] In the United States, the Perot phenomenon attracted great interest, with the possibility (given that at one point Perot claimed 35 per cent support in opinion polls), that an independent might be elected as the president. On the one hand, the types of political participation of Chung Ju-yung and Ross Perot were similar in that both represented a challenge by capital to gain political power, and that they also reflected the popular desire for an 'economic president' in circumstances of economic crisis and mistrust of the existing political machinery.[15] However, on the other hand, as Son Ho-chul pointed out, the Chung Ju-yung phenomenon and the Perot phenomenon were structurally different from each other:

> The Chung Ju-yung phenomenon is related to the reorganisation of the ruling block, and the seeking of total hegemony by monopoly capital, but the Perot phenomenon is an 'abnormal' phenomenon related to the abolition of the New Deal coalition, the decline of the US economy, and the decay of American party politics.[16]

At any rate, the political participation of the *Chaebôl*, represented by Chung Ju-yung, the Hyundai group and the UNP, stirred up a host of political and social disputes.[17] This section will focus on the political aspects.

Since the Unification National Party was formed under the personal leadership of Chung Ju-yung, the party had to weigh carefully his emotions and intentions. Of course, this situation is not without precedent in Korean politics: the UNP has depended on Chung's personal leadership, as the Democratic Liberal Party and the Democratic Party depended upon the personal roles of Roh Tae-woo, Kim Young-sam, Kim Jong-pil and Kim Dae-jung. The only difference between the UNP and the other main parties is that the latter were formed and reorganised by the professional politicians with their political needs, and the former was formed by the more complicated motivations and calculations of a chairman of a *Chaebôl*.

According to Chung's own account of the motivations of his political participation, he felt a need to take a direct political role after bitterly experiencing the might of political power and his helplessness during the period of industrial readjustment which was initiated by the new military junta after the coup on 17 May 1980.[18] The fact that Chung was summoned as a witness during the congressional hearings of the Fifth Republic in 1988 may also have been a contributing factor. Moreover, confronted with the real ownership control policy of 8 May 1990, in which one-third of the land the *Chaebôl* owned was classified by the state as not for business use and was thus required to be sold, Chung may have felt keenly the necessity of framing a shield to protect himself, his family and his company from the influence of the political sphere. As he revealed in an interview in Tokyo after his failure in the presidential election, he took this step 'under the influence of anger because Roh Tae-woo troubled me'.[19] In other words, personal humiliation and abasement may have been a primary factor.

Chung first revealed his intention to participate in politics in a forum held at the Kwanhun Club on 27 November 1990, when he commented that 'we cannot find a capable leader to guide our nation at the moment'.[20] Such remarks were undoubtedly part of a strategy which included the formation of a newspaper, 'the *Munhwa Daily*' on 29 August 1990, by expanding the role of the public relations department in the Hyundai group to conduct an opinion survey in the Chungro area of the capital to form an analysis on the voters' orientation, and by carrying out contacts with politicians of the ruling and opposition parties, and with distinguished persons in the *Chaeya* (the radical opposition). In July 1991, Chung visited China, accompanying 67 other persons in the fields of politics, the economy, academia, the press, the military, culture and art, under the name of 'the Korea–China Non-government Delegates'. He renamed this 'the *Chônji Dongwuhoi* (club)' to form a political consultant group.[21] From this point, Chung began to participate in politics openly, and his intention began to be known to the public.

However, it may be too simplistic to attribute Chung Ju-yung's political participation simply to his personal political ambition or his personal '*Han Puri* (satisfying a grudge)' against the political sphere, without considering some possible socio-political reasons. That Chung was able to form a party within about six months of his decision to do so, and that the party was able to secure some degree of success in the National Assembly election, cannot be simply attributed to Chung's leadership or to the organisational strength of the Hyundai group. It is a general view that the rapid growth of the UNP was possible because there existed mistrust of or disillusion about the established politicians among the public, and because of the relative growth of the social sphere — especially of the business groups — against the state.

The following circumstances contributed to the mistrust of party politics and politicians among the public. On the eve of democratisation in 1980, the two opposition party leaders, Kim Young-sam and Kim Dae-jung, who had long struggled for democratisation in the *Yushin* era, were generally accepted as the leaders who could deliver political democracy to Korea. However, they were soon blamed for not preventing the 12 December

Incident or the 16 May Coup, as a result of their failure to work together. Again, the two Kims blocked the possibility of a peaceful transfer of power and the realisation of civilian politics by failing to agree on a single candidacy in the thirteenth presidential election which was held after the 29 June announcement of 1987. The *yôso yadae* (small government, big opposition) composition of the Assembly following the elections of 1988 was similarly unexploited by these leaders, who remained rivals. Kim Young-sam then participated with Roh Tae-woo in the formation of the ruling Democratic Liberal Party. In spite of its rhetoric — 'it is the decision to save our nation from the total crisis which may cause a suspension of constitutionalism' — the merger in 1990 of the three parties — the Democratic Justice Party, the Reunification Democratic Party and the New Republican Democratic Party — seems to have deepened public disillusion about parties and politicians. Taking advantage of general disillusionment against the two Kims on the one hand, and utilising his nationwide reputation as a successful businessman, his business organisations and enormous political funds on the other hand, Chung was able to adopt the strategy of making a direct challenge for political power.[22]

Of course, public mistrust and disillusion with regard to the existing political system were not limited to the two Kims. Public opinion of the performance of the government became aggravated to the degree that DLP candidates could not enjoy their premium as ruling party candidates in elections, because of the widespread perception that the economic crisis of the Sixth Republic resulted from the internal dispute within the DLP and the indecisiveness of Roh Tae-woo. Disaffection with the ruling DLP may have resulted from its failure to deal with economic problems — for example, the trade balance worsened from a credit of US$9.584 billion in 1987 to a deficit of US$8.827 billion in May 1992, the price of real estate went up an average 2.3 times compared with 1987, and the consumer price increased by 40 to 50 per cent between 1991 and 1992 — so that it had become a general concern that Korea would sink 'from being a dragon of Asia to being an earthworm'.[23] The DLP also failed in fulfilling the eight democratic measures of the 29 June announcement. As a newspaper pointed out, it 'kept the general but failed to fulfil the details'.[24] However, the existing political system revealed the absence of political leadership by its preoccupation with power struggle and regional conflict, instead of trying to resolve concrete difficulties.[25] The absence of political leadership may have been partly responsible for the success of the UNP.

With the erosion of state power, described by one commentator as amounting to the 'privatisation of the state',[26] capital could not be prevented from playing a direct political role. To avoid the split in the ruling coalition which was feared as a consequence, the ruling party could not find an effective way of dealing with the challenge, except by blocking the mobilisation of political funds through the tax investigation of the Hyundai group. Furthermore, even the proper investigation by the Office of Tax Administration and by the Office of Bank Supervision and Examination for the illegal conversion of business funds to political funds was regarded as unfair pressure limited to a particular business or a particular political group, reminiscent of the exercise in the past of state power against organised labour and in favour of the *Chaebôl*.

Although it is apparent that political power now belongs to the professional politicians operating through political parties, some further argue that any group — including the *Chaebôl* — is entitled to participate in politics to speak for its interests, this practice being the very foundation of liberal democracy. Thus Chung's participation in politics as a businessman could be viewed as a counteraction against the politicisation of organised labour (which the *Chaeya* always longed for), realised by the organisation of the People's Party with labour activists as the leadership. The success of the UNP may have been possible on the basis of the logic of procedural democracy — that is, because the UNP was able to justify the political participation of the *Chaebôl* to the public.

Factors which led the *Chaebôl* to participate in politics

The relative weakness of its structure

The Korean *Chaebôl* sector has long enjoyed enormous economic power and significant political influence. However, the Korean *Chaebôl* has been subordinated to the state power, since it has not yet been able to convert its economic power to political power. Suh Jae-jin perceived in this pattern a 'twofold power structure' whereby there was a 'discordance between superstructure and foundation, that is . . . the bourgeoisie controls the foundation but the superstructure is controlled by the political elite'.[27] If such a twofold power structure is viewed from the perspective of the ruled, 'the bourgeoisie and the political elite are one ruling group'; however, if viewed in itself, the ruling group is divided into the bourgeoisie, which has the economic hegemony, and the power bloc, which has the political and ideological hegemony.[28] The Korean *Chaebôl* is allowed to realise its class interest through the state, and at the same time it is checked by the state in the political and ideological fields. On this view, state interference is more acute in the realm of ideology. For example, with an ideology that emphasises the social responsibility of business, the state controls the *Chaebôl*, which in general does not fulfil its social responsibility, by condemning instances of illicit capital accumulation, real estate speculation or the improper use of political connections. As a result, the Korean *Chaebôl* has not yet obtained social hegemony, in spite of its enormous economic power. Hegemonic leadership, as Gramsci pointed out, involves 'developing intellectual, moral and philosophical consent from all major groups in a nation'.[29] It also involves an emotive dimension. From this perspective, the Korean *Chaebôl* cannot claim itself as a hegemonic group as long as it is not widely acceptable that the *Chaebôl* commands the moral and intellectual leadership. What, then is the status of the Korean bourgeoisie in terms of the hegemony?

Compared to the status the *Yangban* (landlord) class enjoyed as a ruling group in the premodern period,[30] the Korean bourgeoisie has not yet become a political and social ruling or hegemonic class. This results from the fact that the Korean bourgeoisie lacks moral legitimacy. Three historic moments can be cited to sketch the process in which the Korean bourgeoisie undermined its own claims to legitimacy.

First, the bourgeoisie was not able to escape from condemnation by virtue of its role as collaborator during the Japanese colonial period. Second, in spite of its role in the import substitute industrialisation program of the Syngman Rhee era,[31] and in the export driving industrialisation process of the Park Chung-hee era,[32] Korean business has not been able to free itself from the distrust or disregard of the general public who consider that it has grown from government largesse as a result of it providing political funds to successive regimes. The government facilitated the capital accumulation of the *Chaebôl* by means of privileged loans or taxes, labour control and protection from outside competition; for their part the businesses provided the political funds needed for prolonging one-man rule. Third, during the Fifth Republic, and especially in the Sixth Republic, the bourgeoisie, who had been subordinate to political power,[33] became direct competitors for power.

As state control over the financial and tax systems loosened in the course of liberalisation from the mid-1980s, the relative autonomy of businesses became highly visible.[34] The partial democratisation at the end of the Fifth Republic and in the Sixth Republic was in essence a liberalisation which denoted the relaxation of state control over civil society. This liberalisation, however, was limited and disproportionate. The voices of the press and of business were strengthened, but organised labour was not yet permitted an express political role. The press became a vehicle for the demands of unsatisfied businessmen, who generally demanded labour controls and the self-regulation of the financial system[35] without addressing their social responsibilities such as the improvement of working conditions, the social welfare of workers and the protection of the environment. Thus the Korean bourgeoisie has been placed in a contradictory position: it still wants to keep the labour sector under some government controls, but it also seeks to free its own affairs from government control. Therefore the Korean bourgeoisie is far from obtaining social hegemony, given its incapacity to mediate the interests of various social groups and to fulfil social responsibilities.

In addition, the Korean bourgeoisie, compared with the same stratum in European countries, has not paid much attention to obtaining ideological hegemony. Ideological hegemony, according to Gramsci, can be obtained when the interest of the ruling class or group corresponds to the interests of the other sectors of the society. As Bocock points out, in order to obtain ideological hegemony, it becomes necessary that 'policies have to be pursued at times which are in the interests of the whole people, the nation, and not in the narrow interests of the bourgeoisie, or some dominant fraction of it'.[36] Viewed from this perspective, the weakest aspect of the Korean bourgeoisie is that it has not played a substantial, and progressive, role in the development of Korean capitalism. In the European countries, the bourgeoisie played a significant historical role, not only in creating the wealth of nations, but also in advocating revolutionary values such as economic and political freedom. The European bourgeoisie was in opposition to and sought to reform the authoritarian system of government, which hindered the development of capitalism. Thus, as long as the bourgeoisie plays some role in a historic time of social transition, even though this may be through considerations of class interest, it may be able to claim its share, and keep its position as a leader in such periods.

However, the Korean bourgeoisie has maintained selectively friendly relations with the authoritarian governments since the 1960s. More recently, the business elite have been concerned about reaping free-rider benefits such as the self-regulation of the financial market, which has become possible because of the partial democratisation obtained by labour and the middle strata. Furthermore, there is an increasing perception that wealth is becoming more maldistributed, and that the wealth of the *Chaebôl* has been accumulated not by productive economic activities but by speculation. Even those philanthropic activities, which some of the *Chaebôl* undertake to deal with such criticism, are not only limited to tax-free social welfare work such as medical, scholarship and cultural funds, but are also controlled by the *Chaebôl* or its nominees. Some critics have even charged that these are undertaken only as a means of legal tax evasion.

In the field of political ideology, the Korean bourgeoisie has not paid attention to infusing its hegemonic ideology. The Yi dynasty was based on the ideology that the *Yangban* class, being schooled in Confucian ethics, was uniquely capable of ruling. However, the Korean bourgeoisie adopted the ideology of liberal democracy, which prescribes the separation of politics and economy, and indirect participation in a political sphere dominated by professional politicians and bureaucrats. Moreover, the traditional political ethos in Korean society — that is, the belief that ruling a nation or the world requires an individual's moral training and family management — hinders political participation of the businessmen, as they are often regarded as having problems with moral training and family management, because of personal scandals or labour disputes within their companies.

What, then, are the reasons why the *Chaebôl* decided to participate directly in politics, in spite of such difficulties and limitations? Of course, as mentioned above, the *Chaebôl*'s political participation resulted partly from the fact that the *Chaebôl* enjoyed a new confidence in its relation to state power. The political participation of the *Chaebôl*, however, is in addition an attempt to make up for its continuing lack of ideological hegemony. Since the 1987 democratic upsurge, as Hong Duk-ryul pointed out:

> the legitimacy of the anti-Communist ideology, the growth ideology with the *Chaebôl* as its core, the low-wage ideology, and the growth-first distribution-later ideology, all began to be questioned . . . and it became hard to realise the interests of the *Chaebôl*, given that the machinery of the state, which has the ultimate responsibility for the maintenance of the ruling structure and in the operation or reproduction of the ruling ideology, became loosened.[37]

In other words, there appeared a conflict between the aims of the *Chaebôl* and of the government, especially after the Sixth Republic began to take an interest in the distributive demands of the growing social movements, as exemplified in the policies adopted by the government which were directed against the real estate speculation of the major business groups. The *Chaebôl*, which had previously enjoyed socio-economic dominance, now recognised the ineffectiveness of their past politico-economic strategies, and thus moved 'to reproduce a stabilised ruling structure by formally participating in the institutionalised state machinery, and by exercising power directly'.[38] In short, the direct political participation of the *Chaebôl* can be seen as a political experiment chosen to make up for the Korean bourgeoisie's lack of relative autonomy — with regard not only to the state power, but also in relation to other social groups such as the middle strata and organised labour.

It is a well-known fact that the lack of relative autonomy of the *Chaebôl* sector has resulted from its heavy reliance on state power to deliver appropriate labour controls and financial supports. This lack of autonomy is more apparent if compared with the political role of the business sector in the Western European countries.[39] In the case of the European countries, the bourgeoisie, which obtained social hegemony or dominance by the bourgeois revolutions, had room for sacrificing its short term politico-economic interests in order to maintain the stability of the capitalist system. However, in case of Korea, which has not experienced a bourgeois revolution,[40] the *Chaebôl* neither has the confidence nor the social hegemony to allow full associational, bargaining and strike rights to labour, nor can it take a consistent attitude towards working condition improvements and wage increases.

However, as Schumpeter pointed out, 'capitalism . . . is by nature a form or method of economic change and not only never is but also never can be stationary'.[41] The process that incessantly destroys the old structure incessantly creates a new one.[42] Because of this process of creative destruction, Korean capitalism is bound to bring the past pattern of economic activities to a close. The present is an era for business to explore ways of self-reliance, liberated from its dependence on state power. At the same time, however, for those businessmen who cannot operate independently, it is plausible that they may wish to assume some direct responsibility for the management of state power. It should be kept in mind that the largest *Chaebôl*, while operating under government patronage, have managed to maintain their operations under high leverage conditions, confident that governments will rescue them if debt levels threaten to undermine their viability. Moreover, changes in the structure of political power, whether by coup or by election, require enormous political donations if new connections are to be forged with a new political elite. Therefore, business may have regarded it as more effective (and cheaper) to take part directly in political power using the money that otherwise would have gone to the politicians.[43] Indeed, some speculate that the political fund of 40 to 50 billion *won* the UNP spent in the Fourteenth National Assembly election may have been far less than Hyundai may have had to provide if the UNP had not been created.

In addition, it seems to me that the direct political participation of the *Chaebôl*, whatever its political outcome, may also have had certain effects on other groups in society. In a period of accelerating democratisation, the bourgeoisie may be pressed to seek occupation of a part of the political sphere in order to expand its political influence. Especially since the June 1987 upsurge, the components of the conservative two-party system have become increasingly sensitive to the intention and interest of the middle strata. The middle strata perceives the need for greater social responsibility and accountability from the wealthy sector.[44] Therefore, further democratisation may result in these demands impinging upon the *Chaebôl's* indirect rule, a development which may even result in a coalition of the middle strata and organised labour.[45] Accordingly, the Korean bourgeoisie not only recognises the necessity of protecting its present, but also the necessity of ensuring some degree of political influence as the process of democratisation proceeds. There may also have been the less clearly calculated considerations that the bourgeoisie is in need of securing political power before the institutionalisation of a labour union based party, a development foreshadowed by the formation of the People's Party which contested (though with poor results) the Fourteenth National Assembly election.

The resources of the UNP: Policies, organisations and funds

The Unification National Party quickly generated a strong popular following. Within a month of its creation, the UNP became a third major party, and became a focus of attention from the press. By whom, then, was the UNP managed, how large were its financial resources, and what was its stand on policies?

The UNP, at first, had some features not be found in other Korean political parties. The UNP was not created by professional politicians or as a result of a coup, or by an ideology, but formed through the dissatisfaction and motivation of a businessman. The UNP was a business-like party, which depended more on efficiency than on democratic procedure, because it was created within the framework of Hyundai, a company group which directly employs more than 140 000 individuals. The party was managed by about 156 Hyundai managerial staff,[46] 30 of whom returned to their respective companies in the group after the Fourteenth National Assembly election. Long discussions or meetings were regarded as unproductive and wasteful, and business-like principles — that with whatever means given tasks had to be accomplished competitively and effectively — were predominant in the UNP.

The UNP also showed ability in promoting its policies and platforms. For the Fourteenth Assembly election, the UNP had large-scale policy advertisements appear in almost every newspaper eight times, emphasising the themes of small business support, bank autonomy, bank interest rate cuts, apartment price reductions, educational reform, cultural support, rural and fishing area revitalisation, and women's status reinforcement. Among these, the party's policy slogan, 'we will supply a large number of apartments at half price', was a popular if controversial one. This advertisement, regardless of its feasibility,[47] was the most seductive election promise, and also appeared to address the failure on the part of the Sixth Republic to control escalating real estate policies and land management scandals.[48]

In addition to his policy pronouncements, Chung Ju-yung seized the interest of the people by a series of well-timed press manoeuvrings. On 18 January 1992, just before the creation of the UNP, Chung revealed his donation of political funds to the Blue House;[49] on 25 February, when there was a widespread suspicion about political pressures on Hyundai, he threatened the bankruptcy of Hyundai;[50] he also exposed the construction expenses of the Blue House and blamed the president for it;[51] and he even disclosed the existence of atomic-bomb storage facilities built by his company.[52] Chung's impromptu and sometimes contradictory remarks also attracted much attention from the press and led to intensive speculation about his real stand on the issues.

At any rate, the main target for the attacks of the UNP was the alleged economic mismanagement of the Sixth Republic. As Chung stated in the forum of the Kwanhun Club on 9 April 1992, he created the UNP and participated in politics 'because he felt that if the Democratic Liberal Party takes power for another five years our nation and people will be ruined forever . . . during the DLP's four year rule our foreign debt reached 40 billion dollars'.[53] The implication was that if the economy had performed well or if Hyundai had had a good relationship with the Sixth Republic, he would not have participated in politics. From this perspective, the UNP was a pragmatic party — formed because there was a specific problem which needed a solution — rather than an ideological party.[54]

However, the UNP can be seen as a party which spoke for 'a fraction of the neo-liberalistic monopoly capitalists',[55] as its promises and slogans remained in the category of superficial welfare promises. In other words, the UNP hardly mentioned such policies as addressing the wealth concentration of the *Chaebôl* — for example, separation of ownership and management, prevention of hereditary transmission of ownership of the *Chaebôl* or its dominance of financial market and strengthening of the fair-trade law — and had no policies furthering political rights such as freedom of association and protest, or the rights of labour. Even the promise of halving the price of apartments, which may have produced the most dramatic effects of all, was not a realistic alternative but rather was used to 'free-ride on the houseless who anyhow wanted a cut in housing price and who were those most dissatisfied with the housing policy of the Sixth Republic'.[56]

As revealed in the results of the Fourteenth Assembly election, the UNP's capacity was considerable but still limited. First of all, the UNP's unexpected success was not based on voter preference for the party itself, but was rather based on the abilities or personal ties of each of its candidates in their respective constituencies, aided by systematic support from Hyundai. As exemplified by the strength of Independents in the election, the UNP's candidates who won seats in the election were basically Independents who already had support bases in their constituencies, although they ran as UNP candidates. The UNP did not have its own class or regional basis. Even though it was called a party of the *Chaebôl*, there was hardly any evidence that it had support from any *Chaebôl* other than Hyundai. As for the other businesses, Chung's political participation was seen as an attempt to 'maintain its vested interests by a diversion of business',[57] because Hyundai had a bad relationship with the government. Therefore, Chung's political participation finished in his retirement from politics because of his failure in securing the leadership and personal network of the *Chaebôl*.

Despite the limitations of its policies and ideology, the UNP had some exceptional characteristics in terms of personal resources, compared with the other parties. There were basically three groups which constituted the UNP. The first group consisted of those who had some connection with Hyundai. Here the UNP absorbed or utilised the experience, the communal obligations and the efficient management skills of company personnel. Given the intimidation of the party by the Sixth Republic, there was a widespread sense of community between Hyundai and the UNP: 90 per cent of the managerial employees and 60 per cent of the workers of the Hyundai group became members of the UNP by March 1992.[58] Through a secret organisation, called 'the System Reform Committee', which campaigned for membership enrolment, the UNP was known to have secured between 200 000 and 300 000 members during the National Assembly election campaign.[59] The organisations of the UNP during and after the election were managed by figures from Hyundai — namely, the deputy secretary general, Chung Chang-hyun (age 53, former president of the *Kûmkang* Development and Industry), the president's special adviser, Park Se-yong (52, president of the Hyundai *Sangsôn*), the president's special adviser, Lee Byung-kyu (39, former chief secretary of the Hyundai group), the special adviser, Song Yun-chae (57, former president of Hyundai Aluminium), the head of the security office, Lee Chin-ho (49, chairman of Hyundai Aluminium), as well as other individuals.[60] Subsequently, it was a matter of wide speculation that Park Se-yong and Song Yun-chae were arrested because of the political intention of the government and the ruling DLP, which attempted to eliminate the main personnel of the UNP, due to be actively involved in the upcoming presidential election campaign.

The second group consisted of those professional politicians who had not been successful so far, who had not yet decided to belong either to the Fifth Republic group or to the Sixth Republic group, or who had lost their places during the alignments of the ruling and the opposition parties. Those politicians were basically conservative, and they did not politically or ideologically object to the *Chaebôl* sector's political participation as they had good relations with it. Among those, Kim Kwang-il, Yang Sun-jik, Park Han-sang and Bong Du-wan were distinguished politicians. The following well known individuals were among those who had served in the government, the press, the judiciary or the army: Lee Yong-jun (former Deputy Minister of the Labour Department), Yun Ha-jong (former Deputy Minister of the Foreign Affairs Department), Park No-kyung (former editorial writer of the *Kyunghyang Daily*), and Lee Kun-young (former commander of the Third Army). There were also politicians who had been elected in the Fourteenth Assembly election — namely, the secretary general of the UNP, Kim Hyo-young; the floor leader, Kim Chung-nam; the chairman of the policy co-ordination board, Yun Young-tak; the chief secretary, Cha Su-myoung; and the party spokesman, Byun Chung-il. In addition, the UNP attempted to increase its influence by recruiting some of the former Democratic Justice Party members such as Lee Jong-chan, Park Chul-un and Kim Bok-dong. Even though this last group was expected to play some political and professional roles for the UNP, it was generally thought that its members had not played much of a role, either in strengthening the political status of the UNP or in contributing to Chung's votes.

Third, there were some well known TV personalities who actively participated in the UNP. This group included Kim Dong-kil, who had been an academic but was known to the public as a media personality, Chung Ju-il (Lee Ju-il), Choi Bul-am, Kang Bu-ja and Lee In-won. Their participation in the UNP was not unexpected, as the Korean broadcast and TV media are maintained by the advertisements of the *Chaebôl* and by the mass consumer culture. However, the emergence of the usefulness of an entertainer and other non-professional politicians in election campaigns may be a new phenomenon of 'a time when expanding pluralism and the absence of popular alternatives was mixed with the growing influence of the media'.[61] In addition to such examples in other countries as Fatma Girik, a Turkish actress who was elected as mayor of Sisli in 1989, and Ricardo Belmont, a Peruvian host of a popular national talk show who became mayor of Lima in 1990, in Korea there have formerly been such cases apart from those in the UNP — the DLP assemblyman Lee Sun-chae, and former assemblymen Bong Du-wan and Choi Mu-ryong. This indicates that 'for growing numbers, the appearance of bonding between voters and new politicians and the ability to communicate to constituents has been enough to win votes —

regardless of the quality of the candidate or the content of the message conveyed'.[62]

The chairman of the UNP public relations board, Chung Mong-jun, once stated that 'politics requires power, and power requires leadership, money, and national organisation'.[63] In the UNP, the leadership belonged to Chung Ju-yung, and the national organisation consisted of the branches which received support from Hyundai. Political funds were, in general, supplied either from below (i.e. by voluntary participation of elements of civil society — for example, through donations — or from above — that is, by state assistance and subsidies.[64] By contrast, the peculiar feature of the political funds of the UNP was that they were supplied from Chung Ju-yung's personal pocket.

The essence of the conflict between the Sixth Republic and the UNP and Hyundai was money.[65] The conflict was at first expressed in the tax debate, in that Chung refused to pay when the Office of Tax Administration levied additional charges of 130 billion and 900 million *won* upon the conclusion of its tax investigations of stock transfers between Hyundai and the Chung family. Money has become an important factor that has affected the very existence of parties and politicians, not to mention the UNP. Since Korean elections have become a contest of personal networks among candidates themselves rather than between parties — in terms of family ties, local ties, school ties, etc. — the amount of money used in election campaigns has become enormous.[66] Because of the importance of political funds, the Sixth Republic government put pressure on Hyundai, the source of the UNP's political funds, in order to restrain the political activities of the party. The conflict concerning the political funds became a debate between proponents of the government's view — that business funds should not be converted to political funds — and Hyundai and the UNP's view — that the UNP's funds were Chung Ju-yung's personal money, and thus government pressure on Hyundai was aimed at restraining the UNP and was also disturbing normal business activities.

At any rate, it was estimated that Chung set aside more than 200 billion *won* — if current assets are included, 500 billion *won* — in cash in preparation for the 1992 presidential election. This was in relation to the sum of his personal assets which he disclosed were 3 trillion *won*. Of these funds, the UNP was estimated to have spent 40 to 50 billion for its branch formation and activities, and for the Assembly election.[67] Of course, the total may have been far more than this if the money Chung had spent in person were added, and if the material and man-power support from Hyundai were calculated into monetary terms. Experts are in general agreed that Chung secured at least 150 billion *won* for the presidential election.

Conclusion: Political significance and influences of the UNP

The background to and the process of the UNP formation, and its material and personal resources, have been reviewed so far. To summarise, the emergence of the UNP has been interpreted as a product of changes in the power structure of Korean society, and as part of the process of democratisation in which social groups seek to translate their socio-economic power into political power. In other words, the launching of the UNP can be seen as a political strategy on the part of the *Chaebôl*, which tried to make up for its excessive dependence upon political power and its lack of ideological hegemony at a time when it was confronted by the demands of the democratisation process.

If the June upsurge of 1987 is regarded as a political expression of the rapidly growing middle strata aimed against authoritarianism, then the political participation of the *Chaebôl*, signified by the UNP, is to be seen as an attempt by the bourgeoisie to hold power directly during the democratisation process. Of course, such participation is partly attributable to the development of state monopoly capitalism, which has had some degree of success in the past 30 years of industrialisation. In other words, the development of state monopoly capitalism provided a support basis and the legitimacy for political participation by major business figures. At the same time as professional politicians could conduct their activities without proper scrutiny, the politicisation of the organised labour which could have balanced the political participation of the *Chaebôl* was obstructed. At the very least, the formation of the UNP can be regarded as an attempt by a specific *Chaebôl* to further its interests using the political process.

Under the effective management of Chung Ju-yung, with enormous political funds, using the organisation of Hyundai, and also taking advantage of the atmosphere of uncertainty which prevailed in the last period of the Roh Tae-woo government, the UNP was formed on 8 February 1992, after a meeting of its promoters on 10 January. The party had unexpected success in the Fourteenth National Assembly election, electing 24 of its candidates with 17.4 per cent of the votes, and winning (under the proportional electoral system) an additional seven seats to bring UNP representation up to 31 seats. By nominating Chung as its presidential candidate at the party convention on 15 May 1992, the UNP launched its presidential election campaign earlier than any other party.[68] The prospect then loomed of the UNP holding a casting vote between the Democratic Liberal Party and the Democratic Party.

However, the relative success of the UNP ended at this point. The limitations of Chung Ju-yung as a political leader which appeared during the presidential election — his lack of experience, poor judgment and a shortage of audacity — at last undermined and exposed as a deviation the political participation of the *Chaebôl*. Chung managed to secure 16.3 per cent of the popular vote in the election, with a particularly strong following only in his native Kangwon province, and in areas near the capital. After this electoral failure, Chung's party fell apart. Leading personalities who had campaigned with him complained of his style and other shortcomings, and even the candidate himself went on record to acclaim the election of Kim Young-sam as the best result for the country.

The author has endeavoured to interpret the political rise and fall of the UNP and Chung Ju-yung in terms of Korea's stage of political development. The party claimed that it could perform a balancing role as a third party, and also facilitate the peaceful transfer of power and elite rotation, but these claims went unfulfilled. Since the establishment of direct rule by the bourgeoisie requires the appropriate socio-economic foundations — but the Korean bourgeoisie has not yet become a unified ruling group within the society as argued above — its attempt at the assumption of a direct political role failed. Because of the fact that there was no real consensus on the part of the *Chaebôl* regarding the capture of political power (although the Korean *Chaebôl* sector has made some common efforts at times when it has faced political and economic threats), the class basis of Chung's challenge was weak. Neither could Chung be regarded as advancing the cause of a section of society which possessed a hegemonic role. Thus the relative success of the UNP cannot be seen as a political expression of the whole *Chaebôl* sector, but rather as the limited success of a fraction of industrial capital which managed to mobilise some support from the middle strata. The UNP's unique resources were also a factor, as was the emergence of popular disillusion amongst social groups with the functioning and fairness of the state machinery.

Notes

1 This paper is an upgraded and abridged version of the paper which originally appeared in *Hankuk kwa Kukje Chôngch'i,* Seoul: Kyungnam Univ. Kûkdong Munje Yônguso, vol. 8, no. 2, Fall–Winter 1992. It has been translated by Bae Sun-kwang and revised by James Cotton.
2 The only difference between Korea and the Third World socialists may be that Korea has gone through 'the way of capitalist development by the state

capitalism' — see Park Dong-chul, 'The May 16 Government and Capital Accumulation in the 1960s' (*5.16 Chôngkwonkwa 1960 yôndae Chabonch'ukchôkkwachông*), in Yang Woo-jin, Hong Jang-pyo et al., *Analysis of Korean Capitalism (Hankuk chabonjuûi bunsôk)*, Seoul: Ilbit, 1991, p. 71 — whereas, as an example, Burma has gone through the way of non-capitalist development.

3 Paek Chong-kuk understands the Chung Ju-yung/Hyundai/UNP phenomenon as a result of 'the latent and exposed contradiction of power, which exists among the [neo-mercantilist] ruling alliance'. In other words, it resulted from 'the fact that there exists conflict between the structure of power distribution, which had been changed, and the unchanging norms of power distribution'. See Paek Chong-kuk, 'The Meaning of the 14th National Assembly Election in the Change of Korean Capitalist System' (*Hankuk Chabonjuûich'eche Byôndonge issôsô 14 Dae Ch'ongsônûi Ûimi*), p. 16.

4 Regarding the distinctive characteristics of the Korean *Chaebôl*, three factors — control by the family or by the relatives, a pyramid organisation of the diversified firms, and the oligopoly status of the large firms — have been generally pointed out. See Yu In-hak, *Anatomy of the Korean Chaebôl (Hankuk Chaebôlûi Haebu)*, Seoul: Pulbit, 1991, p. 34. The author would add another: the factor of close connection between business and politics. According to the classification by the Fair Trade Commission of the Economic Planning Board in 1990, a *Chaebôl* — the large-scale business group — is a business group which has total assets of over 400 billion *won* among the affiliated companies.

5 This paper treats Chung Ju-yung (the chairman of a *Chaebôl*)/Hyundai (a *Chaebôl*)/the UNP (a political party) more or less as a unity. This is because of the author's perception that the basic framework of the UNP's operation and organisation is shaped by a combination of Chung Ju-yung's leadership and political funds, and the personal and material resources of the Hyundai group. This paper also assumes a commonality of interest among the *Chaebôl* and the bourgeoisie.

6 The 29 June announcement is, of course, as Park Yong-suh pointed out, 'an opus of the ruling elite of the Fifth Republic'. See Park Yong-suh, 'Roh Tae-woo, Chun Doo-hwan, and Park Chung-hee: A Study of Presidents' (*Yôkdae Daetongryông Yônku*), *Hankuk Nondan*, May 1992, p. 63 for the skilful dualism and manoeuvres of the 29 June announcement.

7 The fact that none of the candidates who contested the fourteenth presidential election had a military background symbolically speaks for a rapid progress in the democratisation of Korean politics. The election was a contest between four main candidates: two strong (Kim Young-sam, Kim Dae-jung), one in the middle (Chung Ju-yung) and one weak (Park Chan-jong).

8 Park Chan-wook summarised briefly and clearly the nature of the Fourteenth National Assembly election in Park Chan-wook, 'An Analysis of

the 14th National Assembly Election Outcomes' (*14 Dae Kukhoiûiwon Sônkôkyôlkwa Bunsôk*), presented in the workshop, *The Future and the Development of Korean Party Politics*, organised by the Unification National Party, 1–2 May 1992. Because 'in the 14th National Assembly election the pattern of voters' support has not shown a change in terms of the regional alignments of party support', and in that the election was a competition among conservative parties, the election was by no means a 'converting', 'realigning' or 'critical' one. However, he classified the election 'as a "deviating" one, because the ruling party . . . lost its dominant position, which it usually had in the past, and even failed to gain a majority', and concluded that 'the outcome of this election has a significance in its own way, since frequent deviations can be regarded as a realignment in the long run'.

9 Park Kwang-ju argued in his article, 'The Characteristics of Korean State and Prospects for Democracy' (Hankuk Kukkaûi *Sôngkyôkkwa Minjujuûiûi Chônmang*), *Hyôndae Sahoi*, Spring–Summer 1992, p. 81 that 'if the bourgeoisie or the working class, or the *Minjung* (the masses) cannot become a hegemonic group of civil society, the last alternative is the middle class', and observed that this is a natural trend of the industrialised society. However, in my opinion, the relative growth of the middle class would not lead the middle class to a hegemonic position in civil society, and the natural trend is rather a balance of power in the society among the social forces of the bourgeoisie, middle class, and working class.

10 Although most of the responses of the members of the *Chaebôl* sector about the Unification National Party were cautious, there were variations on this response, depending on the *Chaebôl*'s political status and relationship with Hyundai. For example, Lucky-Gold Star observed friendly neutrality, and Samsung an ambiguous neutrality. By contrast, the chairman of Daewoo, Kim Woo-jung, stated that 'it is unfortunate that chairman Chung, who represents economic circles, jumped into politics'. See Park Won-bae, 'Empowerment of the UNP and the Profit and Loss Statement of the *Chaebôl*' (*Kukmindang Dûksewa Chaebôlûi Sonikkyesansô*), *Mal*, May 1992. pp. 84–91.

11 Lee Kuk-young understands the tension and conflict between the state and the *Chaebôl* as a conflict within the power block itself, and that the central point of the conflict is concerned with the method and degree of control over the economy (i.e. 'it is a matter of choice between "the principle of laissez-faire free economy", which capital demands, and "state initiated authoritarian economic control"'. See Lee Kuk-young, 'The Crash between Hyundai and the 6th Republic: Conflict between the State and the Capital' (*6 Kong - Hyundai Kyôkdol, Kukka Kyekûpkwa Daechabonûi Daldûng*), *Sahoi Pyôngron*, June 1992, p. 178.

12 According to Poulantzas, if the capitalist state fulfils its role as a class state, '*the capitalist state assumes a relative autonomy with regard to the bourgeoisie*'.

See Nicos Poulantzas (trans. by Timothy O'Hagan), *Political Power and Social Classes*, London: NLB and Sheed and Ward, 1973, pp. 284–85. From this perspective, the political participation of capital in Korea is due to the fact that the state cannot sufficiently play its role as a class state, and that the state lacks relative autonomy with regard to the bourgeoisie.

13 See Nicos Poulantzas, *Political Power and Social Classes*, p. 284.

14 The Chung Ju-yung strategy was previously employed by Stanislaw Tyminski, an arch-rival of Walesa and a businessman, in the Polish presidential election in 1990. Tyminski 'campaigned for "a democracy of money", a free-market economic policy that he promised would make every Pole wealthy within a month of his inauguration'. See Robin Wright and Doyle McManus, *Flashpoints: Promise and Peril in a New World*, New York: Alfred A. Knopf, 1991, p. 89.

15 On similarities between Chung Ju-yung and Perot, see the *Chungang Daily*, 5 June 1992.

16 See Son Ho-chul, 'Perot Storm' (*Dolpung*), *Kilûl Ch'atnun Saramdûl*, July 1992, p. 83.

17 In general, the view of the *Chaebôl*'s political participation has been negative; cf Kim Chung-sik, 'Tragedy of 'Chung Ju-yung politics' (*Chung Ju-yung Chôngch'iûi Bikûksông*), *Sahoi Pyôngron*, May 1992, pp. 80–89.

18 See Shin Hyun-man, 'Anatomy of the UNP: the Money Politics' (*Kûmkwon Chôngch'iûi Hwasin, Kukmindangûl Haebuhanda*), *Sahoi Pyôngron*, March 1992, p. 87.

19 After the presidential election, Chung Ju-yung stated in a Tokyo interview that 'since he could not stand President Roh Tae-woo troubling the Hyundai group by the excessive tax investigation and taxing' (*Jungang Daily*, 4 March 1993) and 'since he could not fight with Roh as a businessman, he established a political party and became a congressman' (*Segye Daily*, 4 March 1993).

20 See Chun Jin-woo, 'Chung Ju-yung Dash' (*Dolchin*), *Sindonga*, April 1992, p. 158.

21 From among the members of 'the *Ch'ônji* club' — which consisted of several well-known persons in their various fields (e.g. former prime minister Lee Han-been, former vice-speaker of the National Assembly Ko Hung-mun, former commander of the Third Army Lee Kon-young, former president of KBS So Young-hun, president of the Songkyunkwan University Chang Ul-byong, former chairman of the Federation of Small Business Yoo Ki-sun, television personalities Choi Bul-am and Kang Bu-ja), ten of them participated as founding members of the UNP, and nine of them were listed on the proportional election roll of the UNP in the National Assembly elections.

22 This was revealed in the case of Kim Woo-jung, who strongly criticised Chung's participation in the Fourteenth National Assembly election, but himself had once tried to be a candidate of the New Korean Party for the

fourteenth presidential election under the slogan of 'a new leadership in the '50s'. Thus the political participation of the *Chaebôl* was not merely a deviation but actually a trend.

23 The *Donga Daily*, 28 June 1992.

24 The *Donga Daily*, 27 June 1992.

25 Chung Ju-yung sought an excuse for his 'changing position from a businessman to a politician' from the corruption and incompetence of the political system, at the concluding part of his autobiography, Chung Ju-yung, *There Can Be Hardship, but No Failure (Siryônûn Issôdo Silpaenûn Ôpda)*, Seoul: Hyundai Munhwa Sinmun Sa, 1991.

26 Privatisation of the state may imply the rule of 'Patrimonialism', as Weber noted. Other cases might be the Fifth Republic of Korea, the Philippines under Marcos and Nicaragua under Somoza.

27 See Suh Jae-jin, *Korean Capitalist Class (Hankukûi Chabonka kyekûp)*, Seoul: Nanam, 1991, p. 235.

28 See Suh Jae-jin, *Korean Capitalist Class (Hankukûi Chabonka kyekûp)*, p. 235.

29 See Robert Bocock, *Hegemony*, Chichester: Ellis Horwood, 1986, p. 37.

30 See Carter J. Eckert, 'The South Korean Bourgeoisie: A Class in Search of Hegemony', *The Journal of Korean Studies*, vol. 7, 1990, p. 116.

31 See Yu In-hak, *Anatomy of the Korean Chaebôl (Hankuk Chaebôlûi Haebu)*, pp. 41–56; and Suh Jae-jin, *Korean Capitalist Class (Hankukûi Chabonka kyekûp)*, pp. 71–73.

32 The *Chaebôl* in the Park Chung-hee era was able to expand through the importation of foreign capital, government policies on the heavy chemical industry, export or construction abroad, privileged loans and acceptance of state-owned or faltering enterprises. See Yu In-hak, *Anatomy of the Korean Chaebôl (Hankuk Chaebôlûi Haebu)*, pp. 57–87.

33 One of the main reasons for the businesses' subordinate position to political power was that the businesses were not able to maintain their success without co-operating with political power, as the state not only firmly controlled the financial system, but also exercised various forms of preferential treatment, including threats of tax investigation of the Office of Tax Administration.

34 Regarding those factors that resulted in the transfer of the state-initiated economic policies into the private sphere since the Fifth Republic, Suh Jae-jin cited the growth of the capitalist class, the malfunction of the state interference in the economy, international pressures, and the effective lobby of the Federation of Korean Industries. See Suh Jae-jin, *Korean Capitalist Class (Hankukûi Chabonka kyekûp)*, pp. 125–34.

35 The self-regulation of the financial system was in reality 'a response of capital (including the state) which encountered a decline of its capacity in absorbing or converging money at the beginning of the 1980s'. See Kim Sang-cho, 'Structure and Change of the Financial Sector: In Case of the

Supply System of Equipment Financing' (*Kûmyungpumunûi Kuchowa Byônhwa — Wonhwa SôlbiKûmyung Kongkûpch'ekyerûl Chungsimûro*), in Yang Woo-jin, Hong Jang-pyo, et al., *Analysis of Korean Capitalism (Hankuk chabonjuûi bunsôk)*, Seoul: Ilbit, 1991, p. 265.

36 See Robert Bocock, *Hegemony*, p. 45.

37 See Hong Duk-ryul, 'Korean Society and Political Participation of the *Chaebôl*' (*Hankuk Sahoiwa Chaebôlûi Chôngch'i Ch'amyô) Sahoi Pyôngron*, March 1992, p. 26.

38 ibid.

39 A parallel example of the Korean bourgeoisie's failure to obtain hegemonic leadership can be seen in Gramsci's description of the northern Italian bourgeoisie who 'had acted entirely as an economic-corporate interest group and thereby failed to establish hegemonic leadership in the state or civil society of Italy'. See Robert Bocock, *Hegemony*, p. 45.

40 It seems to me that one of the structural reasons which made the *Chaebôl* participate in politics in order to obtain political hegemony was the absence of bourgeois revolution in Korea.

41 Joseph A.Schumpeter, *Capitalism, Socialism and Democracy*, 3rd edn, New York: Harper & Row, 1950, p. 82.

42 ibid., p. 83.

43 The view that the UNP was created to protect the interest of Hyundai (capital) because of the uneasy relationship between Hyundai and the government (between capital and the state) is called an 'Insurance Party' hypothesis. See the *Hankyôre Daily*, 31 March 1992.

44 The social movements of the middle strata in the fields of economic justice and environmental issues are growing rapidly, as shown in the activities of the Association for Economic Justice Realisation or the Association for Pollution Prevention.

45 As Wright and McManus argued, 'demands to make empowerment real through active inclusion of all segments of society and to make authority accountable will be at the center of changes to come': Robin Wright and Doyle McManus, *Flashpoints: Promise and Peril in a New World*, p. 109.

46 The *Hankyôre Daily*, 18 March 1992.

47 In his article, 'The Price of Apartments can be Halved?' (*Apart Kap, Chôlbanûro Naerilsuitna*), *Mal*, May 1992, pp. 76–82, Park Hae-jin argued that the solutions advocated by the UNP were far from achievable.

48 In general, it is thought that this advertisement considerably contributed to the UNP's success in the election. See Park Hae-jin, 'The Price of Apartments can be Halved?' (*Apart Kap, Chôlbanûro Naerilsuitna*), p. 76.

49 In the press interview, regarding the formation of the UNP, at his Ch'ôngun-dong house, he said: 'I had provided for political funds to the presidents twice a year since the Third Republic, and in the Sixth Republic I gave 2 or 3 billion *won* at once, and on the last occasion I gave 10 billion *won* at the end of 1990. . . I donated political funds because I wanted it to be used as

needed.' See Chun Jin-woo, 'Chung Ju-yung Dash' (*Dolchin*), p. 161.

50 To the press, Chung Ju-yung also said that 'if the government pressures on Hyundai continue, Hyundai will be bankrupted, and if Hyundai becomes bankrupt, one-third of our business will be bankrupted one after another'. See Chun Jin-woo, 'Chung Ju-yung Dash' (*Dolchin*), p. 161.

51 At the party convention for the Sanch'ông-Hamyang branch on 27 February 1992, Chung said that 'the government paid only half of the expenses, 45 billion *won*, that the government owed the Hyundai Construction for its Blue House reconstruction': Chun Jin-woo, 'Chung Ju-yung Dash' (*Dolchin*), p. 161.

52 In a meeting at the KDI on 5 March, Chung said that 'Hyundai did the construction, when the US made atomic-bomb storing sites in Korea. Governments in the past called for competitive bids for such secret constructions. However, this government is letting a private contract for constructions to get political funds.': Chun Jin-woo, 'Chung Ju-yung Dash' (*Dolchin*), p. 161.

53 In the presidential candidate forum organised by the *Sisa* Journal, Chung answered the question, 'what do you think about prisoners of conscience?', by saying that 'there is no need of punishment even if he/she is a communist unless his/her activities hurt people', and to the question, 'what do you think about people forming a communist party?', he answered that 'it does not matter as long as it does not hurt people' (The *Donga Daily*, 9 June 1992).

54 See Lee Jae-ho, 'A Study of "Chung Ju-yung's UNP" ('*Chong Ju-young Kukmindang' Yônku*),*Sindonga*, May 1992, p. 165.

55 See Chong Young-tae, 'The UNP, its Peculiarity and Duality' (*Tongilkukmindang, Kû Tûksusôngkwa Yijungsông*), *Sahoi Pyôngron*, May 1992, p. 94.

56 See Park Hae-jin, 'The Price of Apartments can be Halved?' (*Apart Kap, Chôlbanûro Naerilsuitna*), p. 76.

57 See Lee Jae-hyun, '"The Political Wind" of "An Adventurous Businessman"' ('*Dolpungchôch'i'ro kûnnan 'Kyôngchegye Punguna'*), p. 30.

58 See Chun Jin-woo, 'Chung Ju-yung Dash' (*Dolchin*), p. 163.

59 See *Wolgan Chosôn*, '*Chedogaesônuiwonhoiûi Chôngch'ê*', June 1992, pp. 144–49.

60 In addition to these high-ranking personnel, there were also middle ranking managers from Hyundai in the UNP — the first assistant secretary-general, Kim Young-il (49, former manager of the Hyundai department store in *Apkujông*), the second assistant secretary-general, Yun Kuk-jin (48, former manager of the Hyundai Tiger soccer team), the director of the organisation department, Kim Chol-sun (45, former general affairs manager of Hyundai Construction), the director of the planning department, Kang Ku-hyun (42, former personnel manager of Hyundai Construction), the director of the policy department, Kim Kon (46, former research manager of the Hyundai group planning department), the manager of the spokesman's

office, No Chi-yong (40, former financial manager of Hyundai Construction), the director of the publicity department (45, former foreign capital manager of Hyundai Construction), the secretary general of the Kyungnam branch, Do Young-hoi, the UNP candidate in Chongro, Lee Nae-hun, etc. In addition, there were 45 more personnel from Hyundai. See Chun Jin-woo, 'Chung Ju-young Dash' (*Dolchin*), p. 164; Lee Jae-ho, 'A Study of 'Chung Ju-yung's UNP' (*'Chung Ju-yung Kukmindang' Yônku*), pp. 171–72; Chong Sun-koo, 'Hyundai Guerilla in the UNP' (*Kukmindangûi Hyundai Tûkkongdae*), *Mal*, May 1992, pp. 54–58.

61 Robin Wright and Doyle McManus, *Flashpoints: Promise and Peril in a New World*, New York: Alfred A. Knopf, 1991, p. 121.

62 ibid., p. 122.

63 Chun Jin-woo, 'Chong, Ju-young Dash' (*Dolchin*), p. 165.

64 See Park Byung-suk, 'An Institutional Approach to the Problems of Political Funds' (*Chôngch'i Chakûm Muncheedaehan Chôngch'ichedoronchôk Chôpkûn*), unpublished, p. 2.

65 Son Ho-chul developed eight hypotheses about the conflict. From the perspective of state theory, Son comparatively analysed the various aspects of the conflict, and concluded that they were totally intertwined. See Son Ho-chul, 'The Eight Hypotheses on the Conflict between Hyundai and the Sixth Republic: from the Perspective of the State Theory' (*6 Kong-Hyundai Kyôkdol, 8 Kaji Kasôl: Kukkaronûi Kwanjômesô*).

66 See Park Byung-suk, 'An Institutional Approach to the Problems of Political Funds' (*Chôngch'i Chakûm Muncheedaehan Chôngch'ichedoronchôk Chôpkûn*),p. 12.

67 See the *Chosôn Daily*, 7 March 1992; the *Hankuk Daily*, 29 March 1992; the *Donga Daily*, 3 April 1992; and the *Chungang Daily*, 3 May 1992.

68 It was speculated that the early nomination of its candidate by the UNP was based on the calculation that this would block outside pressures which might come to disturb Chung's nomination. See the *Donga Daily*, 18 April 1992; and the *Hankuk Daily*, 16 May 1992.

6

Democratisation and Foreign Policy

Young Whan Kihl

South Korea's Sixth Republic saw impressive gains on two discernible political fronts: democratisation in domestic politics and *Nordpolitik* (or Northern Policy) in foreign relations. In both of these political arenas, President Roh Tae-woo's Administration (1988–93) scored high marks, although in other policy domains such as promoting social welfare and economic growth the gains were not as impressive or consistent as in democratisation and foreign policy.[1] The research question that arises in this regard is: what relationship, if any, exists between democratisation and foreign relations? Is the relationship between the two (domestic politics and foreign policy) coincidental or interactive? Does success in foreign relations depend on success in domestic politics, and vice versa? Is it reasonable to assume, for instance, that Roh's success in foreign policy was facilitated by the progress that his administration made in promoting democratisation and related policy agenda?

The regime type of a developing country such as South Korea seems to have a bearing on the public policy outcome, especially on the economic development policy pursued by the regime.[2] South Korea's status as a newly industrialising economy, for instance, was promoted by the authoritarian regimes in the past: President Park Chung-hee of the Third and Fourth Republics (1963–71, 1972–79) and President Chun Doo-hwan of the Fifth Republic (1980–87). Although South Korea's 'democratising regime' of the

Sixth Republic (1988–93) was not as successful in sustaining high economic growth as its predecessors, it was basically able to fulfil both policy objectives of vigorous diplomacy and a growth-oriented economy. This chapter attempts to evaluate the propositions (1) that South Korea's democratisation and economic growth are not always compatible as policy goals; (2) that the relationship between democratisation and economic growth is, therefore, not always positive; and (3) that political regime type and economic performance will have no bearing on the success or failure of a country's foreign policy.

Foreign policy-making in a transitional democracy: The context

The democratisation drive initiated in 1987 provided the context in which the foreign policy initiative was undertaken by the Roh Tae-woo government. In the external environment, the end of the Cold War era also provided the context in which both the foreign policy and reunification policies of the Roh Tae-woo government were carried out. Since foreign policy-making in a transitional democracy follows its own process and dynamics, it is necessary first to clarify the relationship between regime type and foreign policy. This will be followed by a discussion of the context of democratic transition in South Korea and the conceptual issues relative to foreign policy behaviour in South Korea.

Regime type and foreign policy

The Sixth Republic of South Korea embarked upon the task of democratisation as a consequence of the democratic upsurge of 1987.[3] Confronted with the worsening political crisis, due to an escalating conflict between opposition forces and the Chun regime, the 29 June 1987 declaration of democratic reform was advanced by the then-leader of the ruling Democratic Justice Party Roh Tae-woo as a way of attaining breakthrough and a political settlement for the stalemated issues of conflict. The eight-point declaration of democratisation included such bold and sweeping measures as pledges to restore human rights, freedom of speech, assembly and the press, and to conduct direct presidential elections as well as the release of political prisoners.[4]

Democracy or democracy-building in South Korea is an ideal and an ongoing process, rather than a reality or an accomplished fact. The efforts of President Roh Tae-woo's government in democratic transition will, therefore, need to be placed in their proper historical and theoretical context. It is necessary, for instance, to differentiate between theory and practice — that is, Roh's leadership commitment and policy direction on the one hand, and the regime's tangible accomplishments and institutional gains on the other. Instead of accepting the regime's claims at their face value, the performance and actual record of the regime in implementing reform promises must be used as the criteria for evaluation. From this perspective, then, the task of democratisation has not obviously been completed in South Korea, although great strides and impressive gains have been registered during President Roh's tenure in office, 1988–93.[5]

In retrospect, South Korea's Sixth Republic was neither the authoritarian state of the period prior to 1988, nor a fully established mature democracy as in the West. Instead, South Korea during President Roh's tenure in office may best be termed a 'transitional democracy' — that is, one just emerging from an authoritarian regime but not yet fully institutionalised as a mature democracy.[6] The institutional requirements and political dynamics of this regime type, as a newly democratising polity, are somewhat unique and differ from other regime types, whether authoritarian regimes or more mature and developed democratic states.

During the authoritarian regime era, primary attention was given to the task of economic growth and performance. Technocracy and selected *Chaebôls* were the agents through which the regime pursued its developmental goals, via an export-led strategy of industrialisation of the economy. State autonomy in the Fourth and Fifth Republics was very high as the regime tended, on the view of many critics, to over-reward big business and under-compensate others, including workers. The foreign policy agenda during this era was largely a matter of how to manage the existing security relations and trade ties with allies, principally the United States.

During the democratic transition, civil society became activated and the autonomy of the state was correspondingly constrained.[7] Since the democratising regime could no longer exclude the popular sectors of the labor unions and the working class from the political process, it had to develop popular policies tailored to their needs to solicit their support. Intellectuals became more open in articulating their democratic values and norms, thereby exerting pressures on the regime to incorporate them in the reform agenda. The university students became more vocal in their demands — for instance, for participation in campus governance. Popular elections, both at the national and local levels, were inaugurated so as to choose people's representatives and through them to provide popular input into the policy-making process. With the middle class becoming more vocal and attentive, the democratising regime was pressured more to promote and protect the interest of a large number of constituencies and interest groups.[8] With an activated civil society, the regime began to accommodate a large number of demands placed by interest groups for participation in the policy process.

The logic of democratic transition required the regime to give more attention and priority to 'righting the balance' and 'rectifying the ills' of the past years of authoritarian rule.[9] This type of transition problem, stemming from regime change to democracy, is the 'torturer problem' of 'how to treat authoritarian officials who had blatantly violated human rights' in the past.[10] Under these circumstances, politicians in the democratising regime have had more leeway in leadership and decision-making on foreign affairs. That accrued from the initial expectation and goodwill engendered by democratic transition. They may also have behaved differently, more opportunistically, in order to consolidate the regime's newly acquired legitimacy via electoral contests.

The democratic transition in South Korea during the Sixth Republic has been steady, although somewhat slow in pace and frustrating at times.[11] The leadership of the Roh Tae-woo government, constrained as it was by the exigencies of new rules and expectations, continued to tread along the path towards democracy. On the eve of the 1992 presidential election, Roh announced that he was resigning from the position as president of the ruling Democratic Liberal Party to remove himself, he claimed, from possible partisan entanglement. He then appointed a new prime minister and a neutral cabinet to manage the 18 December 1992 presidential election to choose his successor. This unusual act was an expression of Roh's unflagging commitment to attain a full measure of democracy by means of a smooth and orderly transition of power. Unlike his predecessors' regimes, President Roh wanted to make certain that his successor regime would enjoy full measures of legitimacy accruing from an open and fair election.

The fourteenth presidential election of 18 December 1992, which resulted in the victory of the ruling Democratic Liberal Party candidate Kim Young-sam, strengthened the process of democratisation. The election of a civilian president, the first in 32 years, was certainly a milestone in the constitutional history of restoring democracy and institutionalising the process of an orderly and peaceful transition of power. The new government of President Kim Young-sam has shown that it sees the need to continue the democratic reform agenda initiated by President Roh Tae-woo.

What, then, is the nature of the relationship between democratisation and foreign policy? Foreign policy in established democracies tends to be less warlike and more peaceful. History shows that liberal democratic countries tend to maintain peaceful relations with each other more so than with non-liberal countries.[12] This is generally the case, logically speaking, because liberal and democratic states tend to 'exercise peaceful restraints' and 'negotiate rather than escalate disputes'.[13]

It is unclear whether the foreign policy of democratising regimes or transitional democracies can likewise be said to be 'less warlike and more peaceful'. It is sensible to assume, however, that the regime that is moving away from authoritarianism towards democracy will have an incentive to be more prudent and cautious in its attempt to realise the democratic virtues and values of moderation and harmony of interests. To do otherwise seems to be setting the historical clock backwards in the march towards democracy. The non-democratic authoritarian regimes or totalitarian states, by both logic and implication, would be more risk-taking and warlike in their foreign policy style and behaviour.

The policy implications of the preceding analysis are that, as South Korea continues to move along the path of democratic transition, a scenario of war and lethal conflict with liberal democratic neighbors, such as Japan, is more remote and less likely to occur. Such may not be the case for democratic South Korea in its dealings with North Korea, however, so long as the latter continues to remain as a non-democratic and non-liberal state.[14] President Roh's Northern Policy was an answer by South Korea's democratising regime to confront and to cope with external challenges. It was a strategic move by Seoul's democratising regime to strengthen its diplomatic hand *vis-a-vis* Pyongyang's allies while further isolating North Korea internationally. On the eve of the Seoul Olympics in 1988, North Korea pressured its allies to boycott the Olympic Games; however, it was to no avail because all members of the socialist bloc countries except Castro's Cuba sent their athletes to the Seoul Olympic Games.

In terms of Roh's foreign policy in the Sixth Republic, not all of his diplomatic feats were of his own making. The hosting of the twenty-fourth Olympics in 1988, for instance, was the work of his predecessor, former President Chun Doo-hwan, who had worked hard to prepare for the staging of the Games, through massive construction projects and infra-structure building throughout the country. In this endeavour, the Chun regime acquired international loans and aid including $4 billion from Japan. Roh presided over the Olympic opening and closing ceremonies in his capacity as a newly elected leader of the country that had been set to blaze a new trail in democratic transition. Roh's pledge to support democratisation gave him the right, unlike Chun, to host and preside over the Seoul Olympic Games. It had been rumoured that the 1988 Olympic Games might be moved to an alternative site unless South Korea's political situation became stable and orderly.[15]

On the eve of the Seoul Olympics opening in 1988, the Roh administration took a series of important and bold foreign policy initiatives to enhance its diplomatic status *vis-a-vis* the socialist bloc countries. Before detailing the account of President Roh's foreign policy initiatives — called Nordpolitik or Northern Policy — and its implementation, however, we will need first to examine South Korea's democratic transition in its proper context and to introduce a conceptual framework for analysing South Korean foreign policy behaviour.

Democracy and democratic transition

South Korea's democratic transition, in the broader sense, may be regarded as an expression of the global march toward democracy that has been going on throughout the world in the last quarter of the twentieth century. This includes changes in Southern Europe, South America, the Philippines and the former socialist bloc countries in Eastern Europe. In this sense, South Korea certainly shares a common perspective and common problems with other countries that are also undergoing the process of rapid political change.[16]

South Korea's experience may be unique, however, to the extent that some of the pre-conditions or clusters of variables, noted by Samuel Huntington as relevant to the democratisation process, carry different weight and influence upon the country's political development.[17] The four-fold pre-conditions or requisites for democracy, according to Huntington, include: (1) economic development and equality; (2) pluralistic social structure; (3) external environment and its impact; and (4) political culture and its legacy.[18]

A heightened popular demand for political participation and the external impact of the worldwide trend towards democracy have thus influenced South Korea's political transition in 1987–93. The key to South Korea's initial success in democratisation lies, as James Cotton argues, not only in popular demands for political participation, but also in the willingness of elites to recognise them as unavoidable consequences of socio-economic modernisation.[19] An analysis of the South Korean case of democratisation will therefore require specification of the nature of both the regime and the popular sector as well as their interaction with a view to bringing about political changes. The Korean case is particularly timely and suggestive in illustrating difficulties and dilemmas for a rapidly industrialising country bringing about an orderly and peaceful democratic transition in a timely fashion.

South Korea's presidential election campaign of December 1992 symbolises the coming of age of the Korean people in a thriving, albeit fragile, democracy. With the election of Kim Young-sam, the country's first president without a military background in more than 30 years, South Korea has lived up to the goal of establishing democracy through an orderly and peaceful transfer of power. The democratic reform movement, unleashed by Roh Tae-woo's Sixth Republic, has been completed and South Korea is poised to enter a post-democratisation era of politics and economics. Just as South Korea built an economic miracle, the country has proven that the political miracle of democratic transition is within its reach.

Since democracy as a concept is not always easily defined or uniform in usage, we first need to clarify what is meant by democracy. In defining what democracy is, differentiation is usually made between the substantive and procedural meanings of democracy. Substantively, democracy is a form of government based on the consent of the people and serving the general interest of the governed. Procedurally, democracy is a form of government where the leaders are selected by the people through elections which are 'fair, open and periodic' and candidates are expected to compete for votes.[20]

Two observable and empirical indicators of democracy, as Robert Dahl observed, are the presence in the political system of (1) political contestation; and (2) popular participation in the political process.[21] A political system is democratic, as Samuel Huntington argues, 'to the extent that its most powerful collective decision-makers are selected through periodic elections in which candidates freely compete for votes and in which virtually all the adult population is eligible to vote'.[22] An operational definition of the term 'democracy', therefore, will require the presence of the regime and opposition forces in a society which is governed by the institutional rules and mechanisms for a peaceful and orderly political change via elections and an electoral process.

The democracy movement is a popular campaign to bring about an end to authoritarian rule and the establishment of democracy as a political system. Democratisation is thus the replacement of an authoritarian government by a government selected 'in a free, open, and fair election'.[23] Whereas liberalisation entails a 'partial opening of an authoritarian system', democratisation entails the process of 'choosing governmental leaders through freely competitive elections'.[24] Thus defined, democratisation, understood as the process of popular participation in the political process, is widespread throughout the world. South Korea's democracy movement reached a turning point and acquired potency in the summer of 1987 when protest demonstrations were joined by the middle-class citizenry. Thereafter, however, violent demonstrations died down with the waning support of the middle-class citizens who detested tear gas and violent confrontation in the streets. South Korean democratic transition began with the December 1987 presidential election and climaxed with the December 1992 presidential election, thereby completing the full electoral cycle of an orderly and peaceful transfer of power.

South Korea's 1992 presidential election was less violence-ridden and emotionally charged than the 1987 election. No street protest demonstrations or voter boycotts were noticeable in this election. Perhaps this reflects the growing confidence and maturity of South Korean voters and their resolve to build a newly successful democratic polity. The voter turnout of 81.7 per cent of the eligible voters in 1992 was not as high as that of 89.2 per cent registered in the 1987 presidential election. But this figure is still higher than that in most democracies and is higher than the 80 per cent projected by political pundits before the election of 1992. The voting in 1992 was relatively orderly and peaceful, and there were less frequent charges of campaign excesses and voter irregularities. The ruling and opposition party candidates, for instance, avoided scheduled mass rallies in Seoul, although Chung Ju-yung's third party went ahead with its plans. The losing candidates Kim Dae-jung and Chung Ju-yung made conceding speeches, while the electoral returns were still being counted, to admit their defeat and to congratulate their opponent, Kim Young-sam, on his victory.

South Korea, in February 1993, experienced the first-ever peaceful and orderly transition of power by a popularly elected civilian president in the Republic's 45-year constitutional history. Thus South Korea marked its first full-electoral cycle of a democratic transition of power. This remarkable achievement of democratic transformation was made possible by the twin factors of Roh's steadfast commitment to democracy and the character of the democratising regime of the Sixth Republic. 'The wisdom and guts to move his nation toward democracy and free elections, though this progress gradually eroded his party's power and his own,' as Leslie Gelb observed, shows the quality of Roh's presidential leadership.[25] Moreover, the outgoing president Roh Tae-woo was able to solve what Huntington calls 'the Praetorian problem' of the potential rebellion by the military and its political intervention in the political process. As ex-general turned civilian leader, President Roh was able to curb military power by keeping military factionalism from getting out of hand and by pacifying the military, urging them to remain politically neutral and to pursue professionalism.[26]

Six years before, in 1987, Roh Tae-woo, as then-leader of the ruling Democratic Justice Party and also as a presidential candidate, decided that dramatic measures of political reform were needed to break a stalemate and to avoid a crisis of confrontation between the ruling party and the opposition forces.[27] On 29 June 1987, Roh put his political career on the line and issued an eight-point proposal for democratic reform. His declaration of democratic reforms called for constitutional revision, among other measures, to provide for direct presidential elections, freedom of the press, and other extended protective measures for the civil rights of the citizenry.

The inauguration of President Roh in February 1988 marked the first peaceful transfer of power in the Republic's 40-year history. Roh was an ex-military general and a hand-picked successor to the discredited outgoing president Chun Doo-hwan. But he was elected president in a popularly held national election with a plurality vote of 36.6 per cent of the total votes. This small margin of the electoral vote was due, in large measure, to the split in the opposition camp, produced by the rival candidacies of Kim Young-sam and Kim Dae-jung, who polled between them a total of 55 per cent of the votes, large enough (had they been in co-operation) to win the election. In the 1992 presidential election, Kim Young-sam, now running as the ruling Democratic Liberal Party candidate, received 42 per cent of the popular votes, while the opposition candidates Kim Dae-jung and Chung Ju-yung received 34 per cent and 16 per cent respectively.

During his 1987 campaign for the presidency, Roh made a promise that, if elected, he would do his best to usher in what he called 'a great era of ordinary people'. Although vague, he meant by this promise that he would introduce an era of popular democracy in which all Koreans would have equal access to the political process and the welfare society where all Koreans would be able to enjoy a decent living standard.[28] Roh's vision of promoting the prosperity of the common people has been borne out with the enhanced political status of the middle-class citizenry in South Korea's electoral process as exemplified in the 1992 presidential election.

According to the constitutional provision President Roh Tae-woo could not succeed himself after completion of his five-year term in 1993. President Roh is credited with three major accomplishments during his tenure: democratic reforms, the Northern Policy, and inter-Korean dialogue.[29] Of the three major policies promoted by President Roh, the Northern Policy was the most successful, while in the area of inter-Korean dialogue there was also some success. Democratisation has enhanced Korea's international standing and foreign policy as well.

Since the reunification of the country has not been achieved, it is in this area of inter-Korean relations that Roh wished to see further progress made before he stepped down as president in February 1993. This desire to bring the reunification of Korea closer to reality was the motivating factor behind the signing of a series of agreements with North Korea in 1992. However, the progress in implementing these agreements has been slow. His government's proposal, for instance, to arrive at substantive progress on the Red Cross talks on divided family reunion was not heeded by North Korea. It is important that older Koreans be allowed to travel and meet with their family members across the border before it is too late for this ageing group. This basic humanitarian cause is not solvable, however, because of the intransigent political stance of a North Korea that is intent upon keeping its population isolated from adverse external influences.

Analysing Foreign Policy Behaviour: 'What, how and why' questions

In the study of South Korea's foreign policy, a number of questions arise. First and foremost, what is foreign policy? Second, how do we account for why South Korea acts and behaves diplomatically as it does? Third, who makes foreign policy and who participates in the policy-making process? Fourth, what role does the public play, if any, in foreign policy-making? Does the public participate in the policy process? Some of these questions can be answered by articulating a working definition of foreign policy and the changing context of democratic transition in South Korean politics.

Foreign policy, for the purpose of this study, will mean 'a plan of action (or blueprint) formulated by "authoritative" decision-makers (i.e. President Roh Tae-woo and his assistants) to cope with the situation external to the country (i.e. South Korea)'. The primary actor in South Korea's foreign policy-making, under the constitutional provision, is the president who relies on his staff in the Blue House, the executive mansion of the president, as well as on his Foreign Minister and ministry officials. This means that a foreign policy elite exists in South Korea, although, with the progress of democratisation, it is an elite which is less autonomous and insulated than formerly. The public and interest groups have begun to exert more pressures and influence upon the process of formulating and executing South Korea's foreign policy, including the policy dealing with the country's reunification.

With further democratisation in domestic politics, the public will come to play a greater role and interest groups will come to participate more in the formulation of South Korea's foreign policy agenda. For instance, in the matter of Roh's Northern Policy, a private initiative was undertaken by the nongovernmental group called IPECK (International Private Economic Council of Korea) led by an ex-Deputy Prime Minister, Lee Hahn-been. This promoted trade and cultural exchanges between Seoul and the former socialist countries in Eastern Europe. The KOTRA (Korea Trade Promotion Corporation), although a semi-government body, has also been engaged in promoting trade ties between South Korea and other countries with which Seoul does not maintain diplomatic relations.[30]

From the preceding analysis it is clear that democratisation in South Korea has provided the context in which the foreign policy agenda was formulated and carried out in President Roh Tae-woo's Sixth Republic. The logic of democracy or democratisation underlies the process of South Korea's Nordpolitik and reunification policy. Table 6.1 shows a framework for analysing South Korea's foreign policy behaviour. This shows that foreign policy behaviour, taken as a dependent variable, is influenced by a series of independent variables in the form of the sources and factors of influence as well as the contextual or intervening variables of industrialisation, the democracy movement or democratisation, and reunification.

Foreign policy patterns and determinants

What is clear from the reading of Table 6.1 is that South Korea's foreign policy behaviour can be described in terms of (a) its alignment pattern being either allied, neutral or non-aligned; (b) its scope of action being either global or regional; and (c) its modus operandi being either bilateral or multilateral, or even seeking greater activism and participation in international organisation (IO) activities.

As for the more challenging questions of analysing and explaining South Korea's foreign policy behaviour, one can identify several key determinants of South Korea's foreign policy. These include:

1 the systemic factors, such as the geopolitical location and position of the country;

Table 6.1   *Analysing South Korea's foreign policy behaviour: Conceptual and theoretical framework*

Pattern	Determinants	Context
Alignment Alliance, non-alignment, neutrality	**Systemic** Geography, interactions, links, international system, structure, etc.	**Industrialisation**
Scope Global or regional	**National attributes** Demographic, economic, military, governmental system or forms, etc.	**Democratisation**
Modus operandi Bilateral, multilateral, degree of activism, greater IO partici-pation, etc.	**Idiosyncratic** Leader's traits, personality, temperament,	**Reunification**

2 national attributes, such as governmental forms and economic capability; and
3 idiosyncratic factors, such as leadership personality.

South Korea's governmental system, as a transitional democracy moving away from authoritarianism, may have foreign policy implications in terms of styles in formulating and carrying out policy programs.

South Korea's foreign policy during the Sixth Republic was clearly influenced by such systemic factors as the bipolar structure of the international system which has waned over time and gained greater flexibility, beginning with the new detente between the United States and the Soviet Union following the Malta summit in 1988 and with the eventual passing of the Cold War era due to the demise of communism. The rise of South Korea as a dynamic and newly industrialising economy has also given impetus to the diplomatic activism of President Roh Tae-woo's government. This was sustained and propelled by the favourable image of the country created with the successful hosting of the 1988 Seoul Olympic Games. President Roh Tae-woo's idiosyncratic characteristics as a leader initiating liberalisation and democratisation of politics have also played a role in moulding and shaping the pattern of South Korea's foreign policy during the Sixth Republic.

President Roh's varied style of leadership was noted in his preference for consensus-building. Unlike President Chun Doo-hwan's assertive approach, Roh's was more or less passive, although his foreign policy was more active diplomatically. The image-building of Roh as 'democratic reformer', and his desire to compensate for his domestic policy failures, such as sluggish economic growth, and to be remembered as initiator of the country's reunification process, motivated Roh to be an activist president on foreign policy and on reunification policy.

Ultimately, it was President Roh's own sense of mission and role, or the ways in which he defined national interest and the goals of South Korea's foreign policy, that was responsible for the ways in which the Sixth Republic behaved diplomatically and *vis-a-vis* North Korea on the reunification issue. The subjective determination of Roh's national interest and that of the regime, in addition to the objective factors of systemic and national attribute variables, moulded the pattern of South Korea's foreign policy behaviour during the five-year term of President Roh's administration, 1988–93.

The new government of President Kim Young-sam faced numerous policy challenges in its aspirations to fulfil campaign promises: realising economic deregulation domestically and restoring the sagging trade performance as well as pursuing further expansion abroad. More emphasis on economic agenda and less on foreign policy characterised the 1992 presidential election campaigns in South Korea — in a similar way to what transpired in the United States presidential election of November 1992. During the campaigns, all three leading candidates, Kim Young-sam, Kim Dae-jung and Chung Ju-yung, went on record — with slight variation in emphasis — supporting economic reforms and deregulation of the economy, lessening governmental intervention, and promoting greater business-led growth. They also advocated greater economic justice, financial market reform, an end to land speculation via taxation, more open markets, transparency in policy-making and an end to one-sided favouring of big business.[31]

All of these objectives are admirable, but their attainment will not be easy. If Mr Roh's tenure is an indication, the South Korean public desires irreconcilable roles from its president. The South Korean people's ideal president seems to be one who can advance the cause of democracy and at the same time promote vigorous economic growth by using, if necessary, authoritarian control measures to discipline the economy.[32] The new government, with a plurality of 42 per cent of the popular votes, was not therefore in a position easily to satisfy voters' expectations at home while simultaneously meeting the mounting pressures for trade liberalisation coming from abroad.

The new president, Kim Young-sam, has found it necessary to prove to both the nation and the world that he is capable of building a new national consensus with a clear purpose that is befitting the newly acquired status and reputation of South Korea in the new global and regional order of the post-Cold War era. In the past, Kim Young-sam was sometimes considered to lack not only charisma but also a firm grasp on some important issues, such as national security. He has generally been regarded as a back-room dealmaker, although his role as president now demands a more open posture.

It is clear that the South Korean people's desire for political democracy, commensurate with South Korea's proud accomplishment as a newly industrialised economy, was manifest in the 1993 political transition. In this sense, South Korea in 1993 was a trail-blazer for other East Asian newly industrialising countries in their common journey towards democracy.

Northern Policy (or Nordpolitik) and democratisation

The Northern Policy or Nordpolitik was the most important foreign policy initiative undertaken by the democratising regime of President Roh Tae-woo. Under this policy directive, Seoul successfully negotiated the establishment of diplomatic relations with all the communist countries except Castro's Cuba. South Korea established diplomatic ties first with countries in Eastern Europe, including Hungary, Poland and Yugoslavia in 1989, followed by ties with Czechoslovakia, Bulgaria, Romania, East Germany as well as with Mongolia and the former Soviet Union in 1990, and finally with China and Vietnam in 1992. South Korea also successfully managed to join the United Nations in 1991, while pressuring North Korea to do likewise and become a member of the world body.[33] An analysis of Roh's Northern Policy, in terms of its logic, substance and consequences, will show that it was promoted in part because of domestic political considerations, and will also demonstrate that South Korea's favourable external image as a newly democratising and industrialising country contributed to its successful implementation.

The logic of the Northern Policy

The Northern Policy, or Nordpolitik, as it is sometimes called after West German Chancellor Willy Brandt's Ostpolitik, was the theoretical rationale for the new strategic calculus of President Roh Tae-woo's foreign policy in the Sixth Republic. With the democratisation agenda intact, following his inauguration in February 1988, Roh Tae-woo soon realised that he could no longer rely on 'politics as usual' as a strategy of governing. A new and fresh approach to politics had to be invented, and urgently, as he was searching for a model of effective governing that suited the new era of democratic transition.

During the authoritarian years, the government used the rhetoric of anti-communism to impose tough measures relating to domestic law and order. With the change in the governing system, away from authoritarianism and towards democracy, the old hackneyed practice of crying wolf on communism was no longer suited or credible. A more sensible alternative strategy was, therefore, deemed essential and this eventually took the form of the Northern Policy or Nordpolitik. This new policy was based on the premise that direct confrontation and encounter with communism head-on was the best workable strategy in a time of rapid environmental changes, thereby providing a rationale for seeking normalisation of relations with the allies of communist North Korea.

Seoul's Northern Policy was aimed at achieving the twin objectives of the relaxation of tensions toward North Korea and the improvement of relations with the communist bloc countries of China, the Soviet Union and Eastern Europe. Although it was presented initially as a means of attaining the unification of Korea, the Northern Policy had acquired a *raison d'etre* and rationality of its own. It soon became a major diplomatic tool for promoting the foreign policy objectives of South Korea's democratising regime of President Roh Tae-woo.[34]

The Northern Policy, thus initiated and used by the Roh Tae-woo government, produced domestic political payoffs. Diplomatic success abroad and the opening of new business opportunities in the former communist-bloc countries ended up enhancing the support level of the regime among the population. President Roh was glad to use the success of this policy for promoting the political standing and legitimacy of his democratising regime.

The logic of Northern Policy was already recognised by his predecessor. The seeds of Nordpolitik were sown by former President Park Chung-hee of the Third Republic on 23 June 1973, when he said that his government was willing to establish ties between South Korea and countries with different ideological and political systems. President Park's declaration opened South Korean ports to ships from communist countries and gave them equal access to formerly forbidden parts of the world. But with the turn of events and the freeze in international relations, occasioned by such events as the Soviet invasion of Afghanistan in December 1979 and the subsequent United States military buildup, the Seoul government initiative was sidelined until the advent of a new detente in United States–Soviet relations following the emergence of a reform-minded Soviet leader in March 1985.

The initial statement of the Northern Policy was contained in the inauguration address of President Roh on 25 February 1988: he pledged to pursue a vigorous northern diplomacy by calling on North Korea to 'accept that dialogue, not violence, is the most direct short cut to ending division and bringing about unification'.[35] Other foreign policy agenda items of President Roh's Sixth Republic were laid down in a series of new and imaginative policy initiatives and pronouncements, including: a Special Declaration on National Self-esteem, Unification and Prosperity, on 7 July 1988; Roh's address before the 34th United Nations General Assembly, on 18 October 1988; and his Special Address before the National Assembly concerning National Unification on 11 September 1989. President Roh used public forums both at home and abroad to launch his initiatives on Northern Policy.

The content of northern policy

The gist of the Roh Tae-woo government's Nordpolitik was contained in a six-point policy statement reflected in the Special Declaration on National Self-esteem, Unification and Prosperity of 7 July 1988. Addressing the National Assembly, President Roh made it known to the world that his government would seek:

- to actively promote exchanges of visits between the people of South and North Korea and make necessary arrangements to ensure that Koreans residing overseas can freely visit both parts of Korea;
- to vigorously promote exchange of correspondence and visits between relatives dispersed in both parts of Korea;
- to open trade between South and North Korea;
- not to oppose (friendly) nations trading with North Korea, provided that the trade does not involve military goods;
- to allow contacts between representatives of South and North Korea in international forums and to co-operate in areas of interest to the whole Korean nation; and
- to co-operate with North Korea in its efforts to improve relations with countries friendly to the South.

The timing of Roh's pronouncement of new policy was opportune, because world attention was focused on the events in South Korea. The government's concern was to prevent any domestic political turmoil, such as violent street demonstrations and escalating partisan conflicts, from undermining the forthcoming international festival of the 24th Olympic Games scheduled to take place in Seoul from 2–14 October 1988.

Despite international apprehension, the 24th Seoul Olympic Games were successful. The hosting of this event enhanced the prestige and reputation of South Korea in the eyes of many nations, especially among the communist bloc nations of the Soviet Union, China and Eastern Europe. This accomplishment gave South Korea's democratising regime the necessary psychological boost and self-confidence to resolve to put into practice the overall objectives of Nordpolitik. Immediately after the closing ceremony of the Olympic Games, President Roh left for New York on a diplomatic mission.

Addressing the United Nations General Assembly on 18 October 1988, President Roh Tae-woo now used the world forum to continue his initiative on Northern Policy. He appealed to the world body to assist his government to resolve the problem of Korean reunification. Included in the list of more specific proposals and suggested measures for settling the Korean problem were:

- a six-power consultative conference on Korea to be attended by the United States, the Soviet Union, China, Japan and North and South Korea;
- building a 'city of peace' in the Demilitarised Zone (DMZ) to promote South–North rapprochement; and
- a non-aggression declaration and a summit meeting between South and North Korea to discuss outstanding issues including military matters.

To underscore the seriousness of its intention, the Roh government announced the following specific follow-up measures of its new Nordpolitik. On 10 October 1988, the Economic Planning Board made public a seven-point economic plan to open trade with North Korea by allowing, among other things, South Korean business to trade with North Korea and contact North Korean counterparts in third countries; North Korean vessels carrying trade goods to make port calls in the South; and North Korean businesses to visit the South for economic exchanges. The Ministry of Culture and Information lifted its ban on the public access to information about North Korea and other communist countries. It also announced plans to discontinue propaganda campaigns against the North.[36]

This positive and progressive move toward North Korea's communist regime culminated in the adoption of a new reunification policy for South Korea's democratising regime. Addressing the National Assembly, President Roh Tae-woo unveiled South Korea's new unification plan on 11 September 1989. This new proposal was aimed at building the Korean National Community (KNC) or Korean Commonwealth as an intermediary stage and preparatory step toward an eventual reunification of Korea at a future date. Unlike the previous proposals, Seoul's KNC plan seemed more forward-looking and realistic in terms of stipulating concrete measures and approaches for institution-building towards reunification. It advocated a gradual and evolutionary approach towards an eventual system integration of North and South Korea following the experiment in the larger community-building efforts. Seoul's KNC plan was put forward as a more realistic and feasible alternative to Pyongyang's DCRK (Democratic Confederal Republic of Koryo) plan.

Seoul's Nordpolitik was thus based on a new approach and attitude toward solving inter-Korean problems. It reflected the change in the perception of North Korea on the part of the South Korean elite. For instance, it insisted that North Korea be treated as a brother and a partner rather than an adversary. As a concrete measure, Seoul's new policy contained pledges to stop slander against North Korea and to assist North Korea in moving out of isolation from the rest of the world. Accommodation and working for common prosperity, rather than confrontation, were said to be a preferred strategy for unification and building a single Korean national community.

Evaluation of Northern Policy

In retrospect, these specific suggestions were noble and idealistic, rather than realistic. Since it requires two to tango diplomatically, a great deal of reciprocity and co-operation was needed on the part of the intended partner.

Whether this unilateral move and policy pronouncement by the Seoul side would succeed and bear fruit, of course, depended on how the Pyongyang side responded to Seoul's gesture. Initially, the prognosis based on the lukewarm response by Pyongyang was not too encouraging. Nonetheless, an important fact is that Seoul's 'bold' initiative on Nordpolitik was well received by South Korea's allies and by those targeted countries in the former communist bloc. This suggests that the targeted audience of Roh's Northern Policy was both Pyongyang and Pyongyang's allies in the communist bloc as well as broader audiences at home and elsewhere in the world.

Democratisation in South Korea had some unforeseen positive impacts, not only at home but also abroad. At home, Northern Policy provided an opportunity for South Korean citizens and business to interact with the communist countries. The door was open, especially for progressive groups such as university students, to travel to socialist countries, thereby learning first hand about the reality of deteriorating conditions in these countries and come back with a renewed sense of how superior the capitalist market system is over the centrally planned socialist economic system. Northern Policy was a strong antidote and medicine, therefore, for curing the social disease of rampant radicalism and 'progressive' ideology. Abroad, democratisation enhanced South Korea's foreign policy and international standing among the nations which, in turn, helped enhance legitimacy and consolidate the democratising regime at home. The ROK Ambassador to the United States, Hyun Hong-choo, was right when he claimed that at least in four ways democratisation had worked to assist South Korea's foreign policy and its international standing.[37]

First, political liberalisation had worked to strengthen Korea's alliances with democratic nations, particularly the United States. Second, democratisation had accelerated the establishment of relations between Seoul and former socialist countries. The success of its Northern Policy was thus owed to democratisation at home because the former Soviet Union and countries of Eastern Europe were going through their own reform movements in the late 1980s and those communist countries were favourably impressed by South Korea's success in democratic transition. Third, Korea's experience in democratisation had shown that rapid economic development could go hand-in-hand with political reform and the ROK was viewed as a model for former communist countries themselves. Fourth, South Korea's democratisation had promoted expanded dialogue with the North which subsequently culminated in the signing of a series of inter-Korean agreements in 1992.

With public opinion on his side, President Roh was able to seek and establish high-level official contact with the government in Pyongyang in

1990, whereby the prime ministers of South and North Korea could meet regularly. Until then, North Korea had conducted no serious negotiation and dialogue in inter-Korean relations by refusing to recognise the legitimacy of the South Korean government. South Korea's successful Northern Policy led to strengthening Seoul's diplomatic hand and to further isolation of North Korea which, in turn, attempted its own southern policy of reaching out to improve relations with Japan and the United States.[38] The pressures exerted by South Korea's Northern Policy thus led North Korea to come to the conference table with South Korea on matters of inter-Korean relations and reunification. Seoul openly admitted that Northern Policy was an attempt to reach Pyongyang via the latter's allies in Moscow and Beijing.

The foremost strategic goal of Northern Policy, at the initial stage, was to realise cross-recognition of South Korea by the communist allies of North Korea in exchange for cross-recognition of North Korea by its allies, Japan and the United States, in the belief that such would enhance stability and peace on the Korean Peninsula. With the success in implementing the policy, the scope and task of Northern Policy seemed to have expanded to include a broader set of concerns. Thus the more specific and expanded considerations now seem to include basically three types of political, military and economic goals: enhancing the domestic political status and legitimacy of the Roh government at home, improving military and security postures *vis-a-vis* North Korea, and promoting economic welfare through trade and economic opportunities abroad in the communist countries.

The Northern Policy, although developed as a foreign policy initiative, was also motivated by domestic political considerations. It was invented as a means of consolidating the Roh Tae-woo regime's authority and hold on power. In the first year of the Roh administration, the challenge of a democratising regime lay in consensus-building at home and the broadening of the political support base. In this strategic aim, Roh's foreign policy initiative seemed highly successful and effective. Although Roh's Northern Policy had largely become identified as a diplomatic and foreign policy initiative toward the communist-bloc countries, it was presented initially as a new policy initiative towards North Korea and as a means of bringing Korean reunification closer, as shown in the preceding discussion.

Strictly speaking, therefore, Northern Diplomacy and Northern Policy may be differentiated. Whereas Northern Diplomacy was a move to reach out to the former communist allies of North Korea, in terms of establishing diplomatic ties with them, Northern Policy was a strategic move to force North Korea to abandon its isolation and to open its system to outside forces. Northern diplomacy was a resounding success and an effective policy instrument for achieving the short-term objectives of peace and stability on the Korean peninsula. The United Nations membership of North Korea in September 1991 is one tangible piece of evidence of Seoul's successful Northern Diplomacy. By virtue of its UN membership, North Korea was obligated (as South Korea is) to honour and abide by the UN charter provisions for promoting world peace and harmony, realising peaceful settlement of international disputes, as well as protecting the human rights of the citizenry.

The Northern Policy of inducing North Korea's domestic reform and change in inter-Korean relations was not particularly effective or successful. Nonetheless, the original intent of Northern Policy was to induce change and reform in North Korea and a breakthrough in inter-Korean relations that might be attained in the long run, given the patience and perseverance of an eventual political transition into the post-Kim Il Sung era in North Korea. The signing of the basic agreement on reconciliation, non-aggression and exchanges and co-operation between North and South Korea in 1992, to which we turn next, is a hopeful sign that North Korea may be coming around to accept the reality of the changing world in the post-Cold War era, even if the regime is doing so out of necessity rather than out of conviction.

Inter-Korean relations and rapprochement

Democratisation at home and success in foreign policy abroad led South Korea to seek improved inter-Korean relations and progress towards the reunification of North and South Korea. In conducting inter-Korean dialogue and negotiation, the democratising regime of President Roh Tae-woo was able to capitalise upon its newly acquired legitimacy domestically and enhanced status internationally. Democratisation now assured the Roh regime of favourable public opinion and gave it the moral high ground in dealing with the communist regime in the North. Democratisation also enhanced South Korea's international standing with the successful achievement of its northern diplomacy.

In building its peaceful relations with North Korea's communist regime, the democratising regime of South Korea took certain risks which were inherent in the practice of an open and democratic system of foreign policy-making and implementation. Nevertheless, South Korea's democratic transition gave political legitimacy and moral superiority to the Seoul government *vis-a-vis* its counterpart in the North on matters of conducting inter-Korean negotiations for the future reunification of Korea. To evaluate this positive impact of democratisation on inter-Korean relations, it is necessary first to examine the context of the newly arranged detente and the substance of the new framework for peaceful coexistence between North and South Korea.

The context of a 'new detente'

Inter-Korean relations went through several stages of ups and downs. Prior to 1972, the two Koreas were in violent contact during the Korean War, 1950–53, followed by a period of estrangement and internal consolidation punctured by an occasional clash and North Korean commando raids across the Demilitarised Zone. The major power detente in the early 1970s, with the Sino-American rapprochement in 1972, changed the character of inter-Korean relations from incommunicado to dialogue and negotiation.[39] Nevertheless, subsequent dialogue and negotiation between the two sides did not bear fruit throughout the 1970s and 1980s, with the familiar pattern of an 'on-off' relationship.

A major breakthrough in inter-Korean relations occurred in 1990, however, with the holding of the high-level talks between North and South Korea at the prime ministerial level. The first meeting held in Seoul in September 1990 was historic in the sense of both sides coming to accept each other, for the first time, as legitimate partners in negotiation.[40] The two subsequent meetings held in 1990, however, produced no substantive agreements.

The fourth prime ministers' meeting, scheduled for February 1991, was unilaterally cancelled by Pyongyang in protest over the United States–ROK joint military exercises called Team Spirit 1991. The rescheduled meeting, set for late August 1991, was postponed once again by Pyongyang due to the prevailing uncertain situations following the abortive coup in the Soviet Union. As the meeting finally took place in Pyongyang in October, an agreement was reached on 22 October 1991 that both sides would negotiate for a single text on the North–South agreement on reconciliation and co-operation to be worked out at a subsequent meeting.[41]

It was during the fifth session of high-level talks in Seoul that the two sides successfully negotiated to sign the basic agreement for reconciliation, non-aggression and exchanges and co-operation between North and South Korea on 13 December 1991. This historic agreement was followed by the subsequent signing of a joint declaration on denuclearisation of the Korean peninsula on 31 December 1991. The final ratified documents of these inter-Korean agreements were exchanged during the sixth high-level talks in Pyongyang on 19 February 1992.

Domestic sources of Roh's rapprochement with Pyongyang

The dilemma of a democracy or democratising regime in dealing with a non-democratic dictatorial regime in foreign relations is that its options are limited in conducting negotiation. The reason is that the democratic or democratising regime must heed public opinion both at home and abroad, more so than the dictatorial regime, and evolve foreign policy programs which are often tailored to the needs and interests of constituent groups at home. Under the circumstances, the leadership of the democratising regime relies on the strategy of balancing the broader interest of national security and the more mundane regime interest of survival. This problem was also confronted by the democratising regime of President Roh in its dealings with North Korea's communist regime on matters of the future of inter-Korean relations and reunification.

President Roh was credited as the one who carried out the bold initiative of putting an end to the authoritarian legacy and bringing about the democratic transition in South Korean politics. Although his commitment to the cause of democracy seemed undiminished, he was often criticised by the democratic forces as being too slow and hesitant in carrying out reform measures. Of the eight-point reform package that he announced on 29 June 1987, most of the points, including the freedom of the press, were slow to be implemented. Yet the economic slowdown and rampant corruption led his administration to be subject increasingly to severe criticism for indecisive leadership. Many critics charged that democratic consolidation was slow in coming.

One way to counter criticism was for President Roh to launch an aggressive reunification policy. By taking a bold initiative on the front of North–South relations, President Roh wanted to find an exit from the public preoccupation with the stagnant economy and uncertain democratic consolidation. Clearly he wished to be remembered in history as the one who took a bold initiative on the front of inter-Korean relations and Korean reunification, as was shown in the successful conclusion of the historical reconciliation and non-aggression pact between North and South Korea.

In his 1992 New Year address, President Roh Tae-woo said that '1992 will be remembered as the first year of the concentrated efforts of the 70 million Korean people to accomplish the great task of building a single national community'. He wanted to be the one who took a positive step toward achieving the nationalist aspiration of the Korean people — that is, reunification of the divided nation. To President Roh, reunification, like democracy, was an issue that was foremost in his mind, perhaps to the same degree that economic growth and industrialisation were a goal-driven obsession of the late President Park Chung-hee. In an interview with the *Korea Times* in November 1992, President Roh gave himself a high mark on his accomplishments in diplomacy, pointing out the fact that, during his tenure in office, Seoul opened diplomatic ties with 39 additional countries.[42]

The North–South basic agreement was clearly a compromise between the two divergent approaches and positions held by the respective sides in inter-Korean negotiations. Whereas the North had insisted that the major steps be taken on political and military matters first, so as to forestall the danger of war, the South had advocated confidence-building measures on economic and cultural matters first, so as to foster a climate of mutual trust. The text of the basic agreement is a comprehensive document that incorporates the varying positions of both sides. Although the interpretation of the text might differ between the two sides, thereby providing a new source of contention, the 1991 agreement still constitutes a landmark and watershed in the 46-year history of inter-Korean rivalry and competition.[43]

The basic agreement consists of 25 separate articles, apart from a preamble, that are grouped into four chapters: Chapter 1 (pledges on reconciliation), Chapter 2 (non-aggression provisions), Chapter 3 (inter-Korean exchanges and co-operation matters) and Chapter 4 (amendment and ratification provisions).[44] In the preamble, both sides agree that, since 'their relations constitute a special provisional relationship geared to unification', they will 'exert joint efforts to achieve peaceful unification'. They also agree to 'reaffirm the reunification principles enunciated in the July 4 (1972) South–North Joint Communiqué' — that is, peaceful, independent and national reunification — as well as to 'resolve political and military confrontation and achieve national reconciliation' and to 'promote multi-faceted exchanges and cooperation' so as to 'advance common national interests and prosperity'.

The subsequent high-level talks in 1992 also made some progress along the line of institutionalising the peace process by setting up the machinery needed to carry out the basic agreement. During the eighth high-level talks in Pyongyang on 17 September 1992, for instance, the two prime ministers signed and put into effect three separate protocols to implement the basic agreement:

1 on non-aggression;
2 on reconciliation; and
3 on exchanges and co-operation.

They also agreed to establish a Joint Commission on Reconciliation and, before that, a liaison office in Panmunjom during the seventh high-level talks, held in Seoul in May 1992. Despite this progress, the protocols failed to resolve several other key and controversial issues, such as the recognition of each other's government in the political arena, prohibition of arms buildup along the Demilitarised Zone, and the on-site nuclear inspection guidelines, which were left for future discussion at related joint commissions and other forums.[45]

The significance and limitation of the Basic Agreement

The foremost significance of the basic agreement of 1992 was that North and South Korea finally came to accept each other as 'legitimate' partners in negotiation. Moreover, they accepted, by deed, the underlying premise of the agreement (i.e. that peace and reunification are inter-related and that peaceful coexistence between the two sides must precede the final act of national reunification). Clearly peaceful coexistence between North and South Korea must precede any change in the status quo which reunification of divided Korea will entail and represent. In this sense, the basic agreement is a reflection of political realism because the reunited Korea that both sides will aspire to attain is a future preferred condition that will come about only if they work together as partners rather than as strangers.

The basic agreement also represents a new breakthrough in inter-Korean relations. It reflects the determination of the two Koreas to stay in touch and keep up with the changing time in world politics. The new relationship between them is thus in line with the search for a new world order and Korea's determination to remain relevant in world affairs.

Finally, the basic agreement has provided the framework for co-operation and exchanges between the two sides which can be used to build the foundation for a reunited Korea. Peaceful co-existence between North and South Korea is the necessary condition for maintaining peace and stability in the post-Cold War era. The reunification of Korea is most unlikely without a framework for peaceful coexistence that will eliminate the threat and the use of force in mutual relations and promote co-operation and exchanges between the two sides.

What is the theoretical and practical implication of the 'new detente' between North and South Korea for the peace and stability of the Northeast Asian region? The basic agreement on reconciliation, non-aggression, and exchanges and co-operation was signed and instituted between two regimes which are basically different in type and orientation. Whereas South Korea is a democratising regime, North Korea continues to remain as a communist dictatorship. The question that arises in this regard is how high is the probability of peace and harmony emerging between two diametrically opposed regimes and regime types, despite the public postures and pledges?[46]

The existence of two separate autonomous states dictates the logic of inter-Korean relations and reunification. Reunification is an aspiration of the Korean people that can be realised at a future time, while the divided nation is the reality that prevails in Korea today. How to move from the present divided nation into a future reunited country is a challenge presently confronting the Korean people. The degree of state autonomy is relatively high for both North and South Korea. The regimes have advanced policies to enhance their respective interest. Therefore, the regime interest and the state interest have taken over and these are not always compatible with the national interest of the Korean people. For instance, whereas regime survival dictates the policies of the respective regimes, the broader consideration of the national interest of the Korean people must guide the process of reunification of North and South Korea.

The effect of democratisation on South Korea's foreign policy has been positive and sanguine, thereby enhancing the prospect for peace and harmony of interests between South Korea and the neighbouring countries. Such may not be the case, however, when considering negotiations between the democratising regime of South Korea and the communist dictatorship of North Korea.

This dilemma and the possibility of building peaceful relations across the nation are discussed by Immanuel Kant, the eighteenth century German philosopher, in his famous essay 'Perpetual Peace'. Kant shows 'how liberal republics lead to dichotomous international politics: peaceful relations — a "pacific union" among similarly liberal states — and a "state of war" between liberals and nonliberals'.[47] The effects of democratic republicanism on foreign affairs, therefore, are positive and contributory towards maintaining 'perpetual peace' in Europe. This finding has both practical and policy implications on inter-Korean relations and on reunification, which both North and South Korea are pursuing as their regime strategy, and on foreign policy, as will be shown below.

From the point of view of democracy and foreign policy, the challenge for South Korea in the post-democratisation era lies in how to entice and induce North Korea's dictatorial regime to change its behaviour, by abandoning its bellicose stance and ambition of promoting national liberation and revolution in South Korea. The rhetoric of reconciliation and non-aggression notwithstanding, there is no hard evidence that North Korea has abandoned its ambition of attaining national reunification by fostering national liberation in the South. This remains the policy guideline of the Korean Workers' Party of North Korea, unless and until the KWP party program and constitution are rewritten. Thus, ironically, the vigilance of South Korea's guard against North Korea cannot and will not be lowered.

Conclusion

South Korea since 1987 has undergone a process of political change and democratic experiment proceeding through several steps. First, it adopted bold measures of democratic reform and liberalisation towards the end of the authoritarian regime of the Fifth Republic under President Chun Doo-hwan. Second, it advanced into a democratising regime or transitional democracy in the Sixth Republic under the popularly elected President Roh Tae-woo. Third, with the election of the civilian President Kim Young-sam in the December 1992 presidential election, South Korea completed the process of an orderly democratic transition and has now entered into the politics of the post-democratisation era. During the five-year tenure in office of Roh Tae-woo, 1988–93, South Korea made great strides in realising the political agenda of democratisation or democracy-building, while enhancing its diplomatic stance and status abroad by successfully carrying out an imaginative and activist foreign policy called Northern Policy or Nordpolitik.

South Korea's democratisation during the second phase may be regarded as a case of 'continuous regime change in an autonomous state'.[48] Since South Korea's autonomous state is the legacy of the past years, the Fourth and Fifth Republics, the democratisation experiment during the Sixth Republic has worked to weaken rather than strengthen state autonomy (i.e. the capacity of the state to act without social constraints). With democratisation of politics, the character of the regime has changed, away from the military or military-dominated ruling group towards a civilian and party-centric leadership. The new administration of President Kim Young-sam has restored a civilian-based or dominant tradition of political leadership of the kind that characterised the Korean states in the past, such as during the Choson dynasty (1392–1910).

As South Korea embarks upon a new path in the post-democratisation era, with the inauguration of the civilian regime of Kim Young-sam, it is necessary to ponder upon the regime–state relationship and the role of the state in the economy. It is the role of the state which has changed in South Korea: the state in the democratic transition was not as autonomous and strong as it once was in the pre-democratisation era. In fact, during the 1992 presidential campaigns, all three leading candidates went on record with pledges to reduce the role of government in the economy. This suggests that the state in the post-democratisation era is no longer a developmental state where the government dictates and manages the economy. Instead, the new state in the post-democratisation era will be more of a liberal type where the government plays a minimal role and basically keeps a hands-off stance in the market mechanism. The South Korean economy has become too strong and complex for the government to interfere and dictate its policy. Business–government relations have changed from government directive and intervention in the market to government non-intervention and hands off in the market.

In the context of South Korea's democratic transition, this chapter has advanced three propositions and tested them to see what relationships, if any, prevail among the three factors of democratisation, economic growth and foreign policy. Two of the three propositions regarding economic growth and democratisation have proven to be valid up to a point, whereas the third proposition on regime type and foreign policy has not been validated. The reasons why these propositions hold true or false need to be explored.

The first proposition states that South Korea's democratisation and economic growth are not always compatible as policy goals. This is somewhat exaggerated because the Roh Tae-woo government attained reasonable economic growth during its five-year tenure in office, by more than doubling the GNP per capita from $3110 in 1987 to $6498 in 1991. Although not as high as that achieved by preceding administrations, an average of 7–8 per cent of the annual GNP growth is certainly a high and respectable economic performance measured against the world standard. The reasons for this claim of the incompatibility of democratisation and economic growth are linked to the changing nature of state–society relations and the dynamics of regime change. With democratisation, the state, in the sense of office-holding by the ruling elites, has changed its character and its role in society. State autonomy has now been constrained as civil society has become activated. State intervention in the market process in a democratising country like South Korea's Sixth Republic has been reduced. Democratisation means a 'continuous regime change in an autonomous state' whereby state autonomy, or state capacity for autonomous action, has become constrained by domestic interests and external pressures.[49]

The second proposition states that the relationship between democratisation and economic growth is not always positive. This claim is also somewhat exaggerated, being valid only in some cases. It is assumed that the role of the state in the capitalist market system is different in the authoritarian developmental state as compared to its role in the democratising state. Successful industrialisation during the authoritarian era has led to the rise of new social classes and a new set of interests in addition to the emergence of new elements of civil society occasioned by the democratisation of politics. The new regime must tailor its policy to suit the interests and demands advanced by the newly activated groups and classes in civil society. The new state intervenes in the process of democratisation and economic growth via the middle class citizenry which helps the regime to broaden its basis of political support. In the transition process, middle-class support is the key determinant in democratisation. Yet, in the post-democratisation phase, the middle class desires political stability and a conservative regime that is able to sustain law and order. The role of the state has become more diversified and its policies more multi-dimensional, so that the policy of economic growth is sometimes put on to a backburner by the regime when it is preoccupied with maintaining continuous political stability and the support of the middle class.

The third proposition states that political regime type and economic performance will have no bearing on the success or failure of a country's foreign policy. This statement is proven false in the case of South Korea's experiments in democratic transition. In fact, the causation is the other way around — that is, the regime type, whether authoritarian or democratic, and the economic performance of either high or low growth will affect the success or failure of the regime's foreign policy. Because of South Korea's initiating 'democratisation' and its proven record of 'high economic performance' in the past, the Roh regime was able to launch and succeed in the foreign policy initiatives of both Nordpolitik and new detente with North Korea.

Moreover, with the progress towards democratisation, the middle-class voters are now interested more in the policy issues of economic growth and social welfare. Foreign policy is not the burning issue for the middle class citizenry, which desires economic security and welfare above all else. This is the reason why, during the 1992 presidential election campaigns, neither foreign policy nor unification policy captured the attention of the South Korean electorate. The public was interested more in the economy and leadership and less in foreign policy or unification policy issues. Although all three leading candidates had their own visions and strategies for the kind of Korean reunification they felt should be brought about, they were not quizzed so much on these issues during the presidential campaigns. In fact, the initial enthusiasm for North–South Korean agreements on reconciliation and non-aggression, as well as exchanges and co-operation, died down during the campaign.

The issues of peace and reunification were effectively non-issues during the presidential election campaign of 1992. Just before launching the presidential election campaign, President Roh made his trip to China in November 1992, preceded by a trip to New York to deliver his speech at the United Nations General Assembly in October 1992. Moreover, during the campaign, Russia's President Yeltsin made an official state visit. However, none of these highly visible diplomatic moves acted to influence the presidential election to a measurable degree.

Foreign policy in the post-democratisation era is not likely to capture the centre of attention, nor to emerge as a main focus, during the administration of President Kim Young-sam. The reason is that the domestic policy agenda of economic growth and social welfare seems to be more salient to the middle-class voters, as shown during the 1992 presidential election campaign, than the distant issues of reunification or foreign policy. Another reason is that Roh's Northern Policy has outlived its usefulness. This is in part the result of successes attributed to it. Nordpolitik was, after all, the policy of a past era.

A new foreign policy agenda is being sought by the post-democratisation administration of Kim Young-sam. This appears to entail reassessing South Korea's options and priority in the post-Cold War era and formulating its strategy *vis-a-vis* the major powers in the region. Korea needs to reassess its position in the regional balance of power, especially between Japan and China, now that Seoul maintains normalised relations with all the major powers. Other agenda may include strategies for checkmating North Korea's nuclear ambition and realising denuclearisation of the Korean peninsula through the agreement already made with Pyongyang. Other issues will result from readdressing South Korea's role in the Asia-Pacific regional security and trading systems. The global environment in the post-Cold War era will continue to change and will offer new challenges and opportunities for the newly emerging democratic Korea to confront and exploit.

Notes

1 On some of these failed policies, see N*ot'aeu det'ongryongui 44-kaji jalmot* (44 mistakes of President Roh Tae-woo). Seoul: Wolgan Sahoe Pyongronsa, 1992.

2 A plethora of writings on this subject exists in the literature, considering such topics as the political economy of newly industrialising countries, bureaucratic authoritarianism, institutionalism and economic growth, etc. See, for instance, Frederic Deyo, ed., *The Political Economy of the New Asian Industrialism*, Ithaca: Cornell University Press, 1987, and Robert Wade, *Governing the Market: Economic Theory and the Role of Government in East Asian Industrialization*, Princeton: Princeton University Press, 1990.

3 Ilpyong J. Kim and Young Whan Kihl, eds, *Political Change in South Korea*, New York: Paragon House, 1988.

4 On the background of South Korea's authoritarian rule leading to the 29 July 1987 declaration on democratic reform, see: Hak-Kyu Sohn,

Authoritarianism and Opposition in South Korea, London and New York: Routledge, 1989.

 5 The official account states that more than 98 per cent of Roh's campaign promises on reform have been carried out. On the list of some of these pledges totalling some 459 measures, see 'A Special Focus on Roh's Sixth Republic: Assessment', *Sisa Journal* (Seoul), 26 November 1992, pp. 52–53.

 6 Tun-jen Cheng and Lawrence B. Krause, 'Democracy and Development: With Special Attention to Korea', *Journal of Northeast Asian Studies*, vol. 9, Summer 1991, pp. 3–25.

 7 On the question of the regime type and state autonomy, see James Cotton, *State Determination and State Autonomy in Theories of Regime Maintenance and Regime Change*, Regime Change and Regime Maintenance in Asia and the Pacific Discussion Paper Series, No. 2, Canberra: Australian National University Department of Political and Social Change, 1991.

 8 T.J. Cheng, *Is the Dog Barking? The Middle Class and Democratic Movements in the East Asian NICs*, Research Paper 89-05, San Diego: University of California Graduate School of International Relations and Pacific Studies, 1990.

 9 Cheng and Krause, *Democracy and Development*, p. 6.

10 Samuel P. Huntington, *The Third Wave: Democratisation in the Late Twentieth Century*, Norman: University of Okalahoma Press, 1991, p. 209.

11 For instance, see: Young Whan Kihl, 'South Korea in 1989: Slow Progress toward Democracy', *Asian Survey*, vol. 30, no. 1 (January 1990), pp. 67–73.

12 Michael W. Doyle, 'An International Liberal Community' in Graham Allison and Gregory F. Treverton, eds, *Rethinking America's Security: Beyond Cold War to New World Order*, New York: Norton, 1992, pp. 307–36. See also Michael W. Doyle, 'Liberalism and World Politics', *American Political Science Review,* vol. 80 (December 1986), pp. 1151–69.

13 Doyle, 'An International Liberal Community', pp. 308–9.

14 Based on the historical evidence of almost two centuries, Doyle discovered that 'peaceful restraint only seems to work in the liberals' relations with other liberals' but that 'liberal states have fought numerous wars with nonliberal states'. Moreover, the wars that liberal and democratic states have been drawn in are basically the 'defensive' ones and the ones 'prudent by necessity': 'An International Liberal Community', p. 310.

15 For instance, see: Trevor Taylor, 'Politics and the Seoul Olympics', *The Pacific Review*, vol. 1, no. 2 (1988), pp. 190–95.

16 Samuel P. Huntington, 'Will More Countries Become Democratic?' *Political Science Quarterly,* vol. 99 (1984), pp. 201–16. See also Huntington, *The Third Wave*.

17 On an attempt to apply democratic theory to South Korean Politics, see: S.M. Pae, *Testing Democratic Theory in Korea*, Lanham, N.Y.: University Press of America, 1986, and Chong Lim Kim, 'Potential for Democratic Change' in Kim and Kihl, *Political Change in South Korea*, pp. 44–72.

18 Huntington, 'Will More Countries Become Democratic?', pp. 193–218.

19 James Cotton, 'From Authoritarianism to Democracy in South Korea', *Political Studies*, vol. 37 (1989), pp. 244–59.

20 Philip Schmitter, 'What Is . . . and What is Not Democracy?' *The Journal of Democracy*, vol. 1 (1990). See also Pae, *Testing Democratic Theory in Korea*, pp. 1–14.

21 Robert A. Dahl, *Polyarchy: Participation and Opposition.*, New Haven: Yale University Press, 1971. See also Robert A. Dahl, *Democracy and Its Critics*, New Haven: Yale University Press, 1989.

22 Huntington, 'Will More Countries Become Democratic?', p. 194.

23 Huntington, *The Third Wave*, p. 9.

24 ibid.

25 Leslie H. Gelb, in an editorial for the *New York Times*, praised President Roh Tae-woo's 'good work of matching his word': 'Mr Roh, pronounced No, said yes to the peaceful transfer of power, a basic principle of genuine democracy.': *New York Times*, 24 December 1992, p. A-13.

26 Huntington, *The Third Wave*, pp. 231–50.

27 Young Whan Kihl, 'South Korea's Search for a New Order: An Overview', in Kim and Kihl, *Political Change in South Korea*, pp. 3–21.

28 Kim and Kihl, *Political Change in South Korea.*, pp. 243–51.

29 *Korea Newsreview*, 27 June 1992, p. 4; 22 February 1992, pp. 4–5.

30 This was the case with Vietnam until diplomatic normalisation was established in December 1992.

31 Young Whan Kihl, 'South Koreans Blaze Asia's Democratic Trail', *The Asian Wall Street Journal*, 23 December 1992.

32 Kihl, 'South Koreans Blaze Asia's Democratic Trail'.

33 Until 1991, North Korea was opposed to the simultaneous entry of North and South Korea into the United Nations on the ground that such action would perpetuate the division of Korea. Pyongyang advocated an alternative policy of single UN membership under a confederal scheme or a rotation of jointly held seats between the two sides.

34 Young Whan Kihl, 'South Korea's Foreign Relations: Diplomatic Activism and Policy Dilemma' in *Korea Briefing, 1991*, edited by Donald Clark, New York: The Asia Society and Boulder, Col.: Westview Press, 1992, pp. 57–84. See also Byung-joon Ahn, *South Korea's International Relations: Quest for Security, Prosperity, and Unification*, The Asian Update, New York: The Asia Society, 1991.

35 For the text of Roh's major statements and addresses, see: ROK, *Korea: A Nation Transformed: Selected Speeches of President Roh Tae Woo*, Seoul: The ROK Presidential Secretariat, 1990. Also, for a discussion on South Korea's Nordpolitik and its impact on the major power policies, see: the special issue on South Korea's Nordpolitik, *Asia Pacific Review*, vol. 2, no. 1 (Spring 1990), especially: Young Whan Kihl, 'The United States and South Korea's Nordpolitik', pp. 3–14.

36 *Korea Newsreview*, October 22, 1988.

37 *Korea Newsreview*, 27 June 1992, p. 4. See also 'ROK Celebrates Achievements of 6th Republic', *Korea Update*, vol. 3, no. 4, 17 February 1992.

38 Young Whan Kihl, 'North Korea's Foreign Relations: Diplomacy of Promotive Adaptation', *The Journal of Northeast Asian Studies*, vol. 10, no. 3 (Fall 1991), pp. 30–45.

39 Young Whan Kihl, *Politics and Policies in Divided Korea: Regimes in Contest*, Boulder and London: Westview Press, 1984, pp. 55–59.

40 Young Whan Kihl, *The 1990 Prime Ministers' Meetings Between North and South Korea: An Analysis*, The Asian Update, New York: The Asia Society, 1990.

41 *South North Dialogue in Korea*, no. 53 (December 1991), Seoul: National Unification Board, 1991, p. 78.

42 *Korea Times*, 1 November 1992, p. 2.

43 Dong Won Lim, 'Inter-Korean Relations Oriented toward Reconciliation and Cooperation: With an Emphasis on the Basic South-North Agreement', *Korea and World Affairs*, vol. 16, no. 2 (Summer 1991), pp. 213–23. See also Se-hyun Jeong, 'Legal Status and Political Meaning of the Basic Agreement between the South and the North', *Korea and World Affairs*, vol. 16, no. 1 (Spring 1992), pp. 5-21.

44 For the English text of the agreement, see *Korea Newsreview*, 21 December 1992, pp. 10–11. For a slightly different version of the text, see: *Korea and World Affairs*, vol. 16, no. 1 (Spring 1992), pp. 145–49.

45 Young Whan Kihl, 'New Environment and Context for Korean Reunification', *Korea and World Affairs,* vol. 16, no. 4 (Winter 1992), pp. 621–37.

46 In addition to the regime types, geographic proximity seems to act as another discriminating factor in foreign policy. As Doyle argues, 'the occurrence of a war between any two adjacent states, considered over a long period of time, would be more probable': Doyle, 'An International Liberal Community', p. 309. This will make physical proximity and neighbourliness a discriminating factor in the issue of warlike and peaceful behaviour in foreign policy.

47 Doyle, 'An International Liberal Community', p. 312.

48 Cotton, *State Determination and State Autonomy*, p. 12.

49 Cotton, *State Determination and State Autonomy*, pp. 6–7.

7

The Korean Bureaucratic State: Historical Legacies and Comparative Perspectives

Meredith Woo-Cumings

Introduction

The purpose of this paper is to trace the evolution and structure of the public bureaucracy in South Korea (henceforth Korea) and thus to deepen our understanding of the way in which the relationship between the state and economy is organised and mediated in Korea.

There is general consensus among scholars of the Korean political economy that the state bureaucracy has been particularly effective in negotiating economic development in Korea — up until the 1970s, anyway — and even strident advocates of economic orthodoxy observed that state interventionism might have had salutary consequences.[1] Along with its counterparts in Japan and Taiwan, the Korean bureaucracy holds, then, the key to what Chalmers Johnson once called the 'developmental enigma' in East Asia, by which he meant the combination of an 'absolutist state' and a capitalist economy. Or, to put it in other words, the ubiquitous and highly capable civil servants in the East Asian developmental states are one step ahead of the Weberian bureaucrats on the evolutionary scale: not mere executors of a higher will, the state bureaucrats in East Asia 'set national goals and standards that are internationally oriented and based on non-ideological external referents'.[2]

The recent literature on the Korean political economy has corroborated such a view, by emphasising the state's patronage, monitoring and guidance of the private sector in an intensely goal-oriented economy. The salient economic policies of this 'developmental state' have been distinguished in the following ways: the Korean state's mobilisation and allocation of resources to selected firms and industrial sectors, especially through financial mechanisms (as I have argued elsewhere);[3] also as 'getting relative prices wrong', in Alice Amsden's words, in violation of the holy grail of marginal productivity theory; as the political economy of 'late industrialisation as learning'; and according to the logic of late industrialisation (diversifying into heavy industries in order to catch up), against the logic of the law of comparative advantage.[4] In all of these strategies, the civil bureaucracy is said to have implemented them from above.

Curiously enough, while the formidable power of the public bureaucracy in Korea is increasingly well analysed, the evolution and structure of this remarkable bureaucracy itself have not received much attention outside of Korea. As a consequence, we can understand what the Korean state bureaucracy does in the economy, but not what it looks like, how it is organised or how it got to be the way it is. This is in contrast with Japan, where the bureaucracy, celebrated as the florescence of the rational–legal type of state administration (ironically, the kind Weber thought attested to the utter uniqueness and singularity of European modernity), has received a great deal of academic scrutiny. This paper is an attempt to fill that lacuna in the study of the Korean political economy.

Weber argued that bureaucratic organisation is the most efficient form of organising large-scale administrative activities, and identified a number of critical issues like corporate cohesion of the organisation, unambiguous location of decision-making and channels of authority, and internal features fostering instrumental rationality and activism.[5] We want to know about the organisation of state institutions because the size and the degree of development of the bureaucratic machinery, the availability of expertise and technical personnel to plan, monitor and implement policies are all good indicators of state capacities. But there is another sense in which the study of the structure of public bureaucracy must be an important part of the broader theory of the state: it enables us to assess the degree to which the state is insulated from, or autonomous of, the pressures of private interest.

For instance, Ben Ross Schneider has hypothesised that the state administration was likely to be more autonomous if, as in Japan and France, the patterns of bureaucratic careers revealed that the base of recruitment was narrow, promotion merit-oriented, and that during normal bureaucratic careers, the levels of circulation between public and private employment were relatively low. The pervasiveness of the *amakudari* in Japan or *pantouflage* in France (meaning, in both cases, the parachuting of retired public officials into the private sector) might seem to undercut Schneider's conception and compromise state autonomy, as does the relative inter-departmental immobility of officials, which tends to foster proprietary relations between the bureaucracy and industry.[6] Other scholars, however, have found in this combination of bureaucratic insulation on the one hand, and collaboration with the business sector on the other, a highly effective interventionist combination — what Peter Evans has dubbed the case of 'embedded autonomy'.[7]

The Korean bureaucracy exhibits the same 'embedded autonomy' as its counterparts in Japan and France: it, too, is a meritocracy that is recruited from an elite pool for a career that is lifelong, such that a professional bureaucrat, as Weber acerbically put it, 'cannot squirm out of the apparatus in which he is harnessed'.[8] It also shows the sort of 'embedded' porosity, built into the institutional structure, such that the distinction between public and private often becomes blurred.

How did the Korean bureaucracy come to bear *general* resemblance to other paragons of statist bureaucracies? Bernard Silberman has argued that highly uncertain political environments are conducive to creating an organisationally oriented administration (as in France and Japan), whereas low political uncertainty has led to the development of professionally oriented administrations in the United Kingdom and the United States.[9] The genesis and evolution of the Korean bureaucracy, however, points to the existence of another route: the situation of a post-colonial bureaucracy that inherits an 'over-developed' administrative structure — 'over-developed' in that its basis lies in the metropolitan structure itself, from which it is later separated at the time of independence.[10] In the Korean context, one might say that post-colonial Korea has inherited the 'over-developed' institutional structure from Japan, but combined and altered it in ways that have reflected both Korea's tradition and new political realities.

The thesis advanced in this chapter is that the development of the Korean civil service is explicable in historical terms: the experience of neo-Confucian statecraft and bureaucratic traditions, as well as the impact of Japan, which, through its colonial policies and its postwar development, presented to Korea a kind of template of bureaucratic development. I will argue, in other words, that the rational-legal bureaucracy in Korea developed neither out of functional necessity as Weber saw it, nor out of political necessity as Silberman has argued, but as a legacy of a long tradition of effective bureaucracy, in the *ancien regime* and during colonial rule.

This chapter will also argue comparatively that there is affinity between the military regime that reigned over Korea for nearly three decades and bureaucratic-authoritarian regimes elsewhere — say, in Latin America. A comparative perspective that cuts across world regions emphasises an aspect of the Korean bureaucracy which is markedly different from that in Japan: namely, an unstable political system in Korea, marked by weak political parties, whereby the relationship between civil society and the state mostly dispenses with the mediation of parties. The classic example of this is the bureaucratic-authoritarian politics that swept through much of Latin America, as well as Korea, in the 1970s.

The bureaucratic state in traditional Korea

When the literature on economic development in East Asia touches on culture and tradition, it often tends to explain everything and therefore nothing. Parroting Max Weber, scholars once saw Confucianism as a catch-all explanation for the region's *lack* of development, for the absence of a vibrant capitalism. But even Confucianism has become modernised since then, so that cultural conceptions like 'post-Confucianism', 'aggressive Confucianism', '*samurai* Confucianism',[11] and the like claim some long-overdue credit for the recent economic dynamism in the area.

Regardless of the theoretical status of these cultural categories, it is true that the great strengths of Confucianism, or more precisely neo-Confucianism, historically lay in the institutions of the family, the school and the bureaucracy, and to that extent it is important to pay some attention to the neo-Confucian cultural tradition.[12] In particular, Korea had a venerable bureaucratic culture that is bred in the bones of every official — even if he or she does not know it.

Yet we do not have a clear understanding of the nature of the bureaucratic state in traditional Korea, based as it was on the most thorough adaptation in East Asia of the social institutions and practices recommended by the pre-eminent neo-Confucian Chinese scholar Chu Xi. Scholars in Korea often present a model of an 'organic, unitary, centralized pyramid, with the king at the apex of state institutions',[13] and invoke this tradition to assail what are said to be the worst qualities of the Korean bureaucracy, variously denoted as 'fatalism', 'ritualism', 'authoritarianism', 'factionalism' and 'anti-materialism'.[14] Where civil service tradition is examined in detail, often the focus has been on the ideas of reformers like Cho Kwang-jo, Yi Yi and Chŏng Yak-yong, who tried (in vain) to make the old bureaucratic system more responsive.[15]

In other words, one of the oldest and most sophisticated bureaucratic traditions in the world remains anathema to the people who inherited it. This severance with the past derives in good measure from Korean nationalistic shame — that the traditional agrarian-bureaucratic system, for all its glory, failed to maintain sovereign integrity and keep Japanese imperialism at bay. (Japan colonised Korea in 1910, and foreigners have had trouble grasping that for centuries Koreans considered themselves superior to the Japanese, especially by virtue of Korea being closer to the fount of East Asian civilisation, China. Thus to fall victim to Japanese militarists added insult to injury.) This dubious tradition is also said to be the source of the greatest political conundrum that besets modern Korea: bureaucratic authoritarianism and centralism. Both too feckless and too rigid, then, Korea's long bureaucratic tradition has not provided a usable past, according to many Korean scholars.

Some foreign analysts have agreed. Gregory Henderson, in his book, *Korea: The Politics of Vortex*, characterised Korean politics as an unstable spiral of social mobility connected to an uninterrupted tendency toward bureaucratic centralisation, such that all ambitious people engage in 'upward streaming' towards the bureaucratic apex. This, he wrote, characterised the Yi dynasty (1392–1910), the colonial state which followed after it, and South Korea since 1945: thus, 'the Korean greenhouse has had several gardeners, but its temperatures have been, on the whole, constant'.[16]

Other studies have shown, however, that the statecraft of the neo-Confucian bureaucracy was not so lamentable. Originally started in China to meet the educational needs of an expanding civil service and to reform civil service examinations to provide a relatively open channel for official recruitment, neo-Confucian philosophy spread in the thirteenth to seventeenth centuries, and emphasised educating officials by combining classical study and learning with less esoteric subjects like civil administration, military affairs, irrigation and mathematics. Neo-Confucians called this new kind of learning 'solid', 'real' or 'practical', in contrast to older forms of Confucian scholarship which emphasised scholarship and contemplation — not to mention the Buddhist and Daoist traditions. The practice of neo-Confucian bureaucratic statecraft reached its apex in Korea. (Theodore de Bary notes that, in embracing neo-Confucianism as a complete way of life, Koreans went far beyond anything undertaken by the Chinese themselves.)[17]

Careful scholarship on the bureaucratic state in traditional Korea has also shown that it was not over-centralised, nor was society disrupted by 'upward streaming'. Instead the bureaucracy was dedicated to goals quite different from the modern state. The bureaucracy often acted as a major restraint on royal absolutism, deploying the Confucian doctrine emphasising the minister's right of remonstrance with his prince, and succeeding in institutionalising that in government agencies. James Palais, historian of the Yi dynasty, has argued that this resulted in an intricate network of checks and balances that was responsible for providing a solution to the problem of political stability, and that was well adapted for governing an essentially steady-state economy. This, indeed, is how he explains the dynasty's half-millennial longevity, which was no mean feat.

The political stability in the Yi dynasty was made possible in part by the quality of its bureaucracy, which recruited officials based on rational criteria of talent and merit, even if in the context of the ascriptive system. In order to improve the merit-orientation in recruitment and procedure, the agrarian bureaucracy required, in addition to the civil examination, the supplementary use of personal recommendation to balance the bias of a literary examination; stricter adherence to review procedures prior to appointment, and through the institution of travelling secret censors; and insistence on proper qualifications and prerequisites for certain posts. These procedures were deemed critical to ensure ideological conformity, seniority and routinisation of performance.[18]

In essence, the neo-Confucians believed that a desirable bureaucratic administration was one that reflected the values of the most basic and exemplary East Asian social unit: the family. As in the family, bureaucratic rule had to be based on respect for authority — not just on instrumental reason in Max Weber's sense. Years of philosophical learning preceded the local, regional and national exams for the bureaucracy, learning that began on a grandfather's knee, memorising the first and simplest classics. The exams were then a prelude to years of practical learning and experience in the civil administration. From this discipline came an administrative culture that, like de Bary's neo-Confucian world view, permeated the lives of officials.[19] This culture also bred a deep respect for education, and especially the educated bureaucrat or 'scholar-official'. In the face of imperialism and competition with modern states, however, especially with post-Meiji Japan, the *ancien regime* could not solve the problem of creating adequate authority for the achievement of new, modernising national goals.[20]

A long tradition of bureaucratic statecraft, drawing its legitimacy from the claim that its civil servants were 'the best and the brightest', helps explain the alacrity with which Koreans took to Japanese bureaucratic doctrines. It survived through the colonial period to facilitate the economic transformation of Korea thereafter.

The Japanese bureaucracy in colonial Korea

In spite of Korea's long bureaucratic tradition, modern legal-rational bureaucracy in the Weberian sense was constructed in Korea by the same architect that had designed it for Japan: the Meiji oligarch, Ito Hirobumi. Ito as a young man had been one of the handful of leaders who had helped usher in the Meiji system. He had travelled extensively in Europe, and came away fascinated by Prussian bureaucracy — which he saw as a route to Western rationality and modernity, but which was at the same time an alternative to Anglo-American liberalism. Within Japan, Ito in 1878 had 'led the campaign to make the bureaucracy the absolute unassailable base and center of political power in the state system'.[21]

In 1907, Ito was appointed Resident-General in Korea, in charge of running the protectorate. His actions as the 'uncrowned king of Korea' were swift and decisive: he dismantled the Korean army, co-opted some army officers to a Japanese-controlled gendarmerie, repressed dissenters and forced the Korean monarch to abdicate. In place of the old system, the Japanese instituted a civil service which 'in the main, followed the lines of the Imperial Japanese services. Provision [was] made for a lower and for a high examination of candidates, for salaries and allowances, and for the appointment, resignation, and dismissal of officials.'[22]

Japanese imperialism in Korea, like so many other aspects of Meiji development, was an act of mimesis. The 'opening' of Korea in 1876 was the Japanese version of the Anglo-American 'gun-boat diplomacy' of the 1850s and 1860s; the 'unequal treaty' that would open up trade in Korea was 'free trade imperialism' a la Japan; and the Japanese even spoke about their *mission civilatrice* in Korea.[23]

Much the same could be said about the bureaucracy; no sooner than they absorbed from Prussia the lessons of rational bureaucracy, the Japanese were practising them in Korea. As early as 1894, the Japan program for Korea singled out as the most urgent task the 'creation of a modern specialised bureaucracy, with functionally defined offices filled by technically competent officials, adequately paid and free from abuses of nepotism and the sale of office; a rationalised government structure, centring on a cabinet made up of functionally specialized ministries', as well as a new judicial structure and rationalised systems of government finances and police.[24]

There was one respect, however, in which Japanese imperialism was highly unusual: the massive presence of Japanese bureaucratic personnel. The territorial contiguity of Japanese imperialism and the security concerns that had prompted the annexation in the first place, when combined with the fact that Japan was still a developing country itself, meant that Japanese policy in its colonies would be significantly different from that of, say, Britain (which ruled its colonies with a skeleton crew, compared with Japan). Whereas the globe-trotting British imperium left open the possibility of autonomous development for its various components, Japanese control and use of its colonies was much more extensive, thorough and systematic.[25]

In 1910 there were some 10 000 officials in the Government-General. By 1937 this number had increased more than eight-fold to 87 552, of which 52 270 (or 60 per cent) were Japanese. This contrasted with the French in Vietnam, who ruled a similar-sized colony with some 3000 colonial officials. In other words, there were nearly fifteen Japanese officials in Korea for every French administrator in Vietnam.[26]

The presence of Korean bureaucrats, trained and employed by the Japanese, was also sizeable; nearly 40 000 Koreans qualified as government officials just before the Second World War. While they did not occupy high positions, over the four decades of colonial rule they became an integral part of a highly bureaucratic form of government. Moreover, during the Second World War, as the demand for Japanese officials grew elsewhere, many Koreans moved higher up in the bureaucratic hierarchy. This sizeable cadre of Japanese-trained Korean bureaucrats virtually took over the day-to-day running of a truncated South Korea, first under American military government, and eventually under the independent state formed in 1948.[27]

To understand the 'learning effect' in the Japanese economic bureaucracy, the case of the Industrial Bank of Chosen (IBC) is particularly interesting. The IBC was a major institution of industrial financing, especially towards the last two decades of the Japanese imperium. As such, it was the inevitable reference point for those men who plotted economic development in post-colonial Korea: the similarities in the operation of the IBC and postwar Korean industrial financing are quite remarkable, as I have argued elsewhere.[28] In the early 1940s, more than half of the IBC's regular personnel were Koreans, while one-third of the employees in the Bank of Chosen (the central bank) were Koreans, with many above the clerical level. Such upward mobility for colonial subjects was undoubtedly an artefact of wartime expediency, but even in peacetime, the number was never less than a third of the total bank personnel.

The bureaucracy that the Japanese left behind in Korea also possessed a considerable repressive capacity. Designed on the lines of the Meiji Home Ministry and police system, the national police force, which numbered 6222 in 1910, grew to 20 777 in 1922, and to over 60 000 in 1941. Senior officials were normally Japanese, but over half of the police force was made up of Koreans, often from the lower classes. The Japanese also developed a 'thought police' and a 'spy system' to buttress the civil and police bureaucracy that was 'probably better developed in Korea than anywhere in the world'.[29]

The legacies of civil and military bureaucracy in colonial Korea facilitated the adoption of a particular pattern (or model, or template) in Korean industrial development. The first discernible pattern is one of national industrialisation determined to a significant degree by an East Asian regional economic integration, led by Japan. Whether understood in terms of a regional division of labour, or dovetailing with the product cycle as Bruce Cumings has argued, the Korean industrial structure has historically exhibited a high degree of articulation with that in Japan. We find the genesis and the prototype of this articulation in the colonial experience.[30]

The second pattern is the bureaucracy's role in the comprehensive and semi-coercive channelling of capital to target industries. We find an uncanny parallel to the 1970s in the state's manner of financing industrialisation in the last decade of colonial rule (both periods of military-related heavy industrialisation) and in state creation and utilisation of new breeds of conglomerates (the new *zaibatsu* in the former instance, and the *chaebôl* in the latter) as the spearheads of industrial mobilisation.[31]

Ugaki Kazushige, the Governor-General of Korea from 1931 to 1936, personified the leadership for the kind of industrial task ahead: an ultra-nationalist, he deeply believed in the need for a Japanese imperium of economic autarky and industrial self-sufficiency. Thus, in the 1930s, the real growth of Korea's manufacturing production and value-added would average over 10 per cent per annum, a much greater rate than the one achieved in Taiwan (less than 6 per cent).

Colonial Korea was, in ways that Japan proper was not, a 'capitalist paradise': taxes on business were minimal in order to attract the *zaibatsu*; there was nothing equivalent to the Law Controlling Major Industries that regulated business in Japan proper; legislation for protecting workers was nonexistent; and wages were half of what they were in Japan.

Most critical in the Japanese private sector's decision to invest in Korea, however, were the financial incentives created by the Japanese government and the latter's willingness to share the risk should the investment turn unprofitable. In a situation of excess demand for money that had prevailed since the mid-1930s, the government began intervening heavily in the bank credit allocation process, at first with respect to the Industrial Bank of Japan, and then later the private, commercial banks as well. Through trial and error, the Japanese government devised, over time, ways of channelling capital and credit into war-related heavy industries, and drying up the flow into non-essential industries.[32]

Business and financial interests were not reluctant to go along with the financial policies of the state, for again, any loss suffered by the banks through non-performing loans would be indemnified by the state, which might pay in government securities. In this manner, even short-term credit came under the control of the state.

By the middle of 1940, private banking institutions showed signs of reaching the limit of their ability to expand credit further. Lack of funds forced a number of banks to turn to the Bank of Japan for help, and even several of the 'Big Six' banks, which had traditionally abstained from contracting with the central bank, broke their custom and resorted to it. Once the financial structure became overstretched, the state resorted to centralisation. Given that Japan did not want and could not afford outside capital, and possessed insufficient capital at home, the state had either to utilise its resources or encourage the centralisation of private capital in the hands of financial oligarchs for more efficient use. The effect of this was clearly visible in Korea.

In a relatively short period of time, the grip of *zaibatsu* groups on the Korean economy became tight and concentrated, and by the 1930s they replaced the earlier national policy companies as the spearhead of the industrial expansion drive. Three-quarters of the total capital investment in Korea was estimated to have been made by the leading Japanese *zaibatsu* in 1940, the roster containing names like Mitsubishi, Mitsui, Nissan, Asano, Mori, Riken, Sumitomo and Yasuda.[33]

Thus a civil bureaucracy committed to high levels of national planning and resource mobilisation, abetted by a vast network of police, characterised the political economy in Japan and Korea from the early 1930s until the end of the war. But it also characterised in some sense the political economy of the Republic of Korea from the 1960s through the 1980s.

Korea in the 1960s could not see itself finding a usable past in the wartime industrialisation of the 1930s — indeed, the very idea was and is anathema to Korean patriots. The 1930s bequeathed a set of patterns, a model, that could be the silent companion of Korean development, the parenthetical unspoken force that brings home the truth that people make their own history, but not in circumstances of their own choosing. The Janus-faced legacy of Japanese imperialism was to make of the Korean suffering of the 1930s a usable past for the 1960s onwards. If some recent work has highlighted this important legacy, it has also placed in the shade an age-old bureaucratic culture that was indigenous (as discussed above), and that an independent Korea also drew upon.

We can summarise the model or template from the colonial experience and its application to industrialisation after 1965 as follows: the type of state and its role in the economy; the state's relationship to business, especially the conglomerates; the financial mechanisms peculiar to Japanese development then and Korean development now. Furthermore, there existed a mode of industrialisation connected to security needs and, more broadly, to the harsh requirements of industrialisation in a world that the Western powers dominated, and a domestic social situation making the mobilisation of capital difficult without heavy state intervention, and consequent state direction of funds.

Within these structural constraints, the regime type would oscillate within relatively narrow parameters. In addition to being a praiseworthy 'developmental state', the Korean version shared the authoritarian logic of the prewar Japanese state.[34]

A long interlude

The American military occupation of Korea (1945–48) begat many controversial policies that had long-term consequences, but one thing it did not bring about was a lasting bureaucratic reform. Faced with the choice between the Japanese colonial government and the indigenous, decentralised 'People's Republic' which had spread like wildfire throughout Korea in the aftermath of the Japanese defeat, Americans opted for the former.[35] The Supreme Command of Allied Powers (SCAP), which sent directives from Tokyo, tended to place both Japan and Korea in the same category, and the implementation of its Korea policies was conditioned by the attitudes of the military toward the Japanese occupation, whether these policies had any connection with that operation or not.[36]

In Japan, the SCAP policy toward bureaucratic restructuring sought to increase efficiency and rationality. Beyond that, the bureaucracy was not restructured, but used to rule Japan as an integral component of politics, leaving much of the structure and character of the Japanese national bureaucracy minimally affected.[37] This cut a big contrast with their policy toward politicians and the big business, cameoing by default the enhanced stature of the bureaucracy.[38] Such a permissive attitude towards the Japanese bureaucracy was reflected in Korea as well, such that the military government there often retained civil servants from the Government-General, although sometimes individuals branded as collaborators had to be reassigned to other departments or localities.[39] Even reforms that seemed relatively uncontroversial, such as revision of the system of job classification in civil administration, would be jettisoned as soon as the United States Military Government turned the administration over to the Koreans.[40]

Even in the First Republic of the fiercely nationalistic Syngman Rhee (1948–60), bureaucratic elites who had passed the Japanese Imperial Higher Civil Service Examination and served in the colonial civil service were instrumental in setting forth decrees on government organisation, with the result that the principle and management of civil service remained essentially the same as it was in the colonial period.[41] These bureaucratic elites were distinguishable from the nationalist leaders in having a notably legalistic bent, acquired through their Japanese education with its emphasis on a legalistic curriculum. The technical-legal expertise that they possessed sometimes worked as a check against the politicians, but in general the bureaucracy was not insulated from the politicised environment of the 1950s.[42]

The literature on Korean public bureaucracy generally sees the government structure in the 1950s as an egregious case of an ineffective and tumescent bureaucracy, deeply ignorant and antipathetic toward matters of economic development. Perhaps the best proof for the point is that Rhee's preferred developmental scheme, import substitution, is *ipso facto* seen as a failure. Thus this pause, the 1950s, is precisely that: a blank hiatus between the predatory developmentalism of the Japanese period and the benign miracle of export-led success; nothing remains but an olio of unflattering and contradictory images.

There was, however, method to Rhee's madness. Korea was a key 'containment' country for the United States after 1950, and thus a beneficiary of the *Mutual Security Act* — receiving close to $1 billion a year in economic and military assistance combined. One of the most important foreign policy objectives for Rhee, then, was to keep the American aid spigot open. Through an adroit manipulation of the import substitution industrialisation program and interest rate policies, he rewarded his supporters and built a political coalition.

Rhee commanded the executive and the government with many resources: a strong bureaucracy and police, plus an army that became increasingly bloated by a shower of American military aid; the 'vested' colonial enterprises — that is, firms and factories formerly owned by the Japanese; United States aid money which he knew how to wheedle as well as any national leader; and ubiquitous interventionary power over economic activity in the nation. Using these assets of the state in the economy built a powerful patronage constituency, comprising a select group of old and new entrepreneurs.[43]

The period from independence through the 1950s may be seen as a long interlude between the predatory developmentalism of the Japanese and the benign miracle of the 1960s, a breathing space in which the Korean leadership parlayed its unique geopolitical position into state-building. The civil service that emerged in the process was a politicised one that reflected Rhee's patronage, but many of the future civil servants also cut their bureaucratic teeth there, learning to collaborate with *and* bypass a United

States that had become deeply solicitous of its Korean charge as a result of the Korean War, thus managing the economic reconstruction of their country.

The politics of economic development and the civil bureaucracy in Korea

Much of the acrimonious debate on what the state does in the economy in Japan is replicated in regard to Korea. Many studies of Korean economic development through the 1970s, often under government sponsorship, praised Korea's open economy and free trade policies, whereas the writings of the 1980s often tended to emphasise the reverse: the state's patronage, monitoring and guidance of the private sector in an intensely goal-oriented economy.

These traits are not unique to Korea, and have been attributed to Japan earlier. President Park Chung-hee (1961–79), however, probably overdetermined the influence of the interwar legacy: he was a former officer in the Kwantung Army, which had gained control over much of government policy formation in Manchuria. The enormous military presence was joined by (and often counteracted by) a number of so-called 'new bureaucrats' in the civil agencies, individuals committed to high levels of national planning and resource mobilisation under their own directly supervised lines of authority. Japan's interwar civil and military bureaucracies, like those in Korea from the 1960s to the 1990s, were relatively free of major checks from the electoral or parliamentary sphere. But as T.J. Pempel writes about the interwar Japanese bureaucracy, in spite of nondemocratic elements, 'clarity of vision and technical efficiency were positive counterbalances to the bureaucracy's lack of political responsibility'.[44] The same was true in Korea.

The extent to which interwar Japanese policy was consciously and assiduously emulated in the years of Park Chung-hee remains difficult to assess, since any hint of such emulation was routinely denied. In fact, much of the literature on the reform of civil administration in the early 1960s notes the rather large influence of the United States, citing as evidence the fact that many of the authors of the reform were American educated, and that the reform reflected concern with increasing efficiency and routinisation, as well as supervision.[45]

One could argue, however, that in at least two aspects the new government organisation evoked the colonial pattern: the creation of the Economic Planning Board (EPB), a super-ministry responsible for budget and planning of the national economy, which signalled the beginning of high-level bureaucratic co-ordination and social mobilisation for economic development; and the policy of bureaucratic centralisation which thoroughly denied to local administration any measure of autonomy. (The short-lived Second Republic (1960–61) had sought direct election of local officials as a way to foster democracy in Korea, but the junta immediately reversed the move towards decentralisation to the point where the structure of local administration in Korea remains, to this day, much the same as it was during the colonial period.[46])

There is also evidence that the Korean civil bureaucracy has often resorted to the Japanese precedent in policy formulation. One survey on policy innovation in the Korean civil administration found that 43.0 per cent of the bureaucrats surveyed listed 'foreign examples' as the source of new policy (as versus 21.9 per cent for 'past precedents' and 11.4 per cent for 'original ideas'.) When asked to choose two countries with the most similar policy environment, respondents pointed to Japan (87.7 per cent) and the United States (42.1 per cent), followed by Taiwan (28.1 per cent) and the former West Germany (19.3 per cent). When asked to choose two countries whose policies are most often used as referents, they again pointed to Japan (93.9 per cent), the United States (77.2 per cent), Taiwan (6.1 per cent), the former West Germany (5.2 per cent) and Singapore (2.6 per cent).[47] Thus Korea's civil administrators believe that Korea's policy environment is most like Japan's, justifying their close scrutiny of and learning from Japan. The influence of American public policy, on the other hand, probably owes much to the fact that English is the second language for most bureaucrats, and that many bureaucrats have received higher education and/or training in the United States.

Although Japan provides the most immediate parallel to the policies and structure of the Korean bureaucracy, there are also glaring differences in the two political systems: Postwar Japan has been (until the advent of the Hosokawa coalition) a stable one-party (plus some factions) democracy, and Korea was in the grip of unstable military authoritarian regimes until the late 1980s. Every successive republic until that time either began or ended with civil rebellions or military coups. This difference has often led scholars to compare Korean regimes to those in Latin America, described as 'bureaucratic authoritarian'.

A bureaucratic authoritarian system is a type of authoritarianism characterised by a self-avowedly technocratic, bureaucratic, non-personalistic approach to policy-making and problem-solving. This is said to happen during certain periods of political life when the relationship between civil society and the state seems to dispense with the mediation of parties, and the powerful political and economic interests simply appropriate segments of the state apparatus to defend their interests. In a bureaucratic authoritarian polity, 'bureaucratic rings', which are organised around high officials and articulate the immediate interests of enterprises and government bureaus, substitute for an organisation that is more stable and representative, namely political parties. Particularly when regimes are centralised, these 'bureaucratic rings' end up constituting the form of political linkage that establishes connections between civil society and the state.[48]

Korea, too, had its 'bureaucratic rings', with the military prominently placed within the system. If we venture to take the presence of former military personnel as a rough index of authoritarian inclinations (as opposed to the formal route of bureaucratic recruitment based on civil education, merit and passing the civil service exams), the evidence is strong. Retired military officers were conspicuous in important positions in government and public enterprise. During the Third Republic (1964–72), cabinet ministers with military backgrounds constituted 73 out of the total of 170, claiming a whopping 42.4 per cent of the total; the figure was 45 out of 142 (or 31.7 per cent) for the Second Republic (1973–79), and 37 out of 151 (or 24.5 per cent) for the period 1980–84 under President Chun Doo-hwan. The total for 1964–84, then, comes to 155 out of 465 — that is, for two decades, one out of every three cabinet ministers was a military man. As for the vice-ministers during the same time period, 73 out of 403, or 18.1 per cent, were former soldiers.[49] In certain bureaus and agencies there was even higher representation for the military: in transportation, the tobacco monopoly, labour, taxation, tariffs and patents (whose chiefs were equal to vice-ministers of the core ministries), military officers claimed about 40 per cent for the same time period.[50]

Even for those military officers who took civil service examinations, the favoured route was not the regular competitive civil service examination, but rather a special one that allowed for lateral entry. A 1976 survey of higher civil servants showed that fourteen out of 22 persons who joined the civilian bureaucracy at Grade II were military men, and at least eleven of these did so in the period after 1961. Upward mobility was also shown to be higher among those who came from a military background.[51] Military officers were also sent abroad for professional education under the Military Assistance Program (MAP): in the period between the early 1950s and 1987, some 36 000 officers received short-term training and long-term education, most of them in the United States.[52]

Another aspect of the Korean bureaucratic structure that resembled the Latin American-style 'bureaucratic ring' was the parallel concentration of executive power and technical expertise in the Blue House (Korea's presidential residence), eventually competing with, say, the Economic Planning Board for economic policy-making. For instance, the chief architects and executors of Korea's heavy industrialisation program in the 1970s were not the technocrats of the Economic Planning Board, as might be expected, but rather a nationalistic coterie headed by a political appointee at the Blue House — the First Economic Secretary to the President.

The *raison d'etre* for this team of economic bureaucrats (called the Corps for the Planning and Management of Heavy and Chemical Industries) was the speedy formulation and execution, unfettered by bureaucracy, of policies relating to investments in heavy industrialisation. The Economic Secretariat at the Presidential Palace became firmly ensconced as an important economic decision-making body in the Republic, bypassing and sometimes dictating to the Economic Planning Board and the Ministry of Finance.[53] It enjoyed the confidence of the president, which increased its power and autonomy, and it was able, by participating in various policy co-ordinating forums, to mediate between economic ministries which had conflicting interests.[54] In other words, presidential protection was a critical element in the planning and execution of economic policies, and in this, the pattern of economic policy-making in Korea was not unlike that in Mexico as well as Brazil.

In the end, though, such 'bureaucratic rings' cannot be very stable, since they depend on close association with the top leader, and presidents can be removed (through assassination or popular upheavals in the case of Park and Chun), key officials can be dismissed, and the ring can thereby be broken.[55] In fact, periodic purges conducted in the name of administrative 'reform' — in the early and late 1970s, and in 1981 and 1993 — have tended to disrupt this ring.

What renders permanence to the Korean state structure and its efficacy is, then, the persistence through regime change of a surprisingly robust civil bureaucracy — in spite of its accommodation of the military, political vicissitudes and the occasional emergence of competing policy-making centres.

The persistence of the civil bureaucracy through the political turmoil that has prevailed in Korea for the last three decades might be likened to that noted by E.H. Norman in 1940. Observing that Japan was not swept by a complete fascist mobilisation (as in Nazi Germany), Norman wondered if this insulation against totalitarian extremism had not been largely made possible through that ubiquitous and anonymous body, the bureaucracy, acting often in conjuction with higher court circles. The Japanese bureaucracy was thus a steadying force, a 'shock absorber', with its officials 'act[ing] as mediators who reconcile the conflicts between the military and financial or industrial groups, shifting their weight now to one side and now to the other in order to prevent the complete domination of the military clique and to check big business from controlling politics in its exclusive interest'.[56]

This means that the Korean bureaucracy was no mere possessor of technical information, 'a fox in the position of aping the dignity of a lion', as the old Japanese saying goes. It had to do something more than that — otherwise it would not have been as efficacious as it has been in orchestrating one of the world's most compressed economic development processes. This brings us back to the original contention we started out with: as E.H. Norman, Chalmers Johnson, Bernard Silberman, and other observers of Japanese statism have noted, the efficacy of the bureaucracy ultimately rests on its ability to integrate state and society, or to mediate between the government and the private sector, and that is no less true of Korea.

The pattern of bureaucratic recruitment reflects a great effort to scout talent from the society at large. The educational level of civil servants is high: whereas in 1958 only 15.3 per cent of low-ranking clerks had finished four years of college, more than 70 per cent possessed college degrees in 1988, and one-third of those possessed postgraduate degrees.[57] As for the regular civil service examination in Korea, administered continuously since 1949, it is strictly merit-oriented and highly competitive (although in recent years the ratio of competition has tended to fall). From 1963 to 1981, the rate of competition was anywhere between 50 aspirants to one successful candidate, all the way to 100 to one. In the 1980s, the rate was often over 100 contestants to one, reaching the peak of 164 contestants for every position. Table 7.1 shows the trend for the foreign service and the other lower ranking civil service examinations.[58]

The decline in competitiveness in recent years reflects the increase in attractiveness of the private sector, as well as the difficulty in preparing for state examinations. Whereas examinations for entering a private company

Table 7.1 *Rates of competition for select government examinations*

	1985	1986	1987	1988	1989	1990	1991
Foreign Service Exam	105:1	108:1	103:1	93:1	89:1	52:1	39:1
Level 7 Civil Service Exam (low ranking)	81:1	79:1	116:1	95:1	96:1	55:1	47:1

Source: Kim Hôn-gu, 'Hanengjônggodûnggoshi Kwamok ûi kaep`yoônbangari' [Suggestions for Revising Civil Service Examination Subjects], *Hanguk haengjông hakbo* [Korean Public Administration Review] vol. 26, no. 2, 1992, p. 733.

require preparation of only two to three subjects, Korea's civil service examination requires preparedness in a whopping twelve subjects.[59]

The nature of the expertise mostly valued in Korean civil bureaucracy might be gleaned from the major concentration of the successful contestants in the period 1982–91: economics and/or business (28.9 per cent), public administration (27.5 per cent), followed by law (13.1 per cent), sociology (5.4 per cent) and education (5.2 per cent).[60] This is in marked contrast to Japan, where law graduates are preponderant in the civil service: Table 7.2 shows the number and ratio of the graduates from Seoul National University Law School entering Korea's executive and judicial branches, and compares it with the number and ratio of the graduates from Tokyo University Law School entering their respective services. Whereas the overwhelming majority of Tokyo University's law graduates had prepared themselves for the civil service, the reverse was true for Korea, with less than 10 per cent of law graduates entering into the bureaucracy.

This difference is due to the fact that the Korean civil service examination, which had in its early years inherited the legalistic bent of the Japanese civil service examinations, was considerably changed from the mid-1970s, gradually eliminating the excessive requirement for legal knowledge. Other reasons have to do with the relatively low pay for entry-level civil servants in comparison to that for a newly appointed prosecutor or judge, pushing law school graduates in the direction of the judiciary.

In spite of the relatively slow mobility in the civil service, the growth of bureaucracy has been spectacular. In the aftermath of the Korean War and

Table 7.2 Comparison of graduates from Seoul National University Law School and Tokyo University Law School who have passed government examinations

	1990		1991	
	Seoul	*Tokyo*	*Seoul*	*Tokyo*
Judicial exam	128	46	130	51
	(92%)	(20%)	(89%)	(21%)
Civil Service exam	8	172	14	174
	(6%)	(74%)	(10%)	(72%)
Foreign Service exam	9	14	2	16
	(2%)	(6%)	(1%)	(7%)
Total	139	232	146	241
	(100%)	(100%)	(100%)	(100%)

Source: Kim Hôn-gu, 'Haengjônggodûnggoshi kawamok ûi kaep`yônbangan' [Suggestions for Revising Civil Service Examination Subjects] *Hanguk haengjông hakbo* [Korean Public Administration Review] vol. 26, no. 2,1992, p. 734.

the coup d'etat in 1961, as the need to regulate the civil society increased, the number of civil servants increased rapidly — from 237 476 in 1960 to 596 431 in 1980 and 781 346 in 1989, more than tripling the figure from 1961.[61] The rate of increase for civil servants exceeds the rate for general population growth at 0.66; whereas there were 9.5 civil servants per 1000 population in 1960, it soon became 13.3 per 1000 in 1970, 15.9 in 1980, and 18 in 1991.[62]

Yet the irony of the powerful and ubiquitous bureaucracy in Korea is such that, when all is said and done, the size of the Korean bureaucracy is small relative to other countries. Table 7.3 shows the number of civil servants per 1000 population in Korea, by comparison with the figures for France, the United States, Britain, Japan and Singapore.[63]

Another gauge of the relatively small bureaucracy in Korea is the share of the government budget in GDP. Table 7.4 reveals that in advanced industrial countries government budget as a share of GDP is often between one and a half times and twice that in Korea.[64]

The big power of the small bureaucracy in Korea is attributable in part to the autonomy that the bureaucracy enjoys, especially *vis-a-vis* the legislature. Table 7.5 shows that the majority of parliamentary statutes originated with the bureaucracy and not with the law-makers, and that such tendencies only

Table 7.3 *Number of civil servants per 1000*

	Korea	France	USA	UK	Japan	Singapore
No. of civil servants	18	66	63	63	35	31

Source: Chôn Su-il, 'Kongmunwôn singyuimyong chedo wa ch'ungwôn chôngchaek ûi panghyuang' [Directions for Entry-Level and Supplemental Hirings in Civil Bureaucracy], *Hanguk haengjông hakbo* [Korean Public Administration Review], vol. 26, no. 2, 1992, p. 722.

Table 7.4 *Government budget as ratio of GDP*

	1950	*1970*	*1985*
USA	20.0%	30.3%	36.5%
UK	35.3%	37.1%	47.3%
Sweden	23.6%	37.1%	68.5%
India	5.8%	14.1%	27.9%
Korea	13.4%(1955)	17.85%	22.1%

Source: Pak Tong-sô et al., 'Chakûnjôngbu ûi kaenyôm nonûi,' [Discussing the 'Small Government' Concept], *Hanguk haengjông hakbo* [Korean Public Administration Review] vol. 16, no. 1, 1982, p. 50.

Table 7.5 *Comparison of the ruling party and the government in initiating statues in the National Assembly*

		Ruling party No. of cases	Ruling party %	Government No. of cases	Government %	Total No. of cases	Total %
3rd Republic	6th Congress (1963–67)	185	43.3	242	56.7	427	100
	7th Congress (1967–71)	105	26.5	291	73.5	396	100
	8th Congress (1971–72)	15	13.6	95	84.4	110	100
4th Republic	9th Congress (1973–79)	17	3.4	479	96.6	496	100
	10th Congress (1979–80)	2	1.6	124	98.4	126	100
5th Republic	11th Congress (1981–84)	41	12.5	287	87.5	328	100
	12th Congress (1985–88)	57	25.3	168	74.7	225	100

Source: Yi Shi-wŏn, 'hanguk ŭi tang–chŏng kwangge e keanhan yŏnggu' [A Study of the Party–Government Relationship in Korea], *Hanguk haengjŏnghakbo* [Korean Public Administration Review], vol. 23, no. 1, 1989, p. 62.

accelerated over time.[65] (In this there is much potential for comparison with Japan.) As for administrative policies, they are strictly originated and orchestrated within the bureaucracy itself. Only in a few cases, entailing what is politely called 'political sensitivity', is there consultation with the ruling party — and here conflict is very rarely reported.[66]

The logic follows that the Korean bureaucracy is not accountable to the legislature, either. In parliamentary hearings since 1964, most of the substantive questions directed at the executive branch were from opposition parties (such as they were in Korea), and the responses have often been unhelpful and obfuscating, when they were not insincere. According to one study, negative responses by the administration (including categories of 'no response', 'refusal and denial', 'avoidance or off-the-wall answers') came to 54.5 per cent, versus 45.4 per cent positive responses (including 'explanations and policy suggestions' and 'acceptance and accommodation').[67]

The autonomy as well as insularity of the Korean bureaucracy is reinforced by the various ways in which bureaucratic conflicts get resolved, thus to present a united front to carry out national policies. In cases of inter-ministry conflict there are regular channels to mediate it, including decrees on inter-agency co-operation, various rules governing ministerial meetings and economic policy meetings, committees on industrial policy, as well as a myriad of policy consultation groups set up by various ministries. For economic bureaucracies, the mechanisms for co-ordination and conflict mediation include the Economic Ministers' Conference, the Economic Ministers' Consultative Meeting, the Industrial Policy Deliberation Council, the State Council, the Vice-Ministers' Conference, as well as the Ruling Party–Government Consultation Meetings.

The co-ordination and insulation of the economic bureaucracy is abetted by the fact that vice-ministers of the economic super-ministry, the EPB, have tended to become hoisted as ministers in other economic ministries, leading to quick dissemination of development planning concepts and techniques and to a smoother policy co-ordination among economic ministers.[68] Informal channels include '*hoesik*' (eating-out occasions) and other socialising events that are based on school and hometown connections among the bureaucrats, and during which policy conflicts may be smoothed out.[69]

Intra-agency conflict tends to get muted relatively quickly. In a political culture where conflict and policy difference are seen as negative (at least within the organs of state), not to mention as a proof of a lack of leadership and authority as well, Korean cabinet ministers are wont to resolve any conflict as quickly as possible. There is also a built-in bias against intra-agency conflict; given the policy of divisional rotation, bureaucrats in general eschew offending others in different divisions and bureaus, lest they end up there at some point in their career.[70] The upshot is that the Korean bureaucracy seems to speak uniformly and in unison, at least to outside observers.

Yet another way in which bureaucratic autonomy is preserved is through centralisation. Despite much talk of decentralisation and even some tepid attempts at implementing it, the central bureaucracy in Seoul (and its suburban outskirts) has managed to retain tight control over the provinces through institutional, technocratic and financial co-ordination. Provincial governors, as well as other important local bureaucrats down to the county level, are still appointed from Seoul and are rotated rapidly by the centre. When this feature of the civil bureaucracy is combined with the highly centralised character of public enterprises, decentralisation of the public sector in Korea remains a distant goal.[71] The problem is compounded by the concern that decentralisation might actually deepen the existing regional disparity. (Seoul, for instance, is financially self-sufficient, whereas the self-sufficiency rate for the south-eastern province is only some 26 per cent.)[72]

Another effective policy to ensure bureaucratic autonomy and to make it remain relatively free of corruption is through adequate material compensation of civil servants. The compensation level for Korean civil servants has remained low — at some 70 per cent of the number of private-sector employees of comparable rank — although employees of public enterprises have tended to be better compensated than those in the private sector.[73] But the welfare of civil servants has steadily improved in recent years — to the extent that the notion of a civil servant (*kongmuwôn*) no longer invokes the image of an immiserated and demoralised 'salaryman'. In addition to the rationalisation of official benefits, the Korean government has been active in urging the formation of mutual aid societies for civil servants, aimed at promoting their co-operation and welfare. Japan also has this type of mutual aid association for bureaucrats; in fact, some Korean associations, like that for postal workers, trace their origins to the colonial period.[74] The work that these associations perform ranges from the relatively simple social task of contributing money for weddings, graduations and funerals to providing scholarships, health care, moving services, housing and pensions, as well as, in some instances, providing jobs running enterprises and other positions to retired civil servants.[75]

Democratisation and reform in the bureaucratic sector

Throughout its modern history, what has imparted strength to the Korean state is its formidable power to intervene in the economy. The state has played hard and fast with the rules of the open market, combining *laissez-faire* policies with stringent protection and import-substitution; it has also insulated its small financial market from the world, negotiating and brokering the flow of foreign capital, keeping its Gorgon's eyes on capital flight, and in doing so avoided some of the worst tribulations of dependency. The formidable achievement of the Korean state brought about a backlash from the late 1970s on, however, as it was becoming increasingly clear that the economy had grown too big and become too internationalised to be pampered by an overbearing state: hence, 'economic liberalisation' has become the agenda of the late 1980s and 1990s, even if its implementation has been at a snail's pace. Since 1987, political liberalisation in the direction of democracy has filled out some major changes in the Korean model.

The meaning of economic liberalisation for Korea's bureaucracy is a substantial one of keeping its hands off the market, and not the formalistic one of reducing the absolute size of the government (which is not likely to happen). The concept of 'small government', actively introduced in the fifth Republic under Chun Doo-hwan (1981–88), led to the reduction in the number of junior as well as relatively senior bureaucrats.[76] Unlike in Japan, however, the reforms did not come from within (of course, here the Korean experience is the rule and not the exception for bureaucracies generally), and were instituted from above in an effort to legitimise a highly unpopular regime. In the end the reform did not stick, and the bureaucracy grew back to its former size.

The problem with these politically charged 'reforms' has been the tendency to view corruption and other problems in the civil service as a personalised or individual phenomenon, rather than as an institutional or systemic problem. Hence anti-corruption drives are usually geared towards getting quick results, focusing on weeding out the rotten apples, and not on reforming the system. Therefore, the reforms have tended to be too incidental, episodic and improvisatory.

The current spate of anti-corruption measures, led since early 1993 by the first civilian government in Korea, has enjoyed greater popular support than the ones which occurred in the past, and is aimed at both political legitimation and rooting out the legacy of the worst aspects of bureaucratic authoritarianism: the influence of the military in politics and civil bureaucracy, the monetary link between economic bureaucracies, banks and private enterprises, as well as speculative activities of the bureaucrats. At this early date in President Kim Young-sam's tenure, much has been accomplished in this regard.

The most urgent task for the bureaucracy, however, must be the same one that faces the Korean nation today: democratisation. This means a decentralisation of power, away from the concentration of decision-making in the hands of the executive, to the relevant civil service agencies. It also means a decentralisation that moves away from the centre to the provinces. Finally, such reforms must also be accompanied by a significant reduction in the repressive capacity of the state, by curtailing the power of intelligence and surveillance agencies. These changes now seem possible, however, with the deepening democratic commitment in the political system.

This chapter has argued that the modal bureaucratic form in Korea has been deeply influenced by two legacies: one, which the author construes as salutary and benign, is the indigenous bureaucratic culture deriving from a deep background of neo-Confucian statecraft. The other, seen as salutary for development but malign for political freedom, derives from Korean learning at the knee of a harsh master, colonial Japan. American readers of this essay perhaps will wonder what influence the United States has had on the Korean bureaucratic milieu, since an intense Korean–American relationship began in 1945. The answer from 1945 to 1992 would seem to be 'not much'. But perhaps in the political liberalisation now going on, which promises to be deeper and more long lasting than the somewhat fitful economic liberalisation pursued in the 1980s, the influence of American democratic pluralism may be witnessed. Whatever the democratic future of the Republic of Korea, it can safely be asserted that the civil bureaucracy will persist and accommodate itself to the necessary political realities, as it has for centuries.

Notes

1 See, for instance, the studies on the economic and social modernisation of Korea undertaken jointly by the Harvard Institute of International Development and the Korea Development Institute (KDI): Kim Kwang Suk and Michael Roemer, *Growth and Structural Transformation in Korea*, Cambridge: Harvard University Press, 1979; Leroy Jones and Il Sakong, *Government, Business, and Entrepreneurship in Economic Development*, Cambridge: Harvard University Press, 1970; and Edward Mason et al., *The Economic and Social Modernization of the Republic of Korea*, Cambridge: Harvard University Press, 1980.

2 Chalmers Johnson, 'Political Institutions and Economic Performance: The

Government–Business Relationship in Japan, South Korea, and Taiwan', in Frederic C. Deyo, ed., *The Political Economy of the New Asian Industrialism*, Ithaca: Cornell University Press, 1987, pp. 137, 142.

3 Jung-en Woo, *Race to the Swift: State and Finance in Korean Industrialization*, New York: Columbia University Press, 1991.

4 Alice Amsden, *Asia's Next Giant*, New York: Oxford University Press, 1989.

5 Max Weber, 'Bureaucracy', in H.H. Gerth and C. Wright Mills, eds, *From Max Weber: Essays in Sociology*, New York: Oxford University Press, 1958.

6 Ben Ross Schneider, 'The Career Connection: A Comparative Analysis of Bureaucratic Preferences and Insulation', *Comparative Politics*, vol. 25, no. 3 (1993), pp. 331–50.

7 Peter Evans, 'Predatory, Developmental, and other Apparatuses: A Comparative Political Economy Perspective on the Third World States', *Sociological Forum*, vol. 4, no. 4 (1990), pp. 561–87.

8 Max Weber, 'Bureaucracy', p. 228.

9 Bernard Silberman, *Cages of Reason: The Rise of the Rational State in France, Japan, the United States, and Great Britain*, Chicago: University of Chicago Press, 1993.

10 Hamza Alavi, 'The State in Post-Colonial Societies: Pakistan and Bangladesh', *New Left Review*, no. 74 (1972), pp. 59–90.

11 See Kent Calder and Roy Hofheinz, *The East Asia Edge* (New York: Basic Books, 1982); Lucian Pye, *Asian Power and Politics* (Cambridge, Mass.: Belkap Press, 1985); and Michio Morishima, *Why Has Japan Succeeded?* (Cambridge: Cambridge University Press, 1982).

12 Wm Theodore de Bary, *East Asian Civilizations: A Dialogue in Five Stages*, Cambridge, Mass.: Harvard University Press, 1986.

13 Kim Bun Woong, 'Korean Bureaucracy in Historical Perspective', in Kim Bun Woong and Wha Joon Rho, eds, *Korean Public Bureaucracy*, Seoul: Kyobo Publishing, Inc., 1982, p. 51.

14 Wan Ki Paik, *Korean Administrative Culture*, Seoul: Korea University Press, 1990.

15 Kim Ch'un-shik, 'T'oegye ŭi haengjŏngsasang e kwanhan yŏngu' [A Study of T'oegye's Administrative Philosophy, *Hanguk haengjŏng hakbo* [Korean Public Administration Review] vol. 26, no. 2 (1992), pp. 249–65.

16 Gregory Henderson, *Korea: The Politics of the Vortex*, Cambridge, Mass.: Harvard University Press, 1968.

17 Wm. Theodore de Bary, *East Asian Civilizations: A Dialogue in Five Stages*, pp. 47–48.

18 James Palais, *Politics and Policy in Traditional Korea*, Cambridge, Mass.: Harvard University Press, 1975, pp. 43–57.

19 For further discussion, see Yi Tae-hi, 'Yukyosik haengjŏngmunwha e taehan saeroun haesŏk' [New Interpretations on the Confucian Administrative Culture], *Hanguk haengjŏng hakbo* [Korean Public Administration Review] vol. 25, no. 2 (1991), p. 549.

20 James Palais, *Politics and Policy in Traditional Korea*, Cambridge, Mass.: Harvard University Press, 1975, and 'Stability in Yi Dynasty Korea: Equilibrium Systems and Marginal Adjustment', *Occasional Papers on Korea* no. 3 (June 1975), pp. 1–18.

21 Atul Kohli, 'Where Do 'Developmental States' Come From: The Japanese Lineage of Korean Political Economy', unpublished paper. See also T.J. Pempel, 'Bureaucracy in Japan', *PS: Political Science and Politics* vol. 15, no. 1 (1992), pp. 1–18.

22 Alleyne Ireland, *The New Korea*, New York: E.P. Dutton & Company, 1926, p. 104.

23 Peter Duus, 'The Abacus and the Sword: The Japanese Penetration of Korea', 1895–1910, unpublished manuscript, Chapter 10.

24 ibid., Chapter 3.

25 Jung-en Woo, *Race to the Swift: State and Finance in Industrialization of Korea*, New York: Columbia University Press, 1991, p. 21.

26 Michael Robinson, 'The First Phase of Japanese Rule, 1910–1919', in Carter Eckert et al., *Korea, Old and New*, Seoul: Ilchokak, 1990, pp. 256–57.

27 Michael Robinson, 'The First Phase of Japanese Rule', p. 17.

28 See Jung-en Woo, *Race to the Swift*, especially Chapters 2 and 6.

29 Andrew Grajdanzev, *Modern Korea*, New York: John Day, 1944, p. 55, quoted in Kohli, p. 20.

30 This argument on product cycles is advanced by Bruce Cumings in his 'The Origins and Development of the Northeast Asian Political Economy', *International Organization*, vol. 38, no. 1 (1984), pp. 1–40; on Korean inheritance of Japan's obsolete industries and new regional division of labour, see Andrew Granjdanzev, 'Korea under Changing Orders', *Far Eastern Survey*, vol. 8, no. 25 (1939), p. 295.

31 Jung-en Woo, *Race to the Swift*, p. 20.

32 ibid., Chapter 2, passim.

33 ibid.

34 ibid.

35 See Bruce Cumings, *The Origins of the Korean War*, vol. 1, Princeton: Princeton University Press, 1979.

36 E. Grant Meade, *American Military Government in Korea*, New York: King's Crown Press, Columbia University, 1951, p. 76.

37 T.J. Pempel, 'Bureaucracy in Japan', p. 21.

38 This argument is advanced in Chalmers Johnson, *MITI and the Japanese Miracle*, Stanford: Stanford University Press, 1982.

39 E. Grant Meade, *American Military Government in Korea*, p. 76.

40 O Sôk-hong, 'Hanguk chongbu ûi chikwi pullyu' [The Classification of Positions in the Korean Bureaucracy], in Kim Un-tae et al., *Hanguk chôngch'i haengjông ûi ch'egge* [The System of the Korean Politics and Public Administration], Seoul: Pakyongsa, 1981, p. 201.

41 O Sôk-hong, 'Taehanminguk chôngbu ûi haengjông kaehyôk', [Administrative Reforms in the Government of the Republic of Korea], *Haengjôngronch'ong* [Korean Journal of Public Administration], vol. 28, no.1 (1990), pp. 52–78.

42 Lee Hahn-been, *Korea: Time, Change, and Administration*, Honolulu: University of Hawaii Press, 1968, pp. 98–99.

43 Jung-en Woo, *Race to the Swift*, passim.

44 T.J. Pempel, 'Bureaucracy in Japan', p. 20.

45 O Sôk-hong, 'Taehanminguk chôngbu ûi haengjông kaehyôk', [Administrative Reforms in the Government of the Republic of Korea], p. 62.

46 Cho Sôk-jun, 'Ilbon ûi jedo wa kyunghôm e bichuôbon urinara chibang kongmuwôn jedo ûi panghyang', [The Direction for Korea's Local Administration in Light of the Japanese System and Experience] *Haengjôngronch'ong* [Korean Journal of Public Administration], vol. 26, no. 2 (1988), p. 93.

47 Min Chin, 'Hanguk kongmuwon ûi chôngch'aek kaebaljigak e taehan t'amsaekjôk yônggu', [An Analysis of Policy Innovations in Korean Civil Bureaucracy], *Hanguk haengjông hakbo* [Korean Public Administration Review], vol. 25 (1991), no. 3, pp. 832–33.

48 Fernando Henrique Cardoso and Enzo Falletto, *Dependency and Development in Latin America*, Berkeley: University of California Press, 1979 , p. 215.

49 Kim Kwang-wung, *Hanguk ûi kwallyoje yôngu* [A Study of the Korean Bureaucratic Structure], Seoul: Taeyôngmunhwasa, 1991, pp. 57–58.

50 Kim Kwang-wung, *Hanguk ûi kwallyoje yôngu* [A Study of the Korean Bureaucratic Structure], p. 59.

51 Bark Dong-Suh and Chae-Jin Lee, 'The Bureaucratic Elite and Development of Orientations', in Dae-Sook Suh and Chae-Jin Lee, eds, *Political Leadership in Korea*, Seattle, WA: University of Washington Press, 1976, pp. 109–11.

52 Chôn Chong-sôp, 'Chônmungga yôkwhal kwa yunrijôk ch'aekim', [The Role and Ethical Responsibilities of Experts], *Hanguk minju haengjôngron* [Theories of Democratic Administration], Seoul: Koshiwon, 1988, p. 452.

53 Jung-en Woo, *Race to the Swift*, p. 129.

54 Byung-Sun Choi, 'Institutionalizing a Liberal Economic Order in Korea: The Strategic Management of Economic Order', unpublished PhD dissertation, Harvard University, 1987.

55 F. Cardoso and E. Falletto, *Dependency and Development in Latin America*, p. 215.

56 E.H. Norman, *Origins of the Modern Japanese State*, edited by John W. Dower, New York: Pantheon Books, 1975, p. 313.

57 Chôn Chong-sôp, 'Chônmungga yôkwhal kwa yunrijôk ch'aekim', [The Role and Ethical Responsibilities of Experts], p. 456.

58 Kim Hôn-gu, 'Haengjônggodûnggoshi kwamok ûi kaep'yônbangan' [Suggestions for Revising Civil Service Examination Subjects], *Hanguk haengjông hakbo* [Korean Public Administration Review], vol. 26, no. 2 (1992), pp. 733–34.

59 Kim Hôn-gu, 'Haengjônggodûnggoshi kwamok ûi kaep'yônbangan' [Suggestions for Revising Civil Service Examination Subjects], p. 736.

60 ibid., p. 741.

61 Pak Tong-sô et al., 'Chakûnjôngbu ûi kaenyôm nonûi', [Discussing the 'Small Government' Concept], *Hanguk haengjông hakbo* [Korean Public Administration Review], vol. 16, no. 1 (1982), p. 50.

62 Kim Kwang-wung, *Hanguk ûi kwallyoje yôngu*, p. 88.

63 Chôn Su-il, 'Kongmuwôn singyuimyong chedo wa ch'ungwôn chôngchaek ûi panghyang' [Directions for Entry-Level and Supplemental Hirings in Civil Bureaucracy], *Hanguk haengjông hakbo* [Korean Public Administration Review], vol. 26, no. 2 (1992), p. 722.

64 ibid., pp. 50, 52.

65 Yi Shi-wôn, 'Hanguk ûi tang-chông kwangge e kwanhan yônggu' [A Study of the Party-Government Relationship in Korea], *Hanguk haengjông hakbo* [Korean Public Administration Review], vol. 23, no. 1 (1989), p. 62.

66 Kim Yông-pyông and Shin Shin-u, 'Hangukkwallyoje ûi kikwangaldûng kwa chôngchaek chojông' [Institutional Conflicts and Policy Adjustments in the Korean Bureaucracy], *Hanguk haengjông hakbo* [Korean Public Administration Review], vol. 25, no. 1 (1991), p. 310.

67 Kim Pyông-jun, 'Haengjôngbu e taehan kukhoe ûi yônghyangryôk' [The Influence of the Legislature toward the Executive], *Hanguk haengjông hakbo* [Korean Public Administration Review], vol. 23, no. 1 (1989), p. 10.

68 Byung-Sun Choi, 'Institutionalizing a Liberal Economic Order in Korea: The Strategic Management of Economic Order', unpublished PhD dissertation, Harvard University, 1987.

69 Kim Yông-pyông and Shin Shin-u, 'Hangukkwallyoje ûi kikwangaldûng kwa chôngchaek chojông' [Institutional Conflicts and Policy Adjustments in the Korean Bureaucracy], p. 319.

70 ibid., p. 312.

71 Yi U-jông, 'Ironjôk shigak esô pon chibangbunkwônhwa ûi munje' [The Problem of De-centralization: A Theoretical Perspective], *Hanguk Chôngch'ihakhoebo* [Korean Political Science Review], vol. 24, no. 2 (1990), pp. 193–219.

72 Ilpyong Kim and Eun Sung Chung, 'Establishing Democratic Rule in South Korea', *In Depth*, vol. 3, no. 1 (1993), p. 207.

73 Yu Chong-hae, 'Haengjôngyunri wa pup'ae' [Administrative Ethics and Corruption], *Sahoekwahak ronjip* [Theories in Administrative Science], vol. 23 (1992), p. 67.

74 Cho Sôk-jun, 'Urinara kongmuwôn sangjojojik e kwanhan yônku' [A Study of Mutual Aid Societies for Civil Servants in Korea] *Haengjôngronch'ong*

[Korean Journal of Public Administration], vol. 29, no. 1 (1991), pp. 2, 11.

75 ibid., pp.13–14.

76 ibid., p. 50.

8

Democratic Opening and Military Intervention in South Korea: Comparative Assessment and Implications

Chung-in Moon and Kang Mun-Gu

South Korea has undergone a major political change since June 1987. Massive popular protests put an end to Chun Doo-hwan's authoritarian regime, and radically altered South Korea's political landscape. Symptoms of democratic opening have been pervasive throughout the nation ever since: institutional reforms for greater democratisation, freedom of the press and association, the proliferation of pluralist groups, and the gradual decentralisation of political power through the revival of local autonomy. Nevertheless, the current democratic opening does not necessarily guarantee the transition to a viable and stable democracy. There still exist several barriers to the transition: the unstable conservative ruling coalition, volatile civil society, precarious economic performance and unpredictable military intentions. Of these, the military appears to remain the most critical factor, which could affect the nature and direction of democratisation in South Korea. Given the sheer size of its physical force and strategic position in Korean society, as well as its historical inertia, the South Korean military may well re-emerge as the ultimate spoiler of the democratic opening.

The past history of South Korea's political development shows that the military often played the role of political spoiler at the critical junctures of democratic transition. The military coup staged by Park Chung-hee in May 1961 crushed the democratic opening of the Second Republic which lasted less than a year. The 'Spring of 1980', the period of political *abertura* followed by the assassination of Park Chung-hee on 26 October 1979, was shattered as General Chun Doo-hwan initiated a quasi-military coup and seized political power in May 1980. A notable exception was the third democratic opening of June 1987. Massive popular protests were caused by the perceived illegitimate origins of the Chun regime, abuse of political power by Chun's relatives and arbitrary political rule manifested through his refusal to amend the constitution for a direct presidential election. The popular sector mobilisation eventually paved the way to democratic transition, engendering a prolonged social crisis characterised by labor unrest and student protest. Despite a sequence of social and political events similar to those in 1961 and 1979, however, the military did not intervene in civil politics, and the democratic transition entered a new phase of progress.

The mixed patterns of military intervention and non-intervention raise several interesting questions about the future of democracy and military politics in South Korea. What factors would foster or inhibit military intervention in civil politics? If the military intervenes, under what conditions and through what mechanism? What is the likely impact of military intervention on democratic development? Is the current democratic transition viable? Is it possible to ensure political neutrality of, and civilian control over, the military in the age of democratic transition?

This study is designed to explore these questions by looking into the historical patterns of military intervention in civil politics. We have selected three phases in the history of democratic opening (1960, 1980 and 1987) and traced how the military has played a part in each of them. In analysing the three cases, we have chosen four explanatory variables:

1 the dynamics of intra-military politics involving factionalism, professionalism, and corporate interests;
2 the patterns of interaction between civil-political societies and the military;
3 the overall socio-economic conditions surrounding democratic transitions;
4 the institutional configuration of state–military links, especially in connection with the role of the security/intelligence community.[1]

The dynamics of intra-military politics as push factors: Factionalism, professionalism and corporate interests

Samuel Huntington once argued that 'military explanations do not explain military interventions'.[2] This statement is only partially valid and even misleading. In many cases, military intervention in civil politics is *pushed* initially and primarily by the internal dynamics of military politics. Intramilitary politics are influenced by factionalism, professionalism and corporate interests. The military is endowed with its own distinct interests, such as professional status, career pattern, institutional resources, corporate identity and decision-making autonomy. It is hardly plausible for the military as a whole to share a uniform view over these institutional interests. Divergent views over these interests among military officers often lead to the formation of factionalism. Geographic origin, ideological proclivities and social and educational background also play an important role in shaping military factionalism.

Intra-military factional struggles can easily spill over to the realm of civil politics under two sets of circumstances. First, if factional struggles involve an act of mutiny, the winning faction is most likely to intervene in civil politics in order to manage backlash effects emanating from the mutiny. Second, if the balance of power among contending factions leads to a stalemate within the military power structure, a contesting faction may take circumventive, but pre-emptive, measures by capturing the state apparatus and civil politics through a coup and then dominate the military machinery. In either case, the dynamics of intra-military factional politics can serve as a useful explanatory variable in understanding military intervention in civil politics, especially in the context of developing countries.

The nature of factionalism and its impacts on civil politics are by and large conditioned by the degree of military professionalism. If the military is well trained and disciplined to respect expertise, societal responsibility and corporateness, individual and collective subordination of the military to higher authority is ensured, and military intervention in civil politics becomes less likely.[3] As Alfred Stepan observed in the Brazilian context, however, the diffusion of neo-professionalist norms can precipitate intramilitary factional politics, and ultimately facilitate military intervention in civil politics. Neo-professional norms blur the demarcation between the military and political domains, creating ambiguous spaces for factional contests, and enhance the propensity to engage in civil politics.[4]

Equally critical are the shifting patterns of the military's corporate or institutional interests. Regardless of professional or neo-professional orientations, the military is likely to intervene in civil politics when its collective interests are perceived to be threatened or deprived. Ideological realignments followed by major social and political transformations, which are incompatible with a pre-existing ideology which is widely shared by the military, could invite military opposition and trigger its political activism. Sharp reductions in defence budgets can also antagonise the military as a sectional interest, driving the military to interfere with civil politics. Measures to undermine the military's professional status and career patterns or to deprive the military of its decision-making power in national security affairs could invoke military opposition and subsequently political activism.[5]

The 1961 military coup by Park Chung-hee and his young associates succinctly illustrates how intra-military dynamics, especially factional politics, can push the military to intervene in civil politics.[6] The Student Revolution of April 1960 toppled the authoritarian Rhee regime, and gave birth to the democratic Second Republic. But the Chang Myon government of the Second Republic inherited the military legacy of the Rhee regime, which was laden with 'factionalism and politicking within a subsystem rife with intrigue and corruption'.[7] In the wake of democratic opening, factional strife became overt. Young officers called for purification of the military by targeting the old legacies. Their purification campaign centred around five issues: the investigation and punishment of high-ranking generals implicated in the rigging of the 15 March presidential election; the punishment of officers who had amassed illicit wealth; the elimination of all incompetent and imprudent officers serving in commanding positions; the removal of factionalism; and the improvement of the treatment of military personnel.

The purification campaign made visible the factional struggle between 'old generals' and 'young officers'. Beneath the campaign, however, lay young officers' resentment against their delayed promotion amid the oversupply of generals, by-products of the Korean War. The young officers concerned were mostly from the 8th class of the Korean Military Academy (KMA). Given the old KMA's six-month cycle of enrolment, they belonged to a similar age group as their seniors, and fought the war along with them. However, their promotion was structurally blocked. By removing 'old' generals in the name of purification, they attempted also to achieve a breakthrough in promotional congestion. Park Chung-hee, who himself was a victim of discrimination due to geographic origin and ideological colour, co-opted these young officers and staged the coup.

Apart from the factional struggle, the politicisation of the military served as another impetus. The Korean military in the 1950s possessed neither professional nor neo-professional traits due to its relative infancy, the absence of due education and socialisation, and heavy dependence on the United States. Nevertheless, the military was excessively politicised in terms of competition for loyalty to President Rhee since promotion and appointment were determined by their personal proximity and obedience to Rhee. This politicised personalism of the Korean military in the 1950s bred forces antagonistic to this trend, resulting in a military coup in 1961.[8]

An equally critical factor in pushing the military to venture into civil politics was a newly emerging threat to the military's institutional interests. From its inception, the Chang Myon government faced enormous economic difficulties: a bad harvest, dismal economic growth, rampant inflation, chronic unemployment, and most importantly the reduction of American aid. Moreover, American aid was tied to fiscal discipline. The Chang Myon government sought the solution in the reduction of defence spending, which had been the primary source of fiscal rigidity since the Korean War. Cutting defence spending involved reducing overall force levels; such a movement sent a red signal to the military. Park and his followers successfully exploited this new development, and won a tacit endorsement from a wide segment of the military. In sum, the 1961 military coup was a result partly of the dynamics of intra-military politics involving factional struggle over promotion and partly of resentment against politicised professionalism as well as threats to corporate interests.

Chun Doo-hwan's takeover of political power in 1979 and 1980 can be approached from the same point of view. The assassination of President Park on 26 October 1979 left Korean politics with an enormous power vacuum, a natural outcome of Park's excessive concentration of political power. The vacuum sent shock waves through the military, triggering an intense factional struggle between the old breed and the new breed of generals. The former was led by General Chung Seung-wha, then Chief of the Army as well as the Martial Law Commander. Chung represented a group of generals who graduated from the old (i.e. six-month cycle) Korean Military Academy before or during the Korean War. Major General Chun Doo-hwan, then Commander of the National Military Security Command (NMSC), led the latter. Chun represented the new breed of military officers who graduated from the regular KMA with four years' education in the post-Korean War period.[9]

The factional struggle was a matter of life and death for those involved. Chun, who was in charge of the criminal investigation of Park's assassination, suspected General Chung of being the assassin's accomplice and clandestinely sought to incriminate him. Meanwhile, Chung and his associates were planning to remove Chun and his clique from the military. The 'old' group regarded them as 'politicised' officers who had undermined the internal unity of the military by forming a private faction, called '*Hanahoe*' (the one-heart/

mind society). *Hanahoe* was mainly composed of the regular KMA graduates of Kyongsang provinces. Throughout Park's reign, members of *Hanahoe* were placed in such strategic positions as the Korean Military Security Command, the CIA, and the Presidential Security Office. By pledging personal loyalty to Park, they enjoyed Park's political patronage in promotion and appointment.[10] *Hanahoe* was a source of friction within the military due to this excessive preferential treatment extended to its members. Chung calculated that he could achieve two objectives by removing Chun, who was both president of *Hanahoe* and commander of NMSC. First, Chung could eliminate a personal threat to him stemming from his alleged implication in the assassination. Second, Chung could forge a new unity in the military by getting rid of politically motivated officers.[11]

The Chun faction pre-empted the old breed by staging a carefully planned and orchestrated mutiny on 12 December 1979. The success of the mutiny allowed Chun to control the entire military machinery and the CIA by appointing himself its acting director. This act of mutiny had to be legitimised, however. Chun did it by seizing political power in May 1980.

The origin of the factional struggle can be found in the birth and expansion of *Hanahoe*, which underscored the widespread 'new professionalism' among selected, if not all, young officers. Hanahoe's loyalty centred more on Park than on national defence. To its members, regime security was equated with national security. They were strategically placed in important national security posts and, in the name of national security, they went beyond the traditional boundary of the military's corporate responsibility. The proliferation of this new professionalism was one of the most visible negative legacies of the Park regime. Nevertheless, institutional interests did not serve as a push factor. Under Park, the military enjoyed a privileged position; the defence budget was increased, force modernisation and improvement expanded career opportunities, and there were considerable overall improvements in welfare and wages.[12]

The third democratic opening of 1987 will now be considered. Intra-military politics were devoid of the pressures which might have inclined the military to engage in civil politics. Under the Chun regime, factionalism proved a less salient issue. Divisions existed involving geographic origin (Yongnam versus Honam) and educational and recruitment patterns (Korean Military Academy versus non-KMA), but these were not serious enough to generate such pressures. The elimination of 'old' generals in 1979–80 eased promotional congestion, and the military leadership became more sensitive to previously disadvantaged officers. Furthermore, those who were loyal and close to Chun occupied important posts in the military. The military was also characterised by a relatively high degree of internal unity.

Another important factor impeding military intervention was the revival of professionalism in the military. Under the Chun regime, the military encountered enormous civilian criticism and resentment. Chun's illicit seizure of political power, the deployment of combat units to repress civil unrest in Kwangju in 1980 and frequent mobilisation of the military for political purposes under the Chun and Park regimes all undermined the legitimacy of the military as an institution. The military was portrayed as an unruly political spoiler rather than as the guardian of national defence and security. The spread of anti-military sentiment among ordinary people forged a consensus within the military not to interfere with civil politics. In fact, it was recognised that military interventions in the past rewarded only a tiny segment of politically motivated officers at the expense of the legitimacy of the military as a whole. This new consensus served as an important deterrent to military interference with the democratic opening.[13]

At the time of the third democratic opening in 1987, there were no immediate threats to the military's institutional interests. Despite the drastic surge in the influence of progressive ideology distinctly incompatible with the military, the conservative foundations of the polity remained intact.[14] From 1981, there was a relative decline in defence budgets as a result of stringent macroeconomic stabilisation programs, but the absolute budget allocation was on the rise due to the expanding economy. Although there were complaints regarding the ambitions still harboured by retired officers and generals, they never provoked a military reaction.

This examination of three cases of military intervention reveals that the dynamics of intra-military politics has played an important role in precipitating political activism on the part of the Korean military. The first democratic opening in 1960 evinced the worst combination of intra-military politics: intense factional struggle, pervasive politicised professionalism and explicit threats to the institutional interests of the military. The setback to the second democratic opening was similar to that in 1961 on the first two accounts — factional contestation and new professionalism — but differed in the nature of the threats to institutional interests. In 1979 and 1980, the collective interests of the military were not endangered, but a segment of the military intervened in civil politics to further their own political interests. In 1987, the overall configuration of intramilitary politics was against military interference with civil politics. Judged from the above, unilateral pressures emanating from intra-military politics are important, but they are insufficient conditions for military intervention. Unless there are 'pulling' forces from political and civil society, the internal politics of the military alone seem insufficient to activate its political adventurism.

Political society, civil resistance and the military: Pull factors

Alfred Stepan defines political society as 'an arena in which the polity specifically arranges itself for political contestation to gain control over public power and the state apparatus'.[15] Political parties, elections, electoral rules, and legislatures constitute the core institutions of political society. The more fragmented the political society, the more likely military intervention in civil politics is, and vice versa. The fragmentation of political society often entails institutional deformity and a power vacuum, which in turn creates 'political spaces' in which the military can act. Furthermore, the military can intervene in politics by the 'invitation' of power contenders in the arena of political society. In either case, weak, divisive and uncompromising political society can foster the political intervention of the military.

Equally important is the configuration of social forces. Ideological orientation, organisational strength and relative autonomy of the popular sector are all critical factors in determining the pattern of military intervention. The military can form a coalition with the popular sector, producing a populist regime (e.g. Egypt under Nasser). In most cases, however, the military is more prone to create a conservative and repressive political alliance with the dominant class.[16] The ultimate deterrent to the latter form of political intervention is the nature of civil society. Unified, autonomous, and well-organised civil society can effectively deter military intervention. However, political apathy, ideological divisiveness and organisational weakness on the part of civil society can *pull* the military into civil politics.

The overall configuration of political and civil society in 1960 and 1961 offered a milieu conducive to pulling the military into civil politics. Democratic opening followed by the April Student Revolution of 1960 was preceded by both the fragmentation of political society and the disorganisation of civil society. Internal frictions within the ruling Democratic Party between the 'old' and 'new' factions not only paralysed party politics, but also hindered the effective functioning of the government under the parliamentary system. Chances for political compromise and social stability were critically undermined, heightening the sense of political disorder. Mushrooming progressive political parties, albeit ineffectual, touched the nerve of conservatives, including the military. In the sphere of civil society, the situation was much worse. Political liberalisation was tantamount to opening Pandora's Box, producing all sorts of volatile interest groups. Civil society enjoyed unprecedented autonomy, but lacked ideological cohesion, organisational strength and unity of purpose. The military could easily justify its intervention in the name of purifying corrupt and incompetent politicians as well as stabilising civil society.[17]

The same can be said of military intervention in 1979. Park's sudden death generated a moment of enthusiasm in political and civil society. However, enthusiasm soon turned into disillusion. Political society was divided and characterised by conflict. The ruling Democratic Republican Party was in disarray, while opposition parties failed to form a consensus to turn democratic potentiality into actuality. Excessive contestation among three major political rivals (i.e. Kim Jong-pil, Kim Dae-jung and Kim Young-sam), combined with deepening social and economic crises, crippled political society and disillusioned ordinary citizens. There were no legal, institutional or political deterrents to confine the military to its barracks. A deformed political society provided the military with a timely fissure to penetrate. As in the Second Republic, the popular sector was activated, but its ideological proclivities were unclear, and organisational strength was weak. The unco-ordinated explosion of civil society did not produce a spontaneous reaction. A mirage of opening and liberalisation in the spring of 1980 led to an array of popular protests, labour unrest and street demonstrations. Ironically, it was this popular movement that pulled the military into the political domain, paving a way for another round of military rule.[18]

The democratic opening in 1987, however, differed radically from the previous two cases. The ruling bloc including the Democratic Justice Party was cohesive under Chun's firm leadership, although there were differences on how to deal with popular protests. Opposition political parties were also united in purpose and action programs as far as their struggle against Chun's authoritarian rule was concerned. The opposition party's successful bid in the 1985 general election enhanced the status of the National Assembly. There was little room for military interference. More importantly, civil society posed the most formidable deterrent to military intervention. The popular sector's unity of purpose and its increased organisational strength through horizontal coalition among intellectuals, labour, church and students ultimately deterred the military from meddling with civil politics. The defection of the middle class to the popular sector, which the Chun regime conceived as being the backbone of its political support, particularly offered a decisive turning point in the political drama of June 1987. There were no excuses available to the military in rescuing Chun or staging its own political showdown.

In short, the configuration of political and civil society is critically linked to the pattern of military intervention in civil politics. In 1961 and 1980, fragmented political society and disorganised civil society sent green signals to the military for its political adventurism. In 1987, however, neither political nor civil society allowed the military to interfere with civil politics.

Socio-economic foundation of democratic opening: Facilitative factors

Intra-military politics and the overall configuration of political and civil society do not, however, exhaust the margin of explanation for military intervention in civil politics. Between the two lies a facilitating or inhibiting factor related to the socio-economic foundation of democratic opening. In reality, democratic opening is hardly *sui generis*. It is by and large a dialectical response to the social, economic and political failures of authoritarian regimes. For this reason, a democratic opening is usually burdened with deepening socio-economic crises, which often breed political crises in terms of coalitional uncertainties and rising popular expectations. Transitional democratic regimes are seldom able to cope with these crises effectively due to a weak institutional foundation and limited resources. It is at this juncture that the military intervenes in civil politics. The military equates political, social and economic crises with the crisis of national security, and justifies its political intervention in these terms.[19] In contrast, the military is less likely to intervene in civil politics if democratic opening coincides with enduring social and economic stability. Likewise, socio-economic conditions associated with democratic opening become important indicators accounting for the patterns of military intervention in politics.

The case of the 1961 military coup represents a classic example in this regard. Political liberalisation in 1960 coincided with the worst economic and social crisis. The lingering legacy of the Korean War, the Rhee regime's corruption and economic mismanagement, and dwindling American aid, coupled with a poor harvest, brought about an economic disaster in 1960. Inflation, unemployment and shortage of food deepened economic hardships. The explosion of mass expectation followed by the democratic opening compounded the difficulties. The average frequency of street demonstrations exceeded more than 1000 per day. The Second Republic simply could not manage the economic crisis and chaotic social situation, raising the question of its ability to govern.[20] The military took advantage of this situation. Guarding national security, restoring social stability and liberating the people from poverty and hunger were the justifications offered for the 1961 military coup.[21]

Military intervention in 1980 followed a similar pattern. After almost two decades of economic expansion, the South Korean economy began to falter in 1979. While growth rates averaged 9.9 per cent from 1962 to 1978, they fell to negative rates in 1979–80. Inflation soared to almost 30 per cent from an annual average of 16.1 per cent for the period 1962–78. Real growth in exports fell from 27.4 per cent annual average during 1962–78 to 7 per cent in 1979–80. As a consequence of the economic crisis, the foundations of Korean society were shaken. Labour unrest, student demonstrations and other forms of social discontent peaked in the spring of 1980. The fragile socio-economic foundation of the second democratic opening facilitated military intervention in civil politics. For Chun and his associates, the socio-economic crisis was the crisis of national security, and the civilian government was perceived as being incapable of coping with it.[22] Political intervention was again justified in terms of national security and social stability.

The depiction of the third democratic opening of 1987 is distinct from that of the previous two cases. The social foundation of the democratic transition was similar to that of 1961 and of 1980. Labour's response to the new political climate was swift. In the two months from 4 July to 4 September 1987, there were more labour disputes than had taken place in the previous ten years, and over a thousand new unions were created. New farm groups were formed, and street protests by farmers increased dramatically around the issue of farm debt, taxes and import liberalisation. Student demonstrations were also rampant and more violent than ever before.[23] Nevertheless, the third opening was substantially different from the previous ones in its economic foundation. Since 1986, the Korean economy had shown unprecedented performance. Growth rates were in double digits, balance of payments surpluses achieved record levels, and price stability was consistently maintained. Owing to solid economic stability, social disorder alone could not precipitate the sense of national security crisis, which in turn prevented the Chun regime from declaring martial law and deploying the military. Furthermore, renewed inter-Korean rapprochement and the advent of new detente did not allow the military to intervene in civil politics in the name of national security.

Likewise, intra-military politics and society–military links are not the sole determinants of military intervention. The political activism of the military is conditioned by the prevailing socio-economic foundation at the time of democratic opening. These variables, however, serve to define only the necessary conditions. The nature and pattern of intervention is shaped ultimately by the structure of institutional links between the state and the military.

Institutional links between the state and the military: Conversion factor

The military is by definition a component part of the state apparatus. Nevertheless, such a relationship cannot be taken for granted. Depending on the institutional arrangement, the state and the military can take divergent relationships. First, as in most advanced democratic nations, the military can be placed under total civilian control and command without any significant autonomy. Second, the military can be simply an aggregation of autonomous entities virtually independent of the state apparatus. The Lebanese military is a case in point, where military personnel are recruited along confessional lines, and command and control are also undertaken accordingly. Third, the military may exist as an agent of specific social classes or political groups and leaders. The privatised military under Qaddafi, Duvalier and Marcos belongs to this category. Fourth, the military as an institution can take over the state *per se*. Most military regimes in the context of developing countries take this form of state–military relationship, in which military officers in uniform undertake the day-to-day operation of government affairs. Finally, there are several hybrid forms mixing the above four.

The particular institutional arrangement is a function largely of the dynamic interplay of security threats, institutional or personal networks between the executive and the military, and the characteristics of the security/ intelligence community. The presence of acute external or internal security threats enhances the institutional and strategic position of the military, increasing the potential for military intervention in politics. If executive control of the military is constitutionally or personally guaranteed, however, the likelihood of military intervention in politics is low. The state–military relationship is deeply conditioned by the character of the security/ intelligence community.[24] Depending on how effective the security/ intelligence community is in monitoring and controlling the military and who controls the community, the nature of institutional links between the state and the military varies.

Failure to prevent the 1961 military coup can be attributed in part to the broken institutional links between the state and the military. Simply put, the state under the Second Republic was too fragile to monitor and control the military. Chang Myon's personal links with the military were virtually nil. Chang tried to overcome this weakness by appointing General (Ret.) Lee Jong-chan to the position of defence minister. Lee was highly respected by a wide segment of the military for his discipline and political neutrality. But his tenure lasted only six months, and he was not able to pacify discontented military factions. Even more destructive in its consequences was the deformed military security and intelligence apparatus. Its extensive political use under the Rhee regime led to a sharp reduction in its function and size, undermining attempts to monitor and control the military. Furthermore, around the 16 May coup in 1961, important positions in G-2 at the Army Headquarters were staffed by the accomplices of the coup force. The Military Anti-espionage Command and the Military Police Headquarters, both of which were responsible for detecting and suppressing the coups, were either sympathetic with the coup, or showed an indifferent attitude. This institutional defect was the key factor leading to the success of the Park military coup.

Aware of its political value in sustaining his authoritarian rule as well as monitoring and controlling the military, Park Chung-hee strengthened the security/intelligence apparatus throughout his reign. Park's security/ intelligence community was composed of the Korean Central Intelligence Agency (KCIA), the National Defense Security Command (NDSC), and the Presidential Security Office. Of these, the NDSC played the most important role in monitoring, controlling and manipulating the military. The NDSC penetrated most areas of military life. It was also influential. NDSC reports and assessments were critical in decisions regarding promotion and assignment. After the Yushin coup, the NDSC became the most feared security apparatus among the military, and the political and civil scope of its activities was extensive. The NDSC competed with the CIA and the Presidential Security Office in terms of intelligence-gathering and political judgment, but on military matters, Park gave greatest credence to the NDSC view.

The strengthening of the NDSC contributed significantly to depoliticising the military and to minimising the potential for military intervention in civil politics. Paradoxically, Chun's takeover of civilian politics was facilitated by the very structure of institutional links which were cultivated between the state and the military during the Park regime. The assassination of Park by the chief of the KCIA allowed Major General Chun Doo-hwan, then NDSC commander, to take full control of the entire security/intelligence community including the KCIA. By centralising control of the security community, Chun and his associates could easily stage the mutiny against General Chung, and later take over the entire state apparatus.

Like Park, Chun further strengthened and expanded the NDSC. The KCIA, which was later renamed the Agency for National Security Planning (ANSP), was inferior to the NDSC in terms of access to Chun and consequently political clout. Throughout the Fifth Republic, the NDSC was Chun's most trusted security/intelligence wing. However, an anomaly became evident in the NDSC's posture in the month of June 1987. Facing immense popular protests following Chun's refusal to amend the Constitution in April 1987, the ruling regime became divided as a result of a dispute between the hardliners and the softliners. The majority of civilian officials in the presidential office, the ANSP and the Ministry of Home Affairs took the hard-line position. They argued that popular protests should be physically contained through the mobilisation of the military and that the declaration of martial law and the deployment of the military were essential.[25]

Surprisingly, however, at this critical moment the NDSC did not support the hard-line position. On the contrary, General Koh Myung-seung, then NDSC commander, favoured scrapping the martial law plan and advised Chun to avoid taking a collision course. The NDSC's opposition was based on the following assessment of the situation: first, the scope of popular protests was too pervasive to be controlled by force. Second, the deployment of soldiers could worsen, rather than ameliorate, the situation. The commitment of combat-oriented soldiers to the scenes of popular protest could bring about a situation far worse than the Kwangju incident of 1980. Third, logistic difficulties, especially transportation, posed a major barrier to effective deployment of military forces. Finally, if popular protests should be contained by force, it was advisable for the police to handle them first; if, and only if, the police could not handle the situation, then the military should engage.[26] Chun adopted the NDSC recommendations over those of the hard-liners, and eventually unlocked the gate to democratic opening. It is ironical that the NDSC was responsible for both Chun's seizure of political power and his demise.

In view of the above discussion, it is clear that the nature of institutional links between the state and the military can either block or facilitate the intervention of the military in civil politics. The deformed linkage which existed under the Second Republic permitted the success of the 1961 coup. Nonetheless, close links between the two do not necessarily ensure the blocking of military interference. While those under the Fifth Republic prevented military involvement, the second democratic opening in 1980 evaporated as a result of the merger of the two through Chun's monopolisation of control over the military–security apparatus. Regardless of the impact of the state–military institutional links on the pattern of intervention, the nature of the links, acting as a mechanism of conversion, are crucial. They draw our attention precisely because they offer an important empirical vantage point through which we can map out the entire picture of military intervention.

Conclusion: Comparative assessment and implications for democratisation and military politics

Military intervention in South Korea's civil politics cannot be accounted for by a single variable, but by the dynamic interplay of the four variables discussed above. The direction of causality among these variables is not fixed, but varies depending on the contextuality of democratic opening and military intervention. However, their functioning can be meaningfully approached in terms of push, pull, facilitative (or inhibiting) and conversion factors. Intra-military politics, involving factionalism, professionalism, and corporate interests, tend to *push* the military to interfere with civil politics. The dynamics of political and civil society *pull* the military into the domain of civil politics, while the overall socio-economic conditions serve as *facilitating* or *inhibiting* factors. Finally, institutional links between the state and the military serve as the *conversion* factor.

The democratic setback in 1961 reveals a classical pattern of military intervention in the Third World. While intense military factionalism and perceived threats to institutional interests pushed the military to venture into civil politics, a fragmented political society and disorganised civil society pulled the military into politics. Worsening socio-economic conditions facilitated the intervention by providing the military with justifiable causes. Weak institutional control over the military failed to detect and prevent the coup.

Military intervention in 1979 and 1980 shares several similarities with the 1961 case: socio-economic crises, a fragmented political society, a volatile and disorganised civil society and military factionalism. But they differ in two important ways. First, political intervention during October 1979–May 1980 was undertaken after the young military faction ousted the old one through an act of mutiny and dominated the military machinery. In the case of the 1961 coup, however, Park and his associates were able to control the military machinery only after they captured the state apparatus as a pre-emptive measure to dominate the military through circumventive control of the state apparatus and political power. The second is related to the conversion factor. The strong institutional control over the military, which was cultivated during the Park period, allowed the young military faction to monopolise the security/intelligence community, and ensured the success of mutiny and political intervention.

In 1987, neither intra-military factionalism nor grievance over institutional interests were pronounced. The internal politics of the military did not produce any justifiable causes for political interference. The surge of anti-military sentiment further deterred political actions by the military. Overall socio-economic signals were mixed, but did not facilitate the intervention. Finally, the conversion factor worked against the intervention. The NDSC took the position of protecting the institutional interests of the military as a whole rather than of sustaining the Chun regime.

Having reviewed three historical cases, we can draw several implications for democratisation and military politics in the future. First, as to the push factor, the dynamics of intra-military politics send mixed signals. Factionalism might be of less concern since the Roh Tae-woo regime made strong efforts to eliminate its sources. General Kim Jin-young, who was appointed as Army Chief of Staff in 1991, initiated a public campaign to wipe out private groups in the military. Ironically, Kim was a key member of *Hanahoe*. The Ministry of Defense has also reformed its system of personnel management. Decision-making on promotion is now open to the public, and merit is being more emphasised. Some have still argued that *Hanahoe* has not disappeared and that though reduced in size, it remains intact.[27] Conflicts between the KMA and non-KMA officers, especially those who entered through the ROTC program, also exist, but these potential sources of factionalism would not become the immediate cause of politicising the military. Thus intra-military factionalism is not likely to serve as the key push factor driving the military out of the barrack.

New professionalism, which is deeply rooted in the Korean military, could be a continuing source of civil–military tensions. During the three decades of military dominance in Korean politics, the Korean military has been systematically exposed to neo-professional norms through education, professional orientation and career patterns. A more vigilant civil society, armed with strong anti-military sentiments, however, is pressing the military to reorient its old inertia. Open critiques of the new professionalist tendency have been emerging from the very core of the military circle.[28] The military has also initiated efforts to deprogram those influenced by new professionalist norms. This is a positive development for the political neutrality of the military and for stable democracy.

Behind the two cheers, however, remains one cause of concern and pessimism: growing threats to the institutional interests of the military. There are two types of threat. One involves an anticipated sharp reduction of military budgets. While the advent of the post-Cold War and inter-Korean rapprochement have enhanced public pressure for arms reduction, democratisation has reoriented budgetary emphasis towards the welfare sector. Being supported by various social groups including the powerful Korea Federation of Industries, the Economic Planning Board (EPB) has taken a lead in this move, causing fierce bureaucratic battles with the military. The Ministry of Defense proposed an 18 per cent increase in the defence budget in 1992, but the EPB slashed this to 9 per cent.[29] The military can no longer enjoy political insulation in the area of resource allocation. This new trend could provoke military opposition and in the worst case military intervention in civil politics.

The second involves career patterns of the military. As the government attempts to reduce the size of the force level, two dilemmas have emerged. One is an acute promotional congestion and the forced retirement of active officers. As the 1961 military coup and the 1979 mutiny imply, promotional congestion in the 1990s could pose a new threat to the military and civil politics.[30] The other is the limited ability to absorb those who are coming out of the military. Finding jobs for retired military officers is getting more difficult. According to one statistic, about 46 per cent of retired middle-level officers (Major, Lt Colonel, and full Colonel) were unemployed in 1982.[31] The situation has become worse since then. Nowadays, even retired generals cannot find suitable jobs.[32] Promotional congestion and poor career opportunities for retired officers are likely to generate constant pressures pushing the military to meddle with civil politics.

Democratisation is predicated on the stable institutionalisation of political society and the expansion of civil society. Viewed from the above premise, neither political society nor civil society should permit or tolerate political adventurism by the military. Despite such crucial deficiencies in party politics as personalism, factionalism and fragile organisational structure, party politics in South Korea are unlikely to generate those mistakes of the past which 'pulled' the military into the political domain. Given the still-divided character of the ruling coalition and the existence of military elements in the ruling Democratic Liberal Party, military intervention by 'invitation' (e.g. palace coup) cannot be totally discounted. However, realignment of the ruling party in 1990 through the merger of three parties and Kim Young-sam's new leadership have rendered this course less plausible. With Roh surrendering office to Kim Young-sam, the influence of officers-turned-politicians in the ruling party has diminished further. Moreover, opposition parties' active recruitment of retired military officers has undermined the military's one-sided pledge to the ruling party.[33] In addition, a maturing civil society on constant alert will be the critical deterrent to military intervention in civil politics.

Overall socio-economic conditions do not favour military intervention either. Despite the current difficulties, the Korean economy has become much more mature, and will probably not be subject to the roller-coasting instabilities of the past. Moreover, having experienced a phase of social instability in the late 1980s, Korean society as a whole has become more conservative. Despite sporadic volatility, the labour sector looks increasingly stable. Student radicalism has virtually capsized. If the current social climate continues, the military is highly unlikely to intervene in civil politics. Though perhaps the least possible scenario, one exception might occur if social and economic chaos followed unexpected national unification. A perception of social crisis, coupled with the deprivation of its corporate interests, could facilitate military intervention in civil politics.

Finally, the conversion factor remains another source of concern. Democratisation has entailed two consequences. One is the advent of a civilian president with no substantial prior link with the military. The other has been the progressive restructuring and curtailment of the security/intelligence community. Under these circumstances, it is conceivable that the democratic government might so weaken its capability to monitor and control the military effectively as to encourage political moves by the military.

On 25 February 1993, the first civilian government since the demise of the Second Republic in 1961 was born with the inauguration of Kim Young-sam as new president. Kim's resolve to sever political ties with the military was manifested in the character of his new cabinet. Of the 24 cabinet members, only three were former military officers (Kwon Young-hae for Defense Minister, Choi Chang-yoon for Government Administration Minister, and Rhee Byung-tae for the Commissioner for Patriots and Veterans Affairs). Tough graduates of the Korean Military Academy, they are very much civilianised former officers with virtually no factional ties to the military establishment. More importantly, Kim Deok, a political science professor with no military background, was appointed as new director of the Agency for National Security Planning. Even the position of chief presidential bodyguard, which used to be a position of enormous power and influence monopolised by the military, was given to a civilian. In addition. the Kim Young-sam administration announced that it plans not only to curtail the size of the Agency for National Security Planning as well as the National Military Security Command, but also remove their performance of such functions as political and civilian surveillance.[34] These cabinet appointments and a series of measures to minimise the political profile of the security and intelligence community constitute a radical departure from the practices of the past.

A more drastic measure was taken on 8 March 1993. President Kim dismissed General Kim Jin-young, the Chief of the Army, and Lieutenant-General Suh Wan-soo, Commander of the National Military Security Command, both long before their tenure in those posts was due to expire.

Both generals were closely tied to the *Hanahoe* faction. They were replaced by General Kim Dong-jin and Major-General Kim Don-yoon, who were politically neutral non-*Hanahoe* members. This measure sent shock waves through the military establishment, political circles, and Korean society as a whole. The reshuffle reflected Kim's pre-emptive efforts to discipline and tame the military through the presidential power of appointment, to send a further warning to the members of *Hanahoe*, and more importantly to enhance Kim's image as a devoted democratic reformer.

This development seems to indicate that ongoing civilian control of the military is feasible, and that the military is now unlikely to intervene in civilian politics. Nevertheless, in order to ensure a viable democracy and the political neutrality of the military, the Kim Young-sam administration and its successors should take persistent and systematic measures to minimise intra-military factionalism; to devise a mechanism through which threats to the military's institutional interests can be minimised; to preserve and even strengthen the security community's functions; to monitor and control the military; to enhance the autonomy and strength of the popular sector; and to promote the institutional stability of political society.

Notes

1   Numerous explanatory variables have been suggested in accounting for military intervention in civil politics. They can be grouped into four distinct categories. The first is the motivational explanation focusing on the class origins of the military. See Jose Nunn, 'The Middle Class Military Coup Revisited', in Abraham Lowenthal and Samuel Fitch, eds., *Armies and Politics in Latin America*, New York: Holmes and Meier, 1986; Samuel Huntington, *Political Order In Developing Societies,* New Haven: Yale University Press, 1968; and Manfred Halpern, *The Politics of Social Change in the Middle East and North Africa*, Princeton: Princeton University Press, 1963. The second category regards the corporate interests of the military as an institution as an important determinant of military intervention. See William Thompson, *The Grievances of Military Coup-makers*, Beverly Hills: Sage, 1973; Martin Needler, 'Military Motivations in the Seizure of Power' *Latin American Research Review* , vol. 10, no. 3 (1975); and Anton Bebler, *Military Rule In Africa*, Princeton: Center for International Studies, 1971. Third, the situational explanation looks into socio-economic preconditions existing at the time of military intervention. See Needler, Huntington, and also Guillermo A. O'Donnell, 'Modernisation and Military Coups: Theory, Comparisons, and the Argentine Case', in Lowenthal and Fitch, *Armies and Politics in Latin America*. Finally, the structural explanation is based on the

analysis of structural configuration involving the state, society, international system and the military. See Alfred Stepan, 'The New Professionalism of Internal Warfare and Military Role Expansion', in Lowenthal and Fitch, *Armies and Politics in Latin America,* and Alfred Stepan, *The Military Politics in Brazil,* Princeton: Princeton University Press, 1971; see also O'Donnell, *Modernisation and Bureaucratic-Authoritarianism: Studies in South American Politics,* Berkeley: Institute of International Studies, University of California, 1973; and Karen L. Remmer, *Military Rule in Latin America,* Boston: Unwin & Hyman, 1989. The five explanatory factors used in this paper are derived from the pool of variables suggested in the above literature as they fit the context of military politics of South Korea. For recent works on the analysis of Korean military politics using a combination of the above variables, see J. Samuel Fitch, 'Military Professionalism, National Security and Democracy: Lessons from the Latin American Experience', *Pacific Focus,* vol. 4, no. 2 (1989), pp. 99–148 and James Cotton, 'The Military Factor in South Korean Politics', in Viberto Selochan (ed.), *The Military the State and Development in Asia and the Pacific,* Boulder: Westview Press, 1991, pp. 203–20.

2 Samuel Huntington, *Political Order in Developing Societies,* p. 194.

3 Samuel Huntington, *The Soldier and the State,* New York: Random House, 1957, pp. 7–97.

4 Stepan, 'The New Professionalism', pp. 134–50 and *The Military Politics in Brazil.*

5 Needler, 'Military Motivations in the Seizure of Power'; Thompson, *The Grievances of Military Coup-Makers*; Richard C. Rankin, 'The Expanding Institutional Concerns of the Latin American Military Establishment: A Review Article', *Latin American Research Review,* vol. 9, no. 1 (1974).

6 John Lovell, 'The Military and Politics in Postwar Korea', Edward Wright (ed.), *Korean Politics In Transition,* Seattle: University of Washington Press, 1975, p. 169.

7 Sung Joo Han, *The Failure of Democracy in South Korea,* Berkeley: University of California Press, 1974, p. 176.

8 Se-Jin Kim, *The Politics of Military Revolution In Korea,* Chapel Hill: University of North Carolina Press, 1971, pp. 36–37.

9 Cho Gap-jeh, *Gunbu* (The Military), Seoul: Chogen llbosa, 1988, pp. 109–204.

10 Cho, *Gunbu,* pp. 16–21; Kang Chang-Sung, *Hankuk/Ilbon-Gunbul Chungchi* (Korea/Japan: The Politics of Military Factions), Seoul: Haedongmunwhasa, 1991, pp. 357–78.

11 Cho, *Gunbu,* pp. 160–223.

12 Chung-in Moon and Intaek Hyun, 'Muddling through Security, Growth, and Welfare: The Political Economy of Defense Spending in South Korea', in Steve Chan and Alex Mintz, eds, *Security, Growth, and Welfare,* New York: Unwin & Hyman, 1992.

13 Chung-in Moon, 'Democratization, National Security and Civil–Military Relations: Analytical Issues and the South Korean Case', *Pacific Focus*, vol. 5, no. 1 (1989), pp. 5–22.

14 Kim Young-jin, 'Hankuk Gunbuui Donghyang (Movements of the Korean Military)', *Wolgan Choson* (May 1989).

15 Alfred Stepan, *Rethinking Military Politics: Brazil and the Southern Cone*, Princeton: Princeton University Press, 1988, p. 4.

16 O'Donnell, 'Modernization and Military Coups: Theory, Comparisons, and the Argentine Case'.

17 See Han, *The Failure of Democracy*, and Kim, *The Politics of Military Revolution in Korea*.

18 See Hak-Kyu Sohn, *Authoritarianism and Opposition in South Korea*, London: Routledge, 1989; Young Whan Kihl, *Politics and Policies in Divided Korea*, Boulder: Westview, 1984.

19 J. Samuel Fitch, 'Military Professionalism'.

20 See Han, *The Failure of Democracy*, and Kim, *The Politics of Military Revolution in Korea*.

21 The revolutionary pledges made at the time by the coup leaders underscore this point.

22 See Kihl, *Politics and Policies in Divided Korea,* pp. 80–83.

23 Stephan Haggard and Chung-in Moon, 'The State, Politics and Economic Development in Postwar South Korea', in Hagen Koo, ed., *State and Society in Contemporary Korea*, Ithaca: Cornell University Press, 1993.

24 See Stepan, *Rethinking Military Politics*, pp. 13–29.

25 'Documentary: Gun Samgai Sandanul Tuphara (Deploy Three Combat Divisions)', *Wolgan Choson* (January 1989); Kim Dong-hyun, 'Lee Han-gi Chongriga Malhanun 6.29 Chunya — Gun Chuldong Myungryongun Naeryu Jussussda (The Eve of June 29 — Order to Deploy the Military was in Effect)', *Wolgan Choson* (October 1989). Also see an interview with Kim Choong-Nam in *Weekly Hankuk* (8 September 1992).

26 Interview with General (Ret.) Park Dong-jun, Chief of Staff of the National Defense Security Command under General Koh. Also see General Koh's interview in *Dong-a Ilbo* (7 June 1991).

27 At a recent conference on civil–military relations organised by the Center for International Studies of Inha University, Kang Chang-sung, who investigated Hanahoe during his tenure as the NDSC commander under Park, argued that Hanahoe is still intact with a membership of 250. On conflict between KMA and non-KMA, see Kim Jae-hong, 'Hankuk Gunbuui Suhja — Gapjongganbuwa ROTC', *Shin Donga* (March 1992).

28 Major General Ahn Byung-ho, a Hanahoe member as well as a close associate of Chun, contributed an article to the army's magazine criticising the 1961 and 1979 coups as well as the new professionalist tendency among military officers. See his article, 'Gunui Sae Yisang Junglipae daehan Insikui

Chulbal' (Toward New Thinking on Military Posture), *Yukgun (Army)*, vol. 2 (1991).

29 *Choson Ilbo*, 24 August 1992.

30 Professor Han Yong-won, a retired colonel as well as former chief of intelligence at NMSC, suggests an interesting hypothesis on the relationships between promotional congestion and military intervention. Han hypothesises that the Korean military has faced severe promotion congestion about every ten years since the Korean War. In 1960 and 1980, military coups resolved the problem, while engagement in the Vietnam War resolved promotional congestion in 1970. This ten-year cycle thesis offers interesting implications for the 1990s.

31 Oh Ja-Bok, former Defence Minister, made this point in his masters thesis at the Graduate School of Public Administration, Seoul National University. See his 'A Study of Career Management of Army Officers' (1982). See also Cho, *Gunbu*, pp. 298–99.

32 This is partly due to the oversupply of generals since 1980. Nevertheless, Chun Doo-hwan's lack of support contributed to the phenomenon.

33 Kim Dae-jung's Democratic Party recruited five generals during the 1992 parliamentary election by offering them seats in the National Assembly, while Chung Ju-yung's Unification National Party recruited two. In view of past practices, this is unprecedented.

34 *Hankuk Ilbo*, 26 February 1993.

9

The Political Geography of Transport Infrastructure Development in South Korea[1]

Peter J. Rimmer

. . . the nation should play an important role in the economic sphere by taking advantage of its geopolitical location.
  . . . if the maldistribution . . . of economic growth that occurred among the regions . . . is to be alleviated, development policies must be directed to insure the harmony between growth and welfare as well as balanced regional development. [The Second Comprehensive National Physical Development Plan, 1982–1991] [2]

Introduction

South Korea occupies a pivotal position within an emerging East Asian Corridor which stretches from Nakhodka in Russia to Hanoi in Vietnam. It straddles the first two of the Corridor's three zones — the Japan (Eastern) Sea, the Yellow Sea and the South China Sea. Rapprochement with China and Russia, together with the prospect of 'opening up' the two Koreas, has prompted the South Korean government to re-evaluate its geopolitical position (see Fig 9.1). Much emphasis has been placed on assessing the adequacy of its transport infrastructure as it affects balanced regional development.

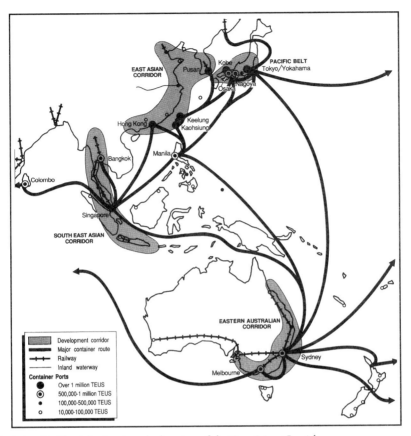

Fig 9.1   *Pacific-Asia showing the location of the East Asian Corridor*
Source: P.J. Rimmer, 'Ports, Inland Transport Linkages and Regional Development: A
Western Pacific Rim Conspectus', in KMI, *The Public Sector's Role in Logistics for the
21st Century*, The 2nd KMI International Symposium, 2–7 July 1990, Seoul: Korea
Maritime Institute, 1990

Since 1961, the outcome of the transport infrastructure developments
during the period of fast economic growth stemming from export expansion
has been to generate 'the high primacy rate of Seoul, vulnerable national
security, extensive regional rivalry and increasing regional disparities'.[3]
Although some uneven regional development is inevitable, given the
distribution of the key factors of production, there is evidence that the
government's transport infrastructural developments have favoured certain
areas at the expense of others. This is best illustrated by comparing the North
and South Cholla provinces with those of North and South Kyongsang —
the former pair comprising almost 20 per cent of South Korea's area and the
latter pair 31.8 per cent. In 1949, the Chollas had almost 26 per cent of the
population, but by the 1990s this had declined to less than 15 per cent. Over

the same period the population of the Kyongsang provinces decreased slightly from 32 per cent to 30 per cent. Strikingly, however, South Kyongsang province increased from 15.9 per cent in 1949 to 17.4 per cent in 1985. Subsequently, attempts have been made to redress this imbalance to take advantage of South Korea's changed geopolitical position. Thus we need to examine whether the transport infrastructure planned for the 1990s will create balanced regional development.

Before proposed transport infrastructure can be discussed, it is necessary to relate past geographical developments to the changing nature of the state over time. Once the importance of the legacy of the Japanese colonial state and developments within the Six Republics since the Korean War is appreciated, the new projects can be examined.[4] Initially, consideration is given to proposals for upgrading the slow-speed transport network. Then the approaches for enhancing the high-speed transport network are studied. Finally, the wider implications of these developments are explored by examining them in terms of South Korea's changed geopolitical position.

Past infrastructural arenas

Transport developments in Korea have reflected the changing nature of the state over time. Historically, three significant Korean states can be recognised:

1 the Early Monarchies (to 1910);
2 the Japanese Colonial Period (1910–45); and
3 the Post-Korean War Period (to 1990).

The thousand-year-old systems of roads and waterways serving the self-sufficient agrarian economy of the Choson Dynasty (1392–1910) and earlier monarchies are of interest to historical geographers. Indeed, the network of arterial roads which radiated from the royal capital of Seoul, together with their procedures for road maintenance and postal services *(yok)* and public inns *(won)* illustrate the administrative aspect of transport. The distribution of *yok* and *won* was concentrated in the populated central and southern provinces — a reflection of the quantity of agricultural production which provided the tax grain and tribute. These roads were complemented by a relatively sparse network of rivers which provided connections to Seoul and, in turn, to the ports of China and Japan. As the resultant pattern of break-bulk settlements did not survive the introduction of modern transport systems it is more appropriate to begin this study with a brief examination of the new networks introduced by the Japanese.

The Japanese Colonial Period, 1910–45

The basic features of the contemporary rail and road networks and associated urban structure were established during Japanese control.[5] Completed in 1899, the first railway line between Seoul and Inch'on, the capital's port of entry, postdated formal Japanese occupation. After Japan's suzerainty was recognised, a cross-shaped rail network was pivoted on Seoul (see Fig 9.2). The Pusan–Siniuju axis linked Japan and China and the Mokpo–Ch'ongjin axis connected the agricultural southwest and the mining areas of the northeast. Subsequent infilling of the network underlined the importance of Seoul as its national hub — its imposing terminal providing a counter-magnet to the old downtown administrative centre. Also, it highlighted the railway's role in supplying internal connections from major ports, notably

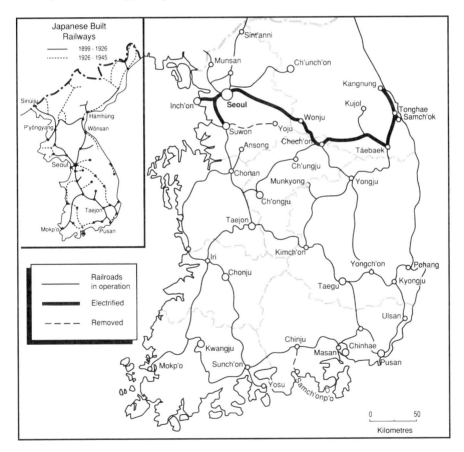

Fig 9.2   *Korea National Railways, 1987, with an inset showing those lines built by the Japanese*
Source: Kim Doojung and Yoo Jea-taik (eds), *Korea: Geographical Perspectives*, Seoul: Korean Educational Development Institute, 1988 p. 390

Pusan, Masan, and Kunsan in the south and Nam'po and Wonsan in the north, and spawning a new set of cities, including the junction towns of Taejon and Iri. Matching these developments, after 1907 a set of new roads was built by the Japanese which, though unpaved, provided the base for the contemporary national system. In 1929, an air cargo service was established between Taegu and Tokyo — seven years before the first domestic passenger service between Seoul and Kwangju was opened.[6]

A series of national surveys of Korea by the Japanese between 1910 and 1944 showed that the paramount political function of the transport system was to provide the colonial power access to areas of prime interest — the southwest's foodstuffs and the northeast's minerals which were shipped to Japan for further processing and consumption. Besides meeting military needs, the Korean peninsula also supplied a bridge between the Japanese archipelago and the puppet state of Manchuria (Manchukuo). During the 1940s, trial borings were made preliminary to constructing a rail tunnel between Shimonoseki and Pusan. Japan's debacle in the Great Pacific War not only resulted in the abandonment of the proposed tunnel but in the loss of Korea. The Korean War (1950–53) and the division of the peninsula led to transport connections being severed. Subsequently, the domestic, passenger and freight movements in South Korea had to be reorganised to adapt to the truncated network, the loss of trade with China and increased interaction with Japan and North America.

Post-Korean War Period

Since 1961, an authoritarian and highly centralised government has controlled and monitored South Korea's export-oriented economic growth which has transformed a poor agricultural country into a semi-industrialised nation. The policy has channelled benefits to large conglomerates (*chaebol*) and to people in particular regions. A recurrent theme is how new transport infrastructural developments — railways, roads and ports — generally have favoured the Seoul–Pusan axis, and the Kyongsang provinces in particular, at the expense of the central-western provinces, the Ch'ungcho'ng and Cholla provinces. Four significant phases, reflecting key development axes, can be identified in this process: the reinforcement of the northeast–southwest axis during the 1960s; the creation of a southern axis during the 1970s; the addition of a western axis together with a proposed northwest–southeast axis as a step towards the creation of a radial–circular transport network during the 1980s; and the inclusion of west–east and eastern axes and strengthening of the original northwest–southeast trunk axis as part of a grid-type network during the 1990s with the northwest–southeast axis still in a planning stage (see Fig 9.3)

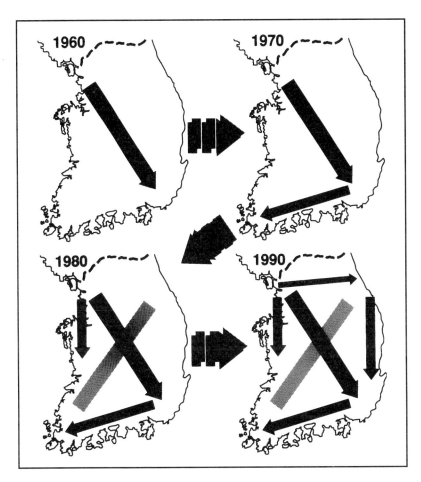

Fig 9.3 *The changing pattern of the main land development axes in South Korea, 1960–1990s*
Source: Kim, Jong-hoon, *Urinarah Chuldo Susong Sanup-yeu Hyeonhwang-gwa Gwajae* [Present Condition and Task of Korea's Railroad Industry], Seoul: Haewoon Sanup Yeonguwon [Korea Maritime Institute], 1991, p. 81

The 1960s

During the early 1960s, under the military government of Park Chung-hee, the provision of transport infrastructure, buoyed by Japanese reparations and United States aid, was conditioned by the need for South Korea to protect its borders against incursions from the north, and to shrug off the imprint of colonial rule and poor resource bases. Underpinned by the rehabilitation and expansion of Korean National Railways (nationalised 1948), particularly into the T'aebaek Mountain region bordering North Korea, there was a pronounced shift from a wet-rice culture to agribusiness and industrial development. Much of the increased workload of the railways came from enterprises on the main trunk line between Seoul and Pusan. Import-substitution industries were focused on the capital city and major port and labour-intensive export industries were also based in intervening cities, such as Taejon and Taegu. Additional activity also stemmed from a string of embryonic port-industrial bases located conveniently for interaction with Japan, notably Ulsan (1962), Yosu (1967) and Pohang (1968), and a flurry of locally inspired industrial estates.[7] Road transport was relatively undeveloped and played a complementary role in providing short-haul feeder services to the long-distance rail network. In 1968, the four-lane, limited-access 35-kilometre Kyong-in Expressway was completed between Seoul and its port at Inch'on. During the following year, the Korean Highway Corporation was established to construct and maintain an expressway system linking key urban centres and industrial areas, and the secondary arterials referred to as national roads.

Preoccupation with industrialisation along the Seoul–Pusan axis reflected the Korean government's bid to maximise national development in the interest of efficiency.[8] One consequence was that previously prosperous agricultural activities within the central-western provinces were neglected. In particular, inattention to upgrading rail services and poorly connected roads disadvantaged the Cholla provinces. Renowned as Korea's 'rice bowl', farmers there were handicapped by their adherence to wet rice cultivation. Initially, South Korea's agricultural economy was devastated by the introduction of farm products from aid-givers and the government's policy of pegging locally grown items to control inflation. This problem was compounded by the small share of national investment afforded agriculture and the lack of reliable access to growing urban markets. Not surprisingly, the Cholla provinces were unattractive to investors. New transport infrastructure developments during the 1970s brought little relief.

The 1970s

In the 1970s, transport improvements proceeded apace with the rapid development of expressways and the electrification of the railways. In 1972, railway electrification was initiated on the Chungang Line between Seoul and the T'aebaek Mountain Ranges. While this boosted the capacity of the railways, spectacular expansion of the expressway network was taking place (see Fig 9.4). In 1970, the 450-kilometre Kyongbu Expressway between Seoul and Pusan was completed using Japanese aid money. Three years later, the Honam Expressway (Chonju–Sunch'on) and the Namhae Expressway (Pusan–Sunch'on) routes were opened. In 1977, the Yongdong (Suwon–Kangnung) and Tonghae (Kangnung–Tonghae) Expressways were finished.

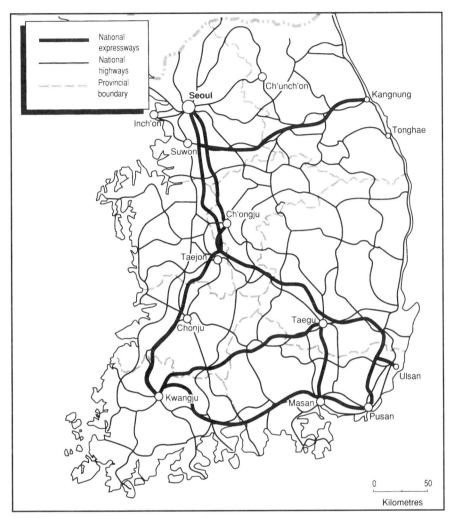

Fig 9.4 Expressways and national roads, 1987
Source: Kim Doojung and Yoo Jea-taik, eds, *Korea: Geographical Perspectives*, Seoul: Korean Educational Development Institute, 1988, p. 393

In the process, the road transport industry — truck and bus — had changed from being complementary to the railway system to being a long-distance competitor.

Most movements on the expanded transport network, apart from the Seoul–Pusan Corridor, stemmed from continued development of the string of port-industrial towns created in the 1960s, notably Ulsan and Pohang. (In 1973, Pohang, for example, received the first large iron and steel mill.) Augmented by Onsan and Ch'ang-won, they were transformed into fully fledged growth poles within the Southeastern Coastal Industrial Belt. As these economic activities spilled over the border of South Cholla, both

Yochon Industrial Complex and Kwangyang were included in the Belt. Offering relative security from North Korea as well as low transport costs, the Belt's ports were those closest to Japan which provided the market for heavily subsidised, capital-intensive, export-oriented heavy and chemical industries (e.g. steel, shipbuilding and petrochemicals). They were designed to make South Korea's defence industries self-reliant — a move prompted by President Carter's decision to withdraw military bases during a deterioration in North–South relations. Thus 'the geography of ports largely determined the location of industries in Korea' during the relatively early promotion of high volumes of heavy industrial exports and imports.

Also in vogue were export industrial estates. They included the free trade zones at Masan (1970) and Iri (1971). In particular, Masan was attractive to Japanese corporations which controlled almost 80 per cent of its firms. Local industrial estates were intended to attract industry from Seoul.[9] The inland centre of Kumi was also selected as the base for a large-scale industrial estates for electronics. This had more to do with the fact that it was the birthplace of President Park than any intrinsic locational advantages. (It was also designated a heavy industrial complex!) Complementing these export-oriented industrial initiatives was heavy expenditure on ports. Since 1970, Pusan has been developed as the major container port. Its purpose-built terminal (Pusan Container Terminal Operation Co.) was opened in 1978 — four years after a specialised berth had been built at Inch'on.[10] These developments resulted in the decline of feeder links with Kobe and Hong Kong and their replacement by mainline services of major shipping companies. Inch'on dock facilities, located one ship-day from the main shipping routes and with a tidal difference of 8 metres, lacked the convenience afforded by the Port of Pusan.

These new transport infrastructural developments bypassed South Korea's west coast. There was no four-lane highway linking Kwangju, South Cholla's capital, to the Kyongbu Expressway. Without a revival in agriculture and in the absence of compensating developments in manufacturing and service employment, it was not surprising that the North Ch'ungch'ong, Kangwon and both Cholla provinces experienced net population losses. The losses from the Cholla provinces, however, were more serious. Migrants from the area moved to Seoul, where surveys show they constitute a disproportionate number of the urban poor (and presumably a small share of the emerging middle class).[11] Alienated from the mainstream of South Korean life, people from the Cholla provinces aligned themselves with the Peace and Democratic Party led by Kim Dae-jung to protect their regional interests.[12] The Kwangju incident in 1980 reinforced their resentment.

The 1980s

During the early 1980s, further improvements were made to inter-city transport connections. These were intended to combat the side-effects of a bi-polarised, regional development pattern.[13] This was reflected in the depopulation of lagging rural regions and the overconcentration of population in Greater Seoul (9.7 million in 1985) and Pusan (3.5 million in 1985) which together monopolised central managerial functions.[14] As most investment was directed to road transport, the railways' position in long distance freight was further eroded (only 14 per cent of the track had been electrified). By 1981, the length of expressways was 1225 km. It was not until 1984, however, that the 88 Olympic Expressway between Kwangju and Taegu was completed — a political gesture to mollify regional antagonisms. Nevertheless, traffic was still concentrated between Seoul and Pusan.

In 1987, congestion between Seoul and Taejon was so severe that the parallel Chungbu Expressway was completed via Inch'on and Ch'ongju. Coupled with the expansion of National Roads, these expressways permitted the government to pursue a multi-centred plan based on 28 integrated service delivery areas. The expanding Port of Pusan, which accounted for over 90 per cent of the containers handled, was at the heart of one area. Other areas were centred on Taejon and Taegu — the former is also the site for South Korea's first technopolis (Taeduk Science Park). Both were alternative bases to suburban Seoul (Suwon) for the development of motor cars, electrical appliances and electronics. In turn, these service areas were incorporated into regional economic clusters in four zones outside the Capital Region. The real need, however, is to deconcentrate political and economic power from Seoul which has been exerted over provincial areas since the Choson [Yi] Dynasty (1392–1910).

By the mid-1980s, both the Ch'ung'chong and Cholla provinces had less than their share of regional output as a proportion of South Korea's population. Their per capita income was only 80 per cent that of the national capital which, in turn, was exceeded by the Kyongsang provinces. Between 1958 and 1983, total employment in the Chollas declined from 13 per cent to less than 6 per cent, whereas the Kyongsang provinces (including Pusan and Taegu) increased from 39 per cent to over 41 per cent. Over the same period, value added in manufacturing within the Chollas decreased from over 10 per cent to 6 per cent, but the Kyongsang provinces increased from 36 per cent to 40 per cent.[15] These figures reflect the low share of the southwest provinces in key industries, such as textiles, machinery, metals and electronics, dominated by Seoul and Pusan metropolitan areas and the Kyongsang provinces. Only the chemical industries were marked in the

Chollas due to location of the country's second largest oil refinery and petrochemical complex at Yochon, which is not renowned as a great employment generator. Although there are strong arguments supporting the cost-effectiveness of the Seoul–Pusan axis, it has resulted in uneven distribution of industry and triggered regional discontent in the Cholla provinces.

These problems associated with South Korea's transport infrastructure have been compounded by the political power structure of the Korean government. According to Chon,[16] President Park Chung-hee drew heavily upon the Kyongsang provinces for army officers and high-ranking bureaucrats. Reinforced by educational and social ties in Taegu, this preferment was intensified by the heads of nine of the top twenty *chaebol* families coming from Kyongsang. Drawing on government privileges available for export activities since the early 1960s, unlimited imports and preferential loans from foreign banks, the advance of the *chaebol* sector has seen economic power become highly concentrated on a few business groups headed by Kyongsang (or Taegu) families. In turn, this web of influence has been heightened by the recruitment of ex-officers into corporations and government (including Cabinet).

Regional antagonisms stemming from the transport and political structure were further aggravated by the realignment of the former opposition leaders Kim Young-sam (from the southeast) and Kim Jong-pil (from the Chu'ngch'ongs) with the ruling Liberal Party under Roh Tae-woo.[17] Hence the provisions of the Second Physical National Development Plan (1982–91) were activated by the Sixth Republic to pursue a more balanced regional development plan. This has meant dispersing industry from Seoul and Pusan and improving accessibility to the Cholla provinces. Simultaneously, the government sought to mitigate the Cholla provinces' alienation from the country's booming economy and to capitalise on South Korea's new geopolitical position brought about by China's 'open door' policy.

In 1988, the Prime Minister's Office established the Standing Committee for West Coast Development. Its main strategy has been to construct a West Coast Expressway from Inch'on to Kwangyang to link six areas designated for capital-intensive agricultural, industrial and high-technology development (see Fig 9.5). Besides double-tracking existing railways, the plan is to develop a new large-scale port at Kunsan and an industrial port at Asan while expanding capacity at Mokpo Port.[18] Connections between existing coastal and inland urban centres are to be upgraded to create two agglomerations — the Kunsan–Iri–Chonju–Chongju T-shaped Axis and the Kwangju–Naju–Mokpo Axis — in a bid to provide higher-level central management services. Other scheduled capital works include an international airport at Kwangju

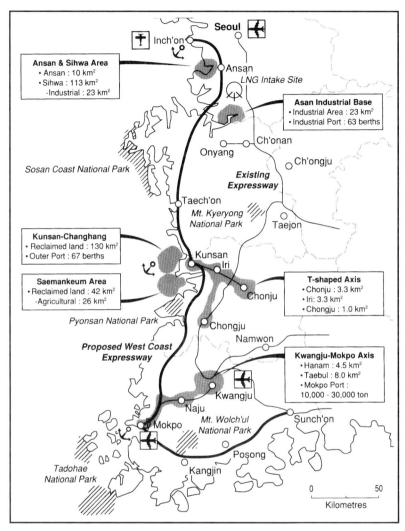

Seoul

Ansan & Sihwa Area
• Ansan : 10 km²
• Sihwa : 113 km²
-Industrial : 23 km²

Inch'on

Ansan
LNG Intake Site

Asan Industrial Base
• Industrial Area : 23 km²
• Industrial Port : 63 berths

Ch'onan
Onyang
Ch'ongju

Sosan Coast National Park

Existing Expressway

Taech'on
Mt. Kyeryong National Park
Taejon

Kunsan-Changhang
• Reclaimed land : 130 km²
• Outer Port : 67 berths

Kunsan
Iri

Saemankeum Area
• Reclaimed land : 42 km²
-Agricultural : 26 km²

T-shaped Axis
• Chonju : 3.3 km²
• Iri: 3.3 km²
• Chongju : 1.0 km²

Chonju

Pyonsan National Park

Chongju
Namwon

Proposed West Coast Expressway

Kwangju-Mokpo Axis
• Hanam : 4.5 km²
• Taebul : 8.0 km²
• Mokpo Port :
10,000 - 30,000 ton

Kwangju
Naju
Mt. Wolch'ul National Park
Sunch'on

Mokpo
Posong

Tadohae National Park
Kangjin

0   50
Kilometres

Fig 9.5 *The West Coast Development Plan*
Source: Choe, Sang Chuel, 'Emerging Spatial Pattern and Coastal Zone Management of the Yellow Sea Rim', in KMI, *East Asian Coastal Area Development and Korea: An Understanding of Common Issues for Promoting Trade*, Seoul: Korea Maritime Institute, 1990, p. 39

and a domestic airport at Mokpo as part of a concerted effort to improve accessibility between the West Coast and other parts of South Korea and the East Asian region as a whole. These attempts to redress this imbalance, and to capitalise on cheap industrial land in the Chollas and the opportunities of trade with China, sent land prices skyrocketing.

Entering the 1990s, analyses of South Korea's domestic transport system pinpointed weaknesses in its infrastructure. Despite heavy investment over the past 30 years, they singled out shortcomings in both South Korea's slow-speed transport network, designed for moving resources and goods, and its high-speed transport network in effecting face-to-face contact between business so that structurally complex information can be transferred. The new infrastructure designed to overcome these problems is discussed by examining slow-speed and high-speed transport networks in turn. Will these developments generate sufficient benefits to appease the Cholla provinces and allow the government to concentrate on the opportunities afforded by South Korea's new geopolitical position?

New slow-speed transport infrastructure

Statistics on internal freight transport within South Korea are not very revealing. They show that road transport dominates followed by rail and sea in tonnes moved (Table 9.1). These positions are reversed in tonne-kilometres with sea leading rail and road. On both counts, air transport makes a negligible contribution. No distinction, however, is made between container and non-container freight. There is not scope here for discussing the transport infrastructure South Korea would require for non-containerised cargo. As illustrated by an analysis of the storage, handling and distribution of grain in South Korea, there are manifest difficulties in handling bulk materials.[19] Nevertheless, the infrastructure necessary for moving containers inland is considered because it is of critical concern for private corporations increasingly dependent on 'outsourcing' products from foreign suppliers.[20] It also provides an opportunity for discussing both rail–road competition and the low priority afforded port development by government.

Table 9.1 Freight transport in South Korea by mode, 1989

Mode	Tonnes million	Per cent	Tonne kilometres million	Per cent
Railway	58.6	18.6	13.6	33.6
Road	199.9	63.7	8.9	22.0
Sea	54.8	17.5	17.8	44.0
Air	0.2	0.2	0.1	0.4
Total	313.6	100.0	40.4	100.0

Source: Song, Hee-hyon, *Dongbuckah jiyeok-yeu susongchaejeh baljeon banghwang: Han, Joong, So-ryl, Jungsim-yeuroh* [Transport system development direction in Northeast Asia: with particular reference to Korea, USSR and China], Seoul: Haewoon Sanup Yeonguwon [Korea Maritime Institute], 1990

Containers

The infrastructure for handling containers in South Korea is inadequate. As shown in Table 9.2, over 90 per cent of the containers are handled at Pusan. In l989, the Port of Pusan handled 2.2 million TEUs — despite its design capacity of only 1.3 million TEUs — which represented a 15 per cent annual growth rate between 1979 and 1989. More than 40 per cent, however, originated or terminated in Greater Seoul, although the capital does not have a container freight station for packing and unpacking. Problems of handling containers stem from two factors: the shortage of port capacity and dispersion and unsystematic operation of off-dock container yards (ODCYs); and the inadequacy of the railways.[21]

Since 1977, 34 ODCYs have been built around the Pusan area to cope with this situation — they store about 80 per cent of the containers handled at Pusan's container terminal. They act as holding areas for both road transport and rail companies. Some containers destined for Seoul are handled at Bugok Container terminal, which is 38 kilometres from the city. Although this terminal is connected to the railway, 90 per cent of the containers arrive or leave by road because of the lack of appropriate handling facilities on the Seoul–Pusan line and the dominance exerted by its leaseholders — sixteen trucking companies. In 1989, less than 30 per cent of the containers were moved by Korea National Railways — two-thirds short of the organisation's capacity. As container trucks aggravate traffic congestion on the Seoul–Pusan Expressway and within the City of Pusan, the extensive use of strike-prone road transport is obviously a less efficient alternative from a national economic perspective than the underused and poorly connected railway system.

In the short term, much emphasis is being placed on expanding and transforming the Bugok Terminal into an Intermodal Container Depot (ICD) under a single owner. Its new function will be to receive and despatch containers by rail to and from Pusan. In 1995, another ICD will be constructed in the area to take the place of the dispersed ODCYs (other ICDs are being considered for Taejon and Kwangju). These ICDs would be linked to the Port of Pusan by Electronic Date Interchange (EDI). In turn, the government boosted the capacity of Pusan by 1 million TEUs in 1991 and is planning to increase it by 1.3 million TEUs in 1994. Even though the Japanese trade has been moved to the neighbouring port of Masan, this expansion will still fall short of demand. By 2001, container throughput at Pusan is expected to exceed 7 million TEUs — an assumption based on attracting transhipments from China, Japan, North Korea, Russia and Taiwan. Because Pusan lacks space for expansion in further handling capacity

Table 9.2 The railways' share of container traffic, 1985–89

Date	(A) Total thousand TEU	(B) Pusan thousand TEU	(C) Seoul sub-total thousand TEU	(D) Seoul railway only thousand TEU	C/A per cent	D/A per cent	D/B per cent	D/C per cent
1985	1259	1155	377	85	29.9	6.8	7.4	22.5
1986	1549	1448	428	147	27.6	9.5	10.1	34.3
1987	1933	1825	710	200	36.7	10.3	11.0	28.2
1988	2217	2065	782	233	35.3	10.5	11.3	19.8
1989	2271	2159	854	247	37.6	10.9	11.5	28.9

Source: Adapted from Chin, 1990b, p. 59

and Inch'on is not favoured as an alternative, the government is planning a new container port in South Cholla.

The new container port is to be built in Kwangyang Bay, some 140 kilometres from Pusan (Fig 9.6). An existing industrial port, related to Kwangyang's steel complex and Yochon's oil and petrochemical developments, it has sufficient land to accommodate a city of 200 000 people, terminals, distribution centres and services such as banking and

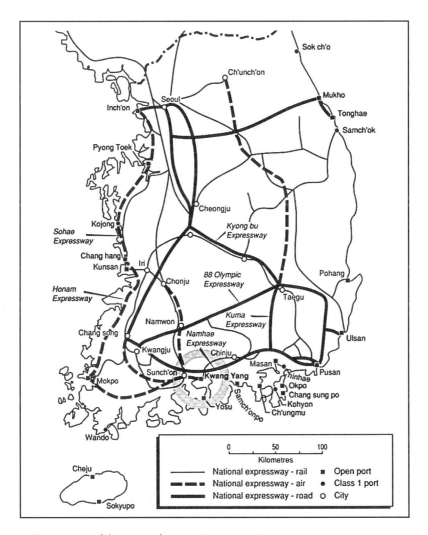

Fig 9.6   Location of the proposed port at Kwangyang Bay
Source: Jun, Il-soo, 'Kwangyang Container Port as an Innovative Structure for Logistics: A Case Study', in KMI, *The Public Sector's Role in Logistics for the 21st Century,* The 2nd KMI International Symposium, 2–7 July 1990, Seoul: Korea Maritime Institute, 1990, p. 80

insurance.[22] Upgrading of expressways and rail connections, however, will be required. By 1996 Kwangyang Bay should have six container berths handling 980 000 TEUs; by 2001, it should have ten container berths and 2.6 million TEUs; and by 2011 it should have twenty container and ten multi-purpose berths and a capacity of 4.8 million TEUs (48 per cent of the Korean total) at a total cost of 388 million *won*. Its location will enable it to serve the major industrial developments on the West Coast, generated by the prospects of trade with China. Proponents of Kwangyang see it becoming a key load centre by handling transhipment cargoes from the East Asian Corridor and its Southeast Asian counterpart stretching from Chiangmai to Bali. Specifically, Kwangyang hopes to benefit from transit trade from Hong Kong once the colony has been returned to China in 1997. Before examining these wider prospects, the proposed high-speed transport network is discussed.

New high-speed transport infrastructure

As noted, the prime purpose of improving the new high-speed transport infrastructure is to facilitate face-to-face business contact as the means of transmitting complex information. Congested highways and limited domestic airports are paramount in arguments for improving high-speed transport. Buyers have difficulty in taking overseas businesspeople to dispersed industrial sites. Most attention has been on high-speed transport, though discussions are also being advanced for an international airport to replace Kimpo. Contrary to the trend towards more balanced regional development, the infrastructure will reinforce existing corridors and population concentrations. Cynics see the high-speed rail as linking government strongholds between Seoul and Pusan.

High-speed rail

A project to build a high-speed railway between Seoul and Pusan is now underway (Fig 9.7). The arguments relating to its construction are elaborated here based on positive material supporting its construction. These have ranged from the pamphlet of the High-speed Railway Business Planning Corporation [23] through a brief study done by the Office of Railways[24] to the more sober treatises of Kim Jong-hoon[25] and the Korea Transport Institute.[26] A brief reference to the opposition to this project is based on discussions with academics, businesspeople and public servants in Seoul.

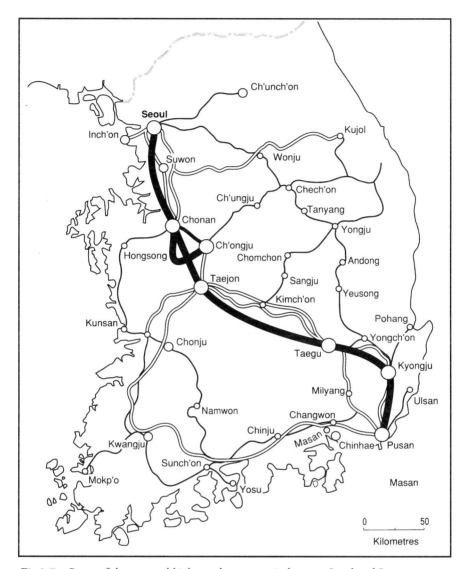

Fig 9.7 *Route of the proposed high-speed express train between Seoul and Pusan*
Source: Kim, Jong-hoon, *Urinarah Chuldo Susong Sanup-yeu Hyeonhwang-gwa Gwajae*
[Present Condition and Task of Korea's Railroad Industry], Seoul: Haewoon Sanup
Yeonguwon [Korea Maritime Institute], 1991, p. 94

Proponents

As the Corridor accounts for almost 68 per cent of South Korea's population,
almost 74 per cent of Gross National Product and almost 84 per cent of
manufacturing employment, the project is seen by its proponents as a new
type of transport, the introduction of which is long overdue. The existing
railways and expressways are saturated. Already the railways are operating at

maximum capacity of 138 passenger and freight trains per day. Further, eight to ten days are required for purchasing a weekday rail ticket and ten days for a weekend one. This situation forces would-be passengers to use private cars or buses. Even if nothing is done to the existing system, an additional 1.5 trillion *won* will be required by the year 2000 to cover the increased costs of transport operations.

Assuming the continuation of present annual growth trends — 3.6 per cent for road and 2.2 per cent for rail — time delays due to traffic congestion will increase on national expressways from 1.3 hours per day in 1990 to 10 hours per day in 2000 (Table 9.3). By then, the cumulative losses due to traffic congestion between 1991 and 2001 will have reached 130 trillion *won*.

Table 9.3 Time lost through traffic congestion, 1990 and 2000

Highway category	1990 (hours/day)	2000 (hours/day)
Expressway	1.3	10
National Highway	1.4	10

Source: Chuldochong [The Office of Korea National Railways], n.p

The choice is between expressway or high-speed rail based on either wheels or magnetic levitation (Table 9.4). Magnetic levitation, however, has been dismissed as a feasible alternative. It is still in an experimental stage in both Germany and Japan. Although it is a safe form of transport, many problems still have to be solved. Not only is it more expensive to build than the high-speed electric train, but it consumes more energy per seat-kilometre. Also, there is a widespread feeling that South Korea should not be used as a test bed for magnetic levitation because of the possibility of accidents. A major drawback is that it would be difficult to link to the existing system. Thus the solution for high-speed inter-city transport devolves on the choice between expressway and high-speed electric railways.

Table 9.4 A comparison between high-speed electric and magnetic levitated trains

Type of train	Construction cost trillion won	Energy consumption kwh/seat km
High-speed electric	4.6	59
Magnetic levitation	5.8	117.5

Note: High-speed train costs based on TGV-A and magnetic levitation train on TransRapid TR-06
Source: Gyotong Gaebal Yeonguwon [Korea Transport Institute], 1991, pp. 19–22

The maximum speed of the high-speed rail is almost three times faster than the expressway (Table 9.5). In terms of construction costs, however, the expressway offers the cheapest short-term solution. Yet its daily capacity is less than half that of high-speed rail.

Table 9.5 *Comparative characteristics of four-lane expressway and high-speed electric railway*

	Construction cost trillion won	Capacity people/day	Speed km/hr
Express electric railway	4.6	520 000	300
Expressway (four-lane)	3.35	250 000	110

Source: Gosock Junchul Saup Gilwoeckdan [High-speed Railway Business Planning Corporation], n.p.

These advantages are offset by maintenance costs (Table 9.6). High-speed electric railways are easier to maintain than expressways. Over time, this margin is progressively increased. In 1998, the margin is expected to be 764 billion *won*. By 2011, it will be 1172 billion *won*.

Table 9.6 *Difference in operating costs between four-lane expressway and high-speed electric railway*

Alternative	1998 billion won	2001 billion won	2011 billion won
Express electric railway	4 598	6 283	15 939
Expressway	5 362	7 147	17 111
Cost saving	764	864	1 172

Source: Gosock Junchul Saup Gihwoeckdan [High-speed Railway Business Planning Corporation], n.p.

Further, no account is taken in these calculations of the costs of expressway externalities (e.g. congestion and pollution). Although the break-even point between a four-lane highway and high-speed rail is 2006 and 'after 2050' respectively, the latter offers a better long-term solution (Table 9.7). Construction of a high-speed railway is inevitable. As a high-quality, high-speed railway is guaranteed for 25 years, the only point at issue is whether it runs at 200 kph or 300 kph.

If a 200 kph train were chosen, the break-even point could be brought

Table 9.7 Comparative characteristics of expressway and high-speed electric railway

Item	Expressway (hours/day)	Express electric railway
Construction cost (billion *won*)	3350	4600
Marginal year	2006	After 2050

Source: Chuldochung [The Office of Korean National Railways], n.d.

back to 2021 (Table 9.8). There is, however, very little difference in cost between the construction of a 200 kph train and a 300 kph train. The latter would undertake the journey in 1 hour and 41 minutes compared with 2 hours and 43 minutes by the former. The more highly rated train would maximise both social and economic efficiency, as the 'life boundary' between Seoul and Pusan would be reduced to a half-day. The flow of goods would be stimulated by the increased activity and the shorter time in transit would reduce operation costs. Given a seven-year construction period, the train should be available to cater for the anticipated escalation in demand by 2001.

Table 9.8 Comparative characteristics of 200km and 300km per hour express electric railways

Item	200km/hr	300km/hr
Construction cost (billion *won*)	4300	4600
Journey time	2hr 43 min	1hr 41 min
Marginal year	2021	After 2050

Source: Chuldochung [The Office of Korean National Railways], n.d.

Table 9.9 Capital cost of proposed Seoul–Pusan Railway

	Capital	
	Billion won	*Per cent*
Land	703	12.0
Civil engineering	2951	50.5
Electricity, signals	871	14.0
Rolling stock	1214	20.8
Others	106	1.8
Total	5846	100.0

Source: Gosock Junchul Saup Gihwoeckdan [High-speed Railway Business Planning Corporation], n.p.

Table 9.10 *Specification of high-speed train between Seoul and Pusan*

Distance	Kilometres	409
Maximum speed	Kilometres per hour	300
Average speed	Kilometres per hour	244
Travelling time	Hour/minutes	1 hour 41 minutes
Capacity	Passengers	1 000
Construction period	Year	1993–98
Configuration cost	Trillion *won*	5.8

Source: Kim, Jong-hoon, *Urinarah Chuldo Susong Sanup-yeu Hyeonhwang-gwa Gwajae* [Present Condition and Task of Korea's Railroad Industry], Seoul: Haewoon Sanup Yeonguwon [Korea Maritime Institute], 1991, p. 78; Gossock Junchul Saip Gihwoeckdan [High Speed Railway Business Planning Corporation].

The total cost of the high-speed railway is estimated at 5846 billion won (Table 9.9). It represents an annual expenditure of 250 billion per year during the 1990s. This figure is only 17 per cent of the annual budget for roads during the 1990s.

Specifications for the train show that it would carry 1000 passengers over the 409 kilometres between Seoul and Pusan every four minutes at an average speed of 244 kilometres per hour (Table 9.10). If construction could be completed by 1998, this would relieve pressure on road transport and allow the existing railways to carry long-haul goods traffic.

The adoption of the 300 kph train would demonstrate high technology. According to the High-speed Railway Business Planning Corporation,[27] the core technology for a high-speed train is beyond the capabilities of South Korean technicians. Although foreign companies will receive 800 billion *won* for their efforts, the benefits will be infinitely greater for local contractors. About 80 per cent of the civil engineering work would be undertaken by local construction companies, and it will have important spin-offs in employment generation. Only the train body has been subject to international competition between the French, German and Japanese producers (Table 9.11). Proponents believe that these international experts should be listened to carefully so that proper assistance and co-operation are provided. Once the technology is appreciated, South Korea will be in a position to develop its own high-speed railway system for export.

Already, the transport problem of travelling between Seoul and Pusan is urgent. If it is tackled, extension of the railway to the East–West and Honam routes could be envisaged and the elusive concept of balanced regional development pursued. Slower speeds, however, are projected on these lines (Table 9.12). Further, the construction of the line from Taejon to Mokpo is subject to a certain level of patronage on the Seoul–Pusan main trunk line being attained.

Table 9.11 Options for the South Korean high-speed railway

	Japan Shinkansen	France Train Grande Vittesse	Germany Intercity Express
Inaugurated	1969	1980	1991
Planned (km)	7200	2071	
Construction	Pre-1969		
Speed (km/hr)	260	300	350
Routes		TGV (PSE) Paris–Lyons (417 km) TGV Atlantique (283 km)	1991: Mannheim–Stuttgart (420 km)
Extension		1993: TGV (PSE) Lyons–Valence (121 km) TGV Nord Lille–London–Brussels–Amsterdam–Koln (388 km)	1991: Wurzburg–Munich; Stuttgart–Munich Koln–Frankfurt
Existing (km)	6786	700	420

Source: Gyotong Gaebal Yeonguwon [Korea Transport Institute}, 1991, pp. 19–22

Opponents' arguments against the high-speed train are not readily available in published form. Discussions with opponents, however, highlight that it will aggravate the concentration of activity in Seoul. For example, one major research institute has reportedly argued that a four-lane expressway would be more economic than a high-speed railway. Other opponents, including the former Chairman of Hyundai, Chung Ju-yung, have contended that the high-speed railway is not urgent compared with other infrastructural tasks — roads and drainage, sewage treatment and expansion of seaports and airports. The high-speed train should wait until South Korea acquires the requisite skills. Already its transport industries are capable of building a 200 kph version.

The new highway will also run counter to plans for balanced regional development. Undoubtedly, it will reinforce the attractiveness of the Seoul–Pusan Corridor. Already it is the prime target of a program for creating technobelts — areas for high-tech research and development. The mix of high-speed transport and R&D will ensure the Corridor's pre-eminence over other areas.

This opposition was unable to dissuade the government from proceeding with the new high-speed rail project. To justify its completion, the

Table 9.12 Proposed high-speed railway lines

	Seoul–Pusan	Seoul–East Coast	Taejon–Mokpo
Characteristics			
Route length(km)	409	240	250–290
Maximum speed (kph)	350	250	180–250
Average speed	—	180	150–180
Construction costs (billion *won*)			
Track	46 320	14 050	—
Rolling stock	12 140	4 150	—
Total	58 460	18 200	—
Schedule			
Basic investigation	1989–90	1988–90	Linked to patronage of Seoul–Pusan line
Design	1990–91	1990–92	
Construction	1993–98	1992–98	

Source: Kim, Jong-hoon, *Urinarah Chuldo Susong Sanup-yeu Hyeonhwng-gwa Gwajae* [Present Condition and Task of Korea's Railroad Industry], Seoul: Haewoon Sanup Yeonguwon [Korea Maritime Institute], 1991, p. 92

government emphasised its importance as a step towards a trans-continental high-speed railway linking Pusan and Paris. In the interim, passengers will have to rely on air transport for high-speed business trips.

New airport

There are three international airports in Korea — Cheju, Kimp'o and Kimhae (Pusan) — with the prospect of an additional one at Chung'ju. Of these, Kimp'o is dominant. Opened in 1953, its facilities were expanded between 1976 and 1980 and between 1983 and 1987 (i.e. prior to the Asian and Olympic Games). A second international airport, however, is contemplated because at Kimp'o the number of landings and take-offs has been restricted to 163 000 per annum because the distance between the two parallel runways is 1200 feet instead of the recommended 4200 feet. Further problems stem from it being too close to military zones and the mountains. Due to built-up areas bordering it, a curfew is in force between 10.00 p.m. and 6.00 a.m. Although it functions as a *de facto* Category III airport, Kimpo's approved visibility and landing heights are still those of Category II facility — hence the proposition for a new 3500 billion *won* international airport at Yong Jong Island, 50 kilometres west of Seoul.

Improved airport infrastructural facilities are vital because South Korea's

13.3 per cent rate of passenger growth between 1979 and 1988 outstripped both the world (7 per cent) and Asia-Pacific (10.4 per cent) averages. Not only will the new transport infrastructure have to cater for business passengers but also for air freight. The growth rate for air freight between 1979 and 1988 was 17.6 per cent — much greater than the world (9.3 per cent), Asia-Pacific (13.8 per cent) and Japan (14.5 per cent). With a new airport, South Korea is poised to be a major linchpin in the intercontinental air express freight market between Europe and North America. This emphasis on investing heavily on nodes offering international access is the government's response to Korea's changed geopolitical position.

Geopolitical implications

Any study of Korea's slow-speed and high-speed transport networks cannot be concentrated solely on internal developments. It must include new transport infrastructure and identify how these will affect ties with North America, within the East Asian Corridor and with Europe.[28]

North America

The mainstream route from South Korea and other East Asian countries to North America has been the pacesetter in establishing new infrastructural requirements.[29] In slow-speed transport, for example, greater use is being made by the leading shipping companies (e.g. American President Line, Sea-Land, Maersk, Mitsui OSK and Nihon Yusen Kaisha) of high-cube and specialised containers, rail feeder networks and inland depots due to carriers seeking economies of scale from newer and larger vessels.[30] These developments mean that major load centres will have the most advanced infrastructure and technology to meet the need for extended depths, super-gantry cranes and extended wharfs. The leading South Korean shipping companies, however, are middle-market competitors offering either minimum cost, port-to-port services (e.g. Hanjin or Hyundai) or round-the-world services (e.g. Choyang). Nevertheless, they have been active in the double-stack rail transfer of containers in the United States, which has prompted demands for investment in South Korean infrastructure.

North America has also been the trendsetter in international air transport. As yet, the international air passenger network is still an immature system. The domestic hub and spoke system developed in the United States is unlikely to find global expression before the middle of the twenty-first century. Superhub status will not be afforded existing airports at Bangkok,

Kuala Lumpur, Manila, Shanghai, Singapore or Tokyo (the New International Airport at Narita) or even planned airports at Hong Kong (1997), Osaka (1993) or Seoul. The basic requirement is that the superhub should be located between 160 kilometres and 800 kilometres from existing population centres. Thus a key problem for the East Asian Corridor is where the superhubs should be located.

East Asian Corridor

South Korea is in a pivotal position with respect to both the heavily populated East Japan Sea and Yellow Sea Economic Zones of Co-operation (Fig 9.8). Within two hours' flying time from Seoul there are 400 million

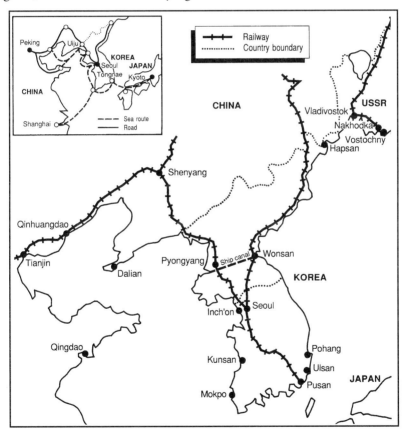

Fig 9.8   *South Korea's pivotal position in the East Asian Corridor. Inset shows the major transport and trade routes of the late Choson Dynasty.*
Source: Rimmer, P.J., 'Ports, Inland Transport Linkages and Regional Development: A Western Pacific Rim Conspectus', in KMI, *The Public Sector's Role in Logistics for the 21st Century*, The 2nd KMI International Symposium, 2–7 July 1990, Seoul: Korea Maritime Institute, 1990, p. 298

people. Previously, political and ideological differences have prevented economic co-operation, but improved economic relations with Korea's neighbours as a result of the government's Northern Policy towards China, North Korea and Russia have changed the situation.[31] South Korea's position would be further strengthened by the 'opening-up' of the two Koreas and the reunification of Korean railways.[32] The end result would be a transport pattern reminiscent of the late Choson Dynasty when Korea provided a bridge from Japan to Northern China.[33]

East Japan Sea Zone

In the Japan Sea Zone there are prospects for South Korean companies entering agreements with Russia to exploit its timber and mineral resources and boost sluggish trade (Table 9.13). Also, closer relations with Russia could lead to forging stronger international rail links with Europe (and pipeline connections to Sakhalin). There is also the prospect of participating in the development of the much-touted site of Hapsan (Hunchun) on the Tumen River near the borders of China, North Korea and Russia.[34] With Japanese involvement, there would be the money, inspiration and confidence to catapult the Golden Delta site into the position of being a second Hong Kong — a supplier of high value services and manufactured products for China and Russia.

Allied to the Hapsan proposition is the prospect of accommodation between Japan and Russia over the disputed Northern Islands which could lead to the accelerated economic development of Sakhalin as a free trade zone. An integrated, internationally oriented South Korean economy offers

Table 9.13   Trade between South Korea and USSR, 1985–90

Date	Export		Import		Total	
	$US mill.	*Per cent*	*$US mill.*	*Per cent*	*$US mill.*	*Per cent*
1985	60		42		102	
1986	65	8.3	68	61.9	133	30.4
1987	67	3.1	866	95.6	200	50.4
1988	112	67.2	133	33.9	290	45.0
1989	208	85.7	178	120.2	600	106.9
1990	485		392		569	

Source: Song, Hee-hyon, *Dongbuckah jiyeok-yeu susongchaejeh baljeon banghwang: Han, Joong, So-ryl, Jungsim-yeoroh* [Transport system development direction in Northeast Asia: with particular reference to Korea, USSR and China], Seoul: Haewoon Sanup Yeonguwon [Korea Maritime Institute], 1990, p. 4

the prospect of blending capital, management and skills with low-cost labour in mooted developments in the Russian Far East and opportunities for rapid economic growth and rising incomes.[35] Much will depend on the quality of the slow-speed and high-speed transport connections being established — a proposition equally applicable to the Yellow Sea Zone.

In the Yellow Sea Zone, South Korea is well situated through its West Coast activities to capitalise on the opening up of China's coastal area and to stimulate trade (Table 9.14). There is the possibility of using China's Special Economic Zones for ventures trading off South Korean technology, capital and management expertise for local raw materials and labour.[36] Already, South Korean interests are targeting the Shanghai and Northeastern Economic Zone, the Beijing–Tianjin–Tangshan area and Shanxi's energy production bases.[37] As noted, South Korea is extending its port capacities for both bulk commodities and containerised feeder cargo. Geographical proximity to China will encourage the import of both coal and iron ore from China at the expense of Australia and other traditional markets.

With its rapid urban and industrial development, the Yellow–North China Seas Zone could become the core of the emerging East Asian Corridor. In China, the prime beneficiaries will be the coastal areas of Shandong, Liaoning and Tianjin provinces bordering the Gulf of Bohai rather than hinterland areas. Within South Korea there is the prospect of promoting the depressed southwest region because the export economy of the southeast coastal region is tied to United States and Japanese markets. As these markets are well serviced, the main problem facing South Korea is its slow-speed transport connections with Europe (see Fig 9.9).

Table 9.14 Trade between South Korea and China, 1985–90

Date	Export		Import		Total	
	$US mill.	*Per cent*	*$US mill.*	*Per cent*	*$US mill.*	*Per cent*
1985	683		478		1161	
1986	715	4.9	621	29.9	1336	15.1
1987	813	13.7	866	39.5	1679	25.7
1988	1700	109.1	1387	60.2	3087	83.9
1989	1438	−15.5	1705	22.9	3142	1.8
1990	1463	1.7	2037	19.5	3500	11.4

Source: Song, Hee-hyon, *Dongbuckah jiyeok-yeu susongchaejeh baljeon banghwang: Han, Joong, So-ryl, Jungsim-yeoroh* [Transport system development direction in Northeast Asia: with particular reference to Korea, USSR and China], Seoul: Haewoon Sanup Yeonguwon [Korea Maritime Institute], 1990, p. 4

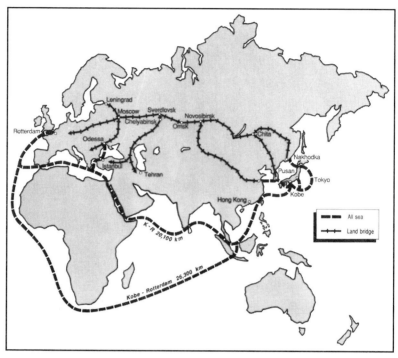

Fig 9.9   *Alternative slow-speed transport routes between South Korea and Europe. Note that the Baikal–AMur–Magistral (BAM) branch of the Trans-Siberian Railway connecting the port of Sovestkaya Gavan is excluded*
Source: Rimmer, 1990, p. 295

Table 9.15 *Freight movements on the Trans-Siberian Railway, 1980–88*

Date	Far East–Europe TEU	Westbound Far East–Middle East TEU	Subtotal TEU	Eastbound Europe–Far East TEU	Total TEU
1980	57 584	20 301	77 885	21 793	99 678
1981	45 060	37 747	82 807	21 037	103 844
1984	42 134	20 950	63 084	25 580	88 420
1985	47 845	11 170	59 015	26 580	85 595
1986	51 380	3 600	54 980	22 522	77 502
1987	39 150	2 710	41 870	20 990	62 860
1988	40 080	2 620	42 700	25 000	67 700

Note: Container throughput is measured in terms of Twenty Feet Equivalent Inits (TEUs)

Source: Song, Hee-hyon, *Dongbuckah jiyeok-yeu susongchaejeh baljeon banghwang: Han, Joong, So-ryl, Jungsim-yeoroh* [Transport system development direction in Northeast Asia: with particular reference to Korea, USSR and China], Seoul: Haewoon Sanup Yeonguwon [Korea Maritime Institute], 1990, p. 9

Table 9.16 Distance, time and cost of moving cargo between Kobe and Rotterdam, 1988

Route	Distance	Time	Cost
Sea (via Suez Canal)	20 100	32	2 300
Trans-Siberian Railway	11 000	25	1 400
Trans-Korean Railway	9 800	23	1 200
Trans-China Railway	8 800	20	1 100

Source: Rimmer, P.J., 'Ports, Inland Transport Linkages and Regional Development: A Western Pacific Rim Conspectus', in KMI, *The Public Sector's Role in Logistics for the 21st Century*, The 2nd KMI International Symposium, 2–7 July 1990, Seoul: Korea Maritime Institute, 1990, p. 296

Europe

With the 'opening up' of Eastern Europe, there has been renewed interest in routes between the Western Pacific Rim and Europe. In the past, the Trans-Siberian Railway has been seen as an alternative to sea transport (Table 9.15). Now attention has been given to connections to the Trans-Siberian Railway through North Korea or the Trans-China Railway — a trend that could lead to an upsurge in the route's flagging fortunes.[38]

Comparing distance, time and cost of moving cargo between Kobe and Rotterdam shows that sea transport is inferior (Table 9.16). Further, the North Korean route is superior to the existing landbridge provided by the Trans-Siberian Railway. The designated Trans-China Railway between Lianyungang and Rotterdam, however, is in the best position. Failing the resumption of through traffic on North Korean railways, South Korea could still concentrate on moving containers by sea to capitalise on the China route's advantages (the shortest distance from the west coast to the Shandong Peninsula is 190 kilometres). Such permutations underline South Korea's key geopolitical position in the East Asian Corridor.

Conclusion

This study has explored the roots of South Korea's uneven regional development. It has assessed the likely contribution of both slow-speed and high-speed transport networks to balanced regional development. Further, it has highlighted how this infrastructure could relate to its changed geopolitical position. Computerised telecommunications (e.g. computers and satellites) must be examined next because seaports or airports-cum-technoports are likely to become pivotal points in economic space within the East Asian Corridor.[39]

The nature and rate of change within the East Asian Corridor is beyond South Korea's control. Decisions must be made about how to keep pace with Corridor developments. Should the South Korean government allow entrepreneurs to locate their firms where they think fit by deregulating government control over regional policy and increasing private participation in providing new transport connections and terminals? Alternatively, should the government take the more difficult option and engage in land use and transport-telecommunications planning to determine how technologies can be used to achieve preferred kinds of society, cities and environments?

These issues for debate have to be matched to an appropriate analytical framework. A study is required of the potential, partial and synergistic impact of the proposed transport (and telecommunications) infrastructure on land use in South Korea during the early years of the twenty-first century. Two polar approaches are preferred. The first looks at how to model the effects of technological changes in transport and communications on land use. The second looks at how they can be created by the judiciously locating new transport and communication infrastructures. Then, assuming limited autonomy, the final issue is: what controls and moves are possible for South Korea within the East Japan Sea and Yellow Sea Zones?

Notes

1 I am indebted to the Korean Links program, Australian National University, for assisting my visit to South Korea in 1991. Lee Deog-an, formerly a Research Scholar, Department of Human Geography, has assisted with translating some material. While in South Korea I had discussions with staff in the Construction Association of Korea, Korea International Freight Forwarders Association, Korea Maritime Institute, Ministry of Transport and Seoul National University. In particular, I am grateful for assistance provided by the president and members of the Korea Maritime Institute in 1990, 1991 and 1992. Barbara Banks and James Cotton made useful comments on the text. The interpretations in this study, however, are those of the author alone.

2 GROK, *Economic Survey: Annual Report of the Korean Economy*, Seoul: Economic Planning Board, Government of the Republic of Korea, 1987, p. 15.

3 Choe Sang-chuel, A Review of Industrial Location Policies and Important Policy Instruments in Korea, unpublished paper presented to a Conference on the Spatial Structure of Industries in Northeast Asia held at Chuo University, Tokyo 21–25 July 1986, p. 1.

4 The first Republic was led by Syngman Rhee; the Second, Third and Fourth by Park Chung-hee; the Fifth by Chun Doo-hwan; and the president of the Sixth was Roh Tae-woo. The military backgrounds of Park, Chun and Roh may explain their penchant for transport infrastructure developments.

5 Kim Doojung and Yoo Jea-taik, eds, *Korea: Geographical Perspectives*, Seoul: Korean Educational Development Institute, 1988, pp. 385–87.

6 Kim Doojung and Yoo Jea-taik, eds, *Korea: Geographical Perspectives,* p. 397.

7 ARC, *A Study of Regional Development in Korea: Ulsan Masan & Jeonju Regions*, Seoul: Asiatic Research Centre, Korea University 1978; Choe Sang-chuel, A Review of Industrial Location Policies and Important Policy Instruments in Korea, unpublished paper presented to a Conference on the Spatial Structure of Industries in Northeast Asia held at Chuo University, Tokyo, 21–25 July 1986; Kim Doojung and Yoo Jea-taik, eds, *Korea: Geographical Perspectives*, Seoul: Korean Educational Development Institute, 1988.

8 Attention is drawn to the rationale used by the South Korean government in justifying the potential, partial and synergistic effects of new transport infrastructure projects. There has been much emphasis on explaining priorities in terms of 'efficiency'. This does not necessarily equate with the 'economic efficiency' concept used by transport economists. Indeed, there is the classic case where economists argued that the Seoul–Pusan Expressway was premature. The then president went ahead regardless of this advice.

9 ARC, 1978. A Study of Regional Development in Korea; Lee Jeong-sik, 'Regional development policies in Korea: retrospect and prospect', *The Korea Spatial Planning Review*, vol. 10 (1986), pp. 79–99.

10 Lee Jeong-sik, 'Regional Development Policies in Korea: Retrospect and Prospect', pp. 79–99.

11 Yu Eui-young, 'Regionalism in the South Korea Job Market', *Pacific Affairs*, vol. 63 (1988), pp. 24–39.

12 Chon Sooh-yun, 'Political Economy of Regional Development in Korea, unpublished paper presented at the Conference on States and Development in the East Asian Pacific Rim, University of California, Santa Barbara, 22–25 March 1990.

13 GROK, *The Second Comprehensive National Physical Development Plan, 1982–1991*; *GROK Economic Survey: Annual Report of the Korean Economy.*

14 KRIHS, *Kookto Jungbo Jaryo* [Land Information Collection], Seoul: Korea Research Institute for Human Settlements, 1986.

15 Kim Doojung and Yoo Jea-taik, eds, *Korea: Geographical Perspectives.*

16 Chon Sooh-yun, Political Economy of Regional Development in Korea, unpublished paper presented at the Conference on States and Development in the East Asian Pacific Rim, University of California, Santa Barbara, 22–25 March 1990, pp. 16–25

17 Kim Jong-pil was alleged to have pressed Roh Tae-woo, who was then president, to upgrade a road running through his home province of

Ch'ungch'ongnam into the status of a highway to be constructed under South Korea's infrastructure program, even though other areas had more pressing congestion problems.

18 ARC, *A Study of Regional Development in Korea*; Choe Sang-chuel, A Review of Industrial Location Policies and Important Policy Instruments in Korea, unpublished paper presented to a Conference on the Spatial Structure of Industries in Northeast Asia held at Chuo University, Tokyo, 21–25 July 1986; Choe Sang-chuel, 'Emerging Spatial Pattern and Coastal Zone Management of the Yellow Sea Rim', in KMI, *East Asia Coastal Area Development and Korea: An Understanding of Common Issues for Promoting Trade*, Seoul: Korea Maritime Institute, 1990, pp. 29–48.

19 Jung Pil-soo, 'Storage, Handling and Distribution of Imported Grains in Korea', in KMI, *The Public Sector's Role in Logistics for the 21st Century*, the 2nd KMI International Symposium, 2–7 July 1990, Seoul: Korea Maritime Institute, 1990, pp. 209–43.

20 KMI, *A Study on Improving Port Efficiency*, Seoul: Korea Maritime Institute, 1987; Haewoon Sanup Yeonguwon [Korea Transport Institute], *Container yeu hang man/nae ruk su song hap ri hwa bang an (Bu Rok)* [Rationalisation scheme of harbour/inland transportation for container (Appendix)], *Yong yeuk bi go seo 018 [Consultant Report No. 18]*, Seoul: Korea Maritime Institute, 1988; Jon Joon-soo, 'Changes in the shipping environment and counter strategies of Korea toward the year 2000', in *Changes in the World Shipping Environment and Counter Strategies Toward the Year 2000*, Seoul: Korea Maritime Institute, 1988, pp. 148–69.

21 Chin Hyung-in, 'An Improvement Plan of Intermodalism in Korea: The Rationalization Scheme of the Integrated Transport System Linking Pusan Port and Bugok Container Terminal', in KMI, *The Public Sector's Role in Logistics for the 21st Century*, the 2nd KMI International Symposium, 2–7 July 1990, Seoul: Korea Maritime Institute, 1990, pp. 110–32; Chin Hyung-in, 'The Development of International Logistics System and the Intermodal System in Korea', in KMI, *East Asia Coastal Area Development and Korea: An Understanding of Common Issues for Promoting Trade*, Seoul: Korea Maritime Institute, 1990, pp. 49–74.

22 Jun Il-soo, 'Kwangyang Container Port as an Innovative Structure for Logistics: A Case Study', in KMI, *The Public Sector's Role in Logistics for the 21st Century*, The 2nd KMI International Symposium 2–7 July 1990, Seoul: Korea Maritime Institute, 1990, pp. 353–87; Jun Il-soo, 'Port Strategy and Planning in Korea: With Special Emphasis on Container Transport', in KMI, *East Asia Coastal Area Development and Korea: An Understanding of Common Issues for Promoting Trade*, Seoul, Korea Maritime Institute, 1990b, pp. 1–28.

23 Gosock Junchul Saup Gihwoeckdan [High-speed Railway Business Planning Corporation], *Gyungboo Gosock Junchul-eun Jigeum Gunsulhaeyah Hapnidah* [Seoul–Pusan High-speed Railway should be Constructed Right Now!], Seoul: Gosock Junchul Saup Gihwoeckdan, n.d.

24 Chuldochung [The Office of Korea National Railways], *Gosockjunchul, Woe Gunsulhaeyah Haneungah?* [High-speed Railway: Why it should be Constructed], Seoul: Office of Railways, n.d.

25 Kim Jong-hoon, *Urinarah Chuldo Susong Sanup-yeu Hyeonhwang-gwa Gwajae* [Present Condition and Task of Korea's Railroad Industry], Seoul: Haewoon Sanup Yeonguwon [Korea Maritime Institute], 1991.

26 Gyotong Gaebal Yeonguwon [Korea Transport Institute], *Gyungboo Gosock Junchul Gunsul-yeu Tadangsung mit Dangweesung* [Appropriateness and Inevitability of the Seoul-Pusan High-speed Railway Construction], Seoul: Korea Transport Institute, 1991.

27 Gosock Junchul Saup Gihwoeckdan [High-speed Railway Business Planning Corporation], *Gyungboo Gosock Junchul-eun Jigeum Gunsulhaeyah Hapnidah.*

28 Rhyu Suck-hyong and Kim Hong-seop, *Soryun Haewoon Sanup-yeu Hyeonhwang-gwa Jeonmang* [Present Situation of and Prospects for the USSR's Shipping Industry], Seoul: Korea Maritime Institute, 1989; Rhyu Suck-hyong and Kim Hong-seop, *Jonggook Haewoon Sanup-yeu Hyeonhwang-gwa Jeonmang* [Present Situation of Prospects for China's Shipping Industry], Seoul: Korea Maritime Institute, 1989; Rhyu Suck-hyong and Kim Hong-seop, *Asia Shinhueng Gongupgoock Haewoon Sanup-yeu Hyeonhwang-gwa Jeonmang* [Present Situation of and Prospects for the Shipping Industry of Asian NIEs], Seoul: Korea Maritime Institute, 1990.

29 Shin Bu-yong, 'South Korea: Course of Remedy', *Intermodal Asia: Supplement to Lloyd's Maritime Asia,* Part One: 34, 38. (1988); USDOA, 'The Korean Maritime Industry', *Far East Port Survey,* Washington DC: Office of Transportation, United States Department of Agriculture, 1988; Jin Hyung-in and Back Jong-sil, *Gookjuck Sunsa-yeu Buckmi Bockhap Woon Song Gangwa Bangan* [The Multimodal Transport Reinforcement Scheme of Korean Shipping Companies in North America], Seoul: Korea Maritime Institute, 1990.

30 P.J. Rimmer, 'Transport and Communications in the Pacific Economic Zone During the Early Years of the Twenty-first Century', in Yeung Yeu-man, ed., *Geography and Development in Pacific Asia in the 21st Century,* Hong Kong: Chinese University Press, forthcoming.

31 Noh Hee Mock, 'The Development of Korean Trade and Investment in the PRC', *Korea and World Affairs: A Quarterly Review,* vol. 13, no. 3 (1989), pp. 421–39; Rhyu Suck-hyong, Rim Jong-kwan and Park Yong-geun, *Pukbang Chung Chack-kwa Haewoon Sanup Bumun-yeu Daewung Pang Hwang* [Northern Policy and the Counter Strategy for the Maritime Industry], Seoul: Haewoon Sanup Yeonguwon [Korea Maritime Institute], 1991.

32 North Korea has constructed an expressway under construction between Pyongyang and Kaesong. This could be linked to the expressway network in South Korea (personal comment). See Rhee Jong-ho, 'Direction for

constructing Eurasia transportation network', in KMI, *Far East–U.S. Symposium on Maritime Development of the Northeast Asian Pacific Rim*, the 4th KMI International Symposium Proceedings August 1992, Seoul: Korea Maritime Institute, 1992) , pp. 67–91.

33 Kim Doojung and Yoo Jea-taik, eds, *Korea: Geographical Perspectives*, p. 384.

34 A.R. Holm, 'Northeast Asia maritime trade and industry', in KMI, *Far East –U.S. Symposium on Maritime Development of the Northeast Asian Pacific Rim*, the 4th KMI International Symposium Proceedings August 1992, Seoul: Korea Maritime Institute, 1992, pp. 197–203; Lee Sang-man, 'Economic Cooperation in Northeast Asia and Economic Exchange between South and North Koreas', pp. 49–58; Ogawa Yuhei, 'Local Economic Exchange and Economic Cooperation in Northeast Asia', in KMI, *Far-East-U.S. Symposium on Maritime Development of the Northeast Asian Pacific Rim*, the 4th KMI International Symposium Proceedings August 1992, Seoul: Korea Maritime Institute, 1992, pp. 17–27.

35 R. Garnaut, *Australia and the Northeast Asia Ascendancy: Report to the Prime Minister and the Minister for Foreign Affairs and Trade*, Canberra: Australian Government Publishing Service, 1989, p. 70; Ishigaki Hiro, 'The Sea of Japan Free Trade Area: Broad Perspectives for the 1990s', in *Japan and the World*, Proceedings of the Seventh Biennial Conference, vol. 1, Canberra: Australia–Japan Research Center and The Australian National University, 1991, pp. 106–11.

36 Noh Hee Mock, 'The Development of Korean Trade and Investment in the PRC', *Korea and World Affairs: A Quarterly Review*, vol. 13, no. 3 (1989), pp. 421–39.

37 Choe Sang-chuel, 'Emerging Spatial Pattern and Coastal Zone Management of the Yellow Sea Rim', pp. 29–48.

38 Other Eurasian landbridges include the Trans-Manchuria Railway from Dalian via Harbin to the Trans-Siberian Railway and the Trans-Mongolian Railway from Tianjin via Beijing and Ulan Bator to the Trans-Siberian Railway. See P.J. Rimmer, 'Ports, Inland Transport Linkages and Regional Development: A Western Pacific Rim Conspectus', in KMI, *The Public Sector's Role in Logistics for the 21st Century*, The 2nd KMI International Symposium 2–7 July 1990, Seoul: Korea Maritime Institute, 1990, pp. 259–312; and Song Hee-hyon *Dingbuckah jiyeok-yeu susongchaejeh baljeon banghwang* [Transport system development direction in Northeast Asia: with particular reference to Korea, USSR and China], Seoul: Korea Maritime Institute, 1990.

39 Kim Young-kon and Yoon Chang-bun, 'Country Strategy for Developing the Information/Communication Technology and its Infrastructure: Korea', *The Korean Journal of Information Society*, vol. 3, no. 1, 1991, pp. 140–88.

10

Korea in Comparative Perspective

James Cotton

This volume has reviewed the transformation of the Korean state. While domestic developments have provided the chief focus for most of the contributors, it is clear that the South Korean political system has not been immune from such major international trends as the transnationalising of capital, information and ideas, the decline of citizenship, the rise of world institutions and cosmopolitan criteria for the assessment of national and international behaviour, and the emergence of new global issues such as the environmental crisis.

   This chapter places this transformation in international and comparative perspective. The experience of Korea will be considered along with that of Singapore and Taiwan (with some references also to Hong Kong, though the colony's early commitment to the market, and the present constraints upon its autonomous political evolution, render it in some respects a case apart). The first argument that is developed is that, into the 1980s, the state remained a useful concept for the analysis of the political and social systems of Korea and the Asian NICs. The second accepts that in some aspects 'the state' has become in the last ten years a less powerful and comprehensive explanatory device. However, developments in Korea and the NICs have been uneven, and from the point of view of international relations — given the rising power and influence of the Asian NICs and their region — more attention rather than less needs to be paid to the NIC state.

Korea and approaches to the Asian NIC phenomenon

Earlier accounts of Korea and the Asian NIC phenomenon adopted either a dependency theory/world systems or a free market approach. Although conceding that the NICs had made rapid progress in some areas of industrialisation, the former maintained that (in the absence of Maoist autarchy) they would never move beyond the semi-periphery and would always remain crucially dependent for capital and markets upon the major capitalist systems.[1] Some authors within this school pointed to such phenomena as the international indebtedness of South Korea (around US$46 billion in the early 1980s) as an indicator of the plausibility of this interpretation. The free market analysts, on the other hand, stressed the correct policy choices — specifically the move from import substitution to export-oriented industrialisation, and the decision to keep the state away from direct management of enterprises — made by the political/economic elites in the NICs.[2] In time, the 'success' of the Asian as opposed to the Latin American NICs seemed to support this latter view, and there even emerged a school with representatives within world financial institutions which advocated an Asian NIC 'model' for the developing world.

By the 1980s, both of these approaches had been largely abandoned by their adherents. The exclusion of multinationals from many sectors of industrial activity, controls on external investment, the development of indigenous technology, and the very limited leverage that the United States was able to exert in redressing adverse trade balances all seemed to point to the inappropriateness of the dependency argument. On the other hand, enough was now known of domestic policy for the 'governed market' hypothesis to gain ground as an influential interpretation of the development of South Korea, and of Taiwan and Singapore (though not Hong Kong).[3]

In addition, at least one school within political science, by stressing those sociological and economic trends (urbanisation, mobility, education) which constituted the main indices of modernisation, seemed also to support the view that the Asian NICs were rapidly joining the ranks of the 'developed' countries. Accordingly, their political systems should come in time to conform more closely to the pluralist prescription.[4]

Approaches to the Asian NIC phenomenon then took an inductive turn. Much of the literature on this question written from the 1980s onwards concentrated upon explicating those significant characteristics which these systems had in common. This literature will be reviewed, paying particular attention to the importance it attributes to the state. Having determined the role of the state in the development of the NICs until recent times, the question will then be posed: to what extent will the state be central to the NICs in the future?

Analysis of Korea and the NICs

The most salient feature of the Asian NICs has been political authoritarianism. Although varying with respect to sophistication, reliance upon force and concessions to the principle of political representation, all have been characterised by political insulation or 'closure'.[5]

The government of Hong Kong remains colonial, though some role (as yet indeterminate) has now been accorded to popular opinion. Even if Governor Patten's present scheme for the reform of the Legislative Council is adopted, the chief executive will remain a powerful and unaccountable office, a structural feature which is likely to persist under post-1997 Chinese rule. Singapore has adapted Westminster institutions, but without permitting sufficient space for a parliamentary opposition. In practice, political activity outside the ambit of the ruling party can be very costly for ordinary citizens, and the divisions between the People's Action Party, the bureaucracy and the government are designedly imprecise. The government states quite specifically at times that it exists as much to mould public opinion as to attend to it, and no detail of social life (from national values to toilet training) is, by convention or definition, beyond its ambit. In Taiwan until 1986, the tutelary role of the Guomindang was explicit, the government in Taibei acting not for opinion on the island to which its activities were curtailed, but for an ideologically defined 'China'. By degrees, the principle of the sovereignty of opinion on Taiwan was accepted, but in practice many of the features of the system which guaranteed the hegemony of the Guomindang remained in place.

Between 1961 and 1987, South Korea was ruled by successive military cliques, and the succeeding government of Roh Tae-woo should be seen as transitional in character, with thorough-going democratic institutions becoming animated as a result of the presidential elections of 1992. Even here, it should be observed that the political coalition now in office still contains elements of the former regime, though much diminished in power as a result of the personnel and structural reforms effected by Kim Young-sam in 1993.

In company with the limited parliamentarianism, or authoritarianism, of the Asian NICs can be observed mechanisms and policies intended to achieve political insulation or pre-emption. Thus social and political interests which might have challenged policies aimed at rapid capital accumulation were weakened (in the case of traditional landlords by land reforms in Taiwan and South Korea) or corporatised (in the case of industrial workers, especially in Singapore and South Korea). The impact of social organisations was also monitored and constrained — for example, religious groups in South Korea and Singapore encountered either obstacles or outright obstruction when they sought to take up issues relating to the rights and conditions of labour.

Indeed, such strategies often lie behind policies which would seem to serve an obvious social purpose. The public housing program of the Singapore government was initiated to alleviate the acute residential shortage of the 1960s. But now that around 80 per cent of the population live in government housing, not only does the overall operation provide an operating surplus but it also presents mechanisms and opportunities for social control.[6] Public housing complexes provide the geographical and organisational foundation for the network of Citizens Consultative Committees which is co-ordinated (ostensibly in a non-partisan spirit) by the Prime Minister's Office. Regulations have also been introduced to guarantee a mixing of the races in public housing, and the ruling party has even stated that the refurbishment of public housing will occur last, all things being equal, in those places where opposition support is strongest. The government's Central Provident Fund, though instituted for social security purposes, may actually be regarded as a mechanism which forces savings for development purposes.[7]

Authoritarianism by itself is not necessarily consonant with industrialising policies, as the experience of much of the South attests. A notable feature of the Asian NICs has been the domination of their regimes by a developmental coalition, comprised of military/political, bureaucratic and business figures.[8] Not only in South Korea, but also in Taiwan, the military had a major voice early in the formation of the system; in Singapore their voice has grown more important with time. In all three systems, the principals of security agencies (most notably the Korea CIA) have intermittently been important actors. Bureaucrats — in Taiwan often engineers by training, in South Korea more usually lawyers or economists — have also been more than agents of rule. The increasing sophistication and complexity of the NICs has accorded them an ever-freer hand, and ultimately bureaucrats have risen to prominence in the upper echelons of the hegemonic political parties and movements which have emerged as the NICs reached middle age. While some have interpreted Singapore as a dictatorship of the middle class, an equal claim could be made for its characterisation in the Goh Chok Tong era as a system in which the bureaucracy is predominant.[9] A similar view could be taken of Taiwan under Lee Teng-hui, though this would obscure the important internal differences which now threaten the solidity of the Guomindang.

The importance of the role of business in these developmental coalitions is a more contentious issue. It is undoubtedly the case that the NICs have comprised, in important respects, the cutting edge of capitalism in the Asia-Pacific region in the last two or three decades. Especially with regard to Korea, the business groups that have been the vehicle and beneficiary of NIC development have prospered mightily, so much so that some at least are now familiar brand names across the world. In very recent times also in Korea, the divergence of view between at least some of the business groups and the government has been a matter of public and political concern, with Hyundai Honorary Chairman Chung Ju-yung running for the presidency in the elections of 1992. However, it is difficult to sustain the hypothesis that the NIC state has been the creature of capitalist interests.

A number of studies of the Korean case have shown how dependent the business groups were, even into the 1980s, for concessionary finance, local oligopoly, export support and government contracts.[10] In Singapore, the government has traditionally performed, through such quasi-government agencies as Temasek Holdings, many of the functions of the entrepeneur. Local capital, dwarfed in any case by the presence of major trans-national companies, has been held at a disadvantage lest the government's monopoly of power be contested by local capitalists or their nominees.

The literature on the Asian NICs also emphasises the role of particular instruments, agents and structures. As Chalmers Johnson points out, following the model of Japan's Ministry of International Trade and Industry, each developed its own commanding agency, staffed by the best talents the system could produce, and accorded prestige and given considerable discretion to plan for and oversee rapid growth.[11] Peak organisations in the business sector were also organised to secure the concurrence of entrepreneurs with rapid development. In the societies at large, the 'right' kind of training (engineers rather than pure scientists, computer specialists rather than lawyers) facilitated the institutional capacity of private and public bureaucracies.

It is important to grasp, given the authoritarian nature of each of the NIC political systems, that these instruments and structures have not functioned simply in a top-down fashion. The early political and developmental goals of these regimes lacked complexity and thus merely enjoined compliance, but over time further development became a complex affair which heavy-handed direction could well have upset. Each of the NICs responded by attempting to emulate elements of the model of government–business co-operation so successfully practised in Japan in the 1960s and early 1970s. Far from diminishing the power of the state, this power was actually enhanced, as policy-makers were able to adjust their objectives to changing conditions and secure the comprehensive co-operation of the industrial conglomerates and the bureaucracy.

Such attention to domestic institutions and forces should not obscure the role of international linkages. In one sense at least, these have been crucial. None of the NICs would have come into existence if the political and security policies of metropolitan powers, the United States in the case of Taiwan and Korea, and Britain in the case of Singapore and Hong Kong, had been different. As it was, the Korean War almost annulled those policies, and the government of Singapore itself sought to reverse them in the period 1963–65. Taiwan's claims to be 'The Republic of China' (in the United Nations as such as late as 1971) could never have been sustained without the political support of Washington, as well as the Washington–Taibei strategic alliance.

If the Asian NIC project was begun by the metropolitan powers, it was also sustained by them, the United States in the 1950s giving more civil and military aid to Korea and to Taiwan than to any other two systems. The NICs benefited from market access, patents, technology and capital, and booming world trade and the small size of their economies as compared to the economy of the United States led to an almost complete lack of complaint about the less than free NIC trade practices. In a later phase and perhaps in a less benign spirit, Japan began to fulfil some of the functions of regional hegemon.

It should not be supposed that in sustaining the Asian NICs, the metropole necessarily determined the particularities either of their development or of their state structures. In the Korean case outstandingly so, in the case of Taiwan more selectively, the state functioned more or less successfully as gatekeeper. Only in Singapore was the decision made to embrace unconditionally trans-national capital. This gatekeeping role has fulfilled political as well as economic objectives. State supervision of injections of foreign capital ensured that government development priorities were observed; the penetration of the economy by Japanese capital — given Japan's former colonial role in Korea, an outcome which Park Chung-hee and his associates wished to avoid — was also constrained. And, again most clearly in the Korean case, the political elite sought and derived rent (typically in the form of political funding) from this activity. Even Singapore's policy had clear political dimensions. Only the vigorous pursuit of international investment would raise the city-state from the status of a regional entrepôt, a status which, after the expulsion of Singapore from Malaysia in 1965, Lee Kuan Yew and his associates sought to escape.

It should also be pointed out that the Asian NICs were major beneficiaries of the war in Vietnam: Korean construction companies were given concessions to build much of Vietnam's infrastructure, and the battlefield participation of Korean troops was supported by generous subventions from Washington. In addition, Taiwan and Singapore in the 1960s rapidly expanded their trade with a South Vietnamese economy inflated with American funds.

It has been Stephan Haggard's particular contribution to this debate to underline the fact that the NICs have managed to turn external adversities which have developed in their relationships with the metropoles to their advantage.[12] The export-oriented industrialisation programs of South Korea and also of Taiwan were in part a response to sharp reductions in United States assistance; the contemporaneous program in Singapore was a clear response to the divorce from Malaysia. In the 1970s, the turn towards heavy and chemical industries in Korea and Taiwan, whatever its economic logic, was intended to offer greater self-sufficiency at a time when the security relationships with the United States — following the Nixon doctrine, Washington's rapprochement with Beijing and Taiwan's expulsion from the United Nations — could no longer be assured. It is also noteworthy that all of the Asian NICs have had to contend with continuing security uncertainties, Korea especially so.

A minority, but still a significant number, of commentators on the Asian NIC phenomenon also include cultural factors in their accounts.[13] Confucianism, once the ideological factor which was supposed to have retarded China's modernisation, has now become for some an essential element in the rapid transformation of the Asian dragons. However, if we examine Weber's account of Confucianism, his assessment of it as a comfortable and conformist creed which raised no tension between its practitioners and the world was almost inevitable given his very imperfect sources, but was perhaps also a consequence of his particular comparative project. Now that Confucianism is much better understood, this interpretation is evidently flawed. Without reviewing this argument, it is sufficient to observe here that many of the social characteristics of Korea as well as of the Asian NICs are consonant with long-standing Confucian patterns — the prestige accorded to bureaucracy, the respect for education, the stress upon self-cultivation, the centrality of the family, frugality and political authoritarianism itself. A complete analysis of Korean political culture in particular needs, however, to include a consideration of the significant (and in important respects anti-Confucian) role of shamanism, and the growing influence of Christianity.

The state in Korea and the NICs

It is evident that the points brought up during what I have called this inductive turn in the analysis of the Asian NICs are consistent with more than one approach to political and social phenomena. Without attempting to reduce them to a single approach, it is sufficient for the purposes of this chapter to indicate that most of them acknowledge the centrality of 'the state'. By the state I would like to offer the following provisional definition.

The term 'state' I understand here to embrace all those individuals or office-holders (the distinction between the two is important, but in some systems fluid) in positions of 'authority' or effective power, the specific purpose of the offices they hold being to make and/or see implemented authoritative policies binding upon all the members of the society at large, and who may in the implementation of such policies have recourse to the ultimate sanction of force. In addition to the government — defined strictly and perhaps formal–legally as the holders of specific executive offices, usually 'elected' and thus in the conventional sense political figures — the state therefore includes key members of the bureaucracy, of judicial and financial institutions, and of the coercive and security organs. The activities of the state are normally co-ordinated by an executive and expressed through formal institutions; they are also both constrained and informed by institutional memory in its various aspects (from archives to deliberative procedures).

The criteria to be satisfied here are both empirical and formal–legal. In settled and institutionalised political systems, formal–legal criteria might well be the best guide to formulating a hypothesis as to the membership of the 'state', but even in such cases only studies of actual instances of policy-making (where they can be conducted) permit the testing of such a hypothesis. To some extent, this membership is bound to be fluid, as different policy agendas are considered and personalities enter and leave crucial offices. In less institutionalised systems, the fact of state membership is likely to be somewhat unclear, though in principle not unknowable.

In order for this term to be used coherently, it is important that the institutional aspect of the state be taken seriously. If this requirement is ignored, membership of the state is enlarged (by definition, as it were, rather than as a result of empirical inquiry) to embrace articulators of economic and social interests, and influence-wielders of every variety. Such a notion of the state is amorphous, and prejudges the issue of the possibility of the effective independent power and interests of state formations (an independence seemingly manifest in the history of states from Chinggis Khan to Kim Il-sung). At the same time, the possibility of any given state lacking independent power need not and should not be excluded.

Working with this provisional understanding, the notion of the insulation or closure of the state in Korea and the NICs makes sense. The relevant individuals and office-holders — the core of which is the 'development coalition' — have been able to pursue political (regime maintenance) and economic (rapid export-led industrialisation) policies relatively unconstrained by domestic forces. As to their international environment, though it has been possible even to apply the (international relations theory) notion of the hegemon to the NIC phenomenon, the NIC state has been crucial in refracting and constraining the influence of and linkages with the metropole. So far, 'the state' would seem to be a necessary category for any discussion of the development of the Asian NICs.

From one perspective, the only part of the inductive ensemble reviewed here which does not rest upon some notion of the state is the cultural factor of Confucianism. 'Confucianism', from this perspective, is an ideology or part of some deep cultural baggage, and thus perhaps (as Lucian Pye would argue)[14] even a determining factor in the development of the NICs. However, without discussing this topic exhaustively, I would like to suggest that Confucianism is not a coherent notion without the state, any more than the belief system of Islam is coherent without the idea of a community of believers.

In practice, 'Confucianism' is not a body of ideas so much as a set of social and political practices. Although there are many books which expound Confucianism, their logic is doxographical; all that the major texts and thinkers of the school have in common are certain slogans which actually have a variable meaning. This observation is justified if one considers the vague boundary line between 'Confucianism' and 'East Asian Political Thought'. Turning to the relevant practices, it can be seen that 'the state' is a central notion in them all. Authority relations in the units of the nation and in the nation as a whole have the same character: the state is the family writ large (an idea implicit in the East Asian word for 'state' *kukka/guojia*, the etymology of which thus bears no relation to the English term). Even folk religion (in Korea shamanism, in Chinese cultures a variety of folk cults) often contains the shades of emperors and officials. In short, taking this and the preceding point together, it can be said that 'the state' has been a necessary conceptual category for the analysis of the Asian NICs.

The state and the future of Korea and the NICs

Recent writing on the NICs is generally concerned with one of two issues. The first is economic liberalisation, the second is political liberalisation (or democratisation).

It is often argued that the 'governed market' phenomenon is on the wane as a result of the new international environment as much as of economic changes within the NICs. As to the former, the sluggish growth in world trade, the difficulties now being experienced in the American economy, the greater attention being paid to the GATT, and the fact that the size of some of the NIC economies make them in the 1990s significant world actors, all constrict state policy. The publicity given by the Korean government to its liberalisation policies, as much as Taiwan's attempts to lessen its trade surplus with the United States, may be taken as evidence of these trends. Regarding the latter, it is argued that the greater complexity of the NIC economies, the exigencies of the product cycle, the trans-nationalising of NIC capital itself and the increasing vocalisation of consumer demands constitute domestic trends working to free government controls over the economy.

Though it is clear that the heyday of the governed market is over, the evidence for liberalisation is mixed. South Korea is a singular example in this regard. A flurry of economic measures were announced by the new Kim Young-sam administration; in June 1993 a lengthy statement on economic reform outlined the government's objectives in the medium term. In this statement, the government embraced the need for deregulation of the still very considerable controls that are held over economic activity. However, the statement included no concrete timetable for reforms in such crucial issues as government requirements for banks to issue 'policy loans' at low interest to the big conglomerates, nor regarding the lifting of exchange controls to make the Korean currency internationally convertible.

Viewed comparatively, the situation in the other NICs is instructive. Though a very much more open economic system exists in Singapore, the 'privatisation' policies announced in 1986–87, and the more recent campaign to encourage local entrepreneurship to take up the spaces being vacated by the state, have left many of the essentials of the interventionist model still in place. In the currency area, for example, the Monetary Authority of Singapore still regulates the value of the Singapore dollar, and national savings are still dominated by the operations of the Central Provident Fund which (compulsorily) absorbs a proportion of all wages and salaries paid in the city-state.

Even greater attention has been paid to the development of political liberalisation in Korea and the NICs. Here, so the argument goes, democratisation is leading to a widening of the developmental coalition, and a weakening of its singular policy thrust (in the name of welfare and other forms of distribution). Representative institutions are transforming the function of political parties from mobilising to interest aggregation, and voluntary organisations, perhaps worthy of the description 'civil society', are emerging to educate the citizenry and enlarge the political agenda. Thus the post-1985 movement towards democracy in the case of Korea as well as of Taiwan (and the upsurge in the expression of popular opinion which occurred in Hong Kong between the Tiananmen incident and the Legislative Council elections of 1991) has been explained as a consequence of the waning influence of those factors which formerly made state autonomy possible and sustainable.

Without necessarily disputing this characterisation, some caution is required lest an excessive weakening in the role of the state is found both in the process of democratisation and in its results.

Explanations of transitions to democracy are couched either in terms of preconditions or processes. Either democracy is the consequence of social and economic pressures, usually generated by rising income levels and attendant increases in the numbers of those claiming 'middle-class' status, or it is a matter of negotiation between ruling and opposition groups or evolution within a formerly dominating political party or movement. Either way, a likely outcome is a diminution in the role of the state. Here we will consider the emergence of preconditions and the operation of process in Korea and in the other NICs.

It is well known that Korea has undoubtedly experienced rapid and profound sociological transformation since Park Chung-hee's military clique seized power in 1961. The role of the middle class in the political upheaval of 1987 (which forced Park's successor, Chun Doo-hwan, to proceed with democratisation) is also widely acknowledged. Has the political/sociological foundation therefore been laid for a pluralist Korea, with a reduced role for the state and greater space for individual and voluntary activities? So far, the evidence here is not clear. It is a singular fact that the most powerful predictive factor in voting behaviour is regional affiliation.[15] Such affiliation, indeed, may not refer to present area of residence, but that place which parents or grandparents regarded as home. It may be supposed, therefore, that with regard at least to the promotion of regional identity and interests, Korean citizens still have high expectations of the state, and are consequently prepared to accord it a major role. In other respects, too, the political culture of modern Korea exhibits some differences from the pluralist norm. On the other hand, the beginnings of a Korean civil society — addressing issues new to the Korean political agenda such as the environment and human rights, and employing non-conventional strategies to put pressure upon decision-makers — may be discerned.[16]

The actual path taken by Korean democratisation demonstrates that, by themselves, sociological factors provide at best a background for the pacts and bargains which have accompanied political transition. In the period

1987–92, two developments stand out. The first is the fact that the division of the opposition permitted Chun Doo-hwan's chosen successor to carry over significant elements of his regime into the era of representative institutions. The second is the political realignment of 1990 which brought together Roh Tae-woo's military/regional group and the former opposition forces of Kim Young-sam, thereby securing the election of the latter as president in 1992. It is difficult to see either of these as immanent in Korea's political sociology. Again, the point for the argument here is that developments at the summit of the state, and especially bargains and pacts among various of the key actors, have continued to deliver outcomes unanticipated (but in a sense subsequently ratified) by Korean voters. Democratisation has not yet given us a truly compliant state. In the longer term, of course, it may be that with the further development of the political system, such compliance will emerge. The beginnings of a Korean civil society — addressing issues new to the Korean political agenda such as the environment, the status of women, and human rights, and employing non-conventional strategies to put pressure upon decision-makers — have been discerned by some commentators.

The situation in Taiwan is not dissimilar. A number of scholars have shown that in Taiwan rising expectations accompanying growing affluence and a trend towards social pluralism have provided the background to the political change of the last ten years. But these sociological trends have had only a limited political expression.[17] Although the leadership of the opposition is predominantly from the new middle class, many of its followers, as well as being almost exclusively Taiwanese (as opposed to mainland China born) are poorer members of society. And the issues that have undoubtedly galvanised the opposition parties have been the perennial questions of national identity and the dominance of the people of the island by mainlanders, issues which have little connection with social change. Again, the most powerful variable in the explanation of voting behaviour is regional affiliation, in this case Taiwan versus mainland. As to the process of democratisation, once more the state has been crucial: the post-1986 decision by the ruling Guomindang to steal the opposition's clothes by reconstituting the political system independent of any more than a nominal attachment with China has delivered to them, at least for the present, a predominant role. And neither the Guomindang nor the opposition can be well understood without resorting to a patron–client model of political relations.

In Singapore we have an even clearer demonstration that the NIC state can retain its dominance despite sociological transformation.[18] Education, urbanisation, the development of the 'new middle class' and extensive external information and financial linkages have made the most progress in Singapore. These trends are reflected in the evolution of the ruling party and of its chosen instruments for mobilisation and control. The People's Action Party now practises a form of politics which is avowedly meritocratic rather than ideological, and consensual rather than mobilising and confrontational. And it is undoubtedly the case that the managed social change of the last three decades has largely removed the destabilising influence of communalism, an influence which much early PAP policy was designed to counter. However, Singapore still lacks a coherent opposition politics. The recent split in the largest opposition party has delayed even further that democratic transition which has generated so much new analysis of South Korea and Taiwan. The state's ambitions to corporatise and constrain all social activity remain large, and considerable resources have even been devoted to the scrutiny of the activities of Singaporeans abroad.

If we turn from institutions and structures to political culture, what can be said of the future of Confucianism? Here Gilbert Rozman and Ezra Vogel may be contrasted on the prognoses they offer for the future role of the Confucian societies.[19] In the perspective he offers on the present, Rozman has discerned an increasingly self-confident and self-referencing, and to this extent 'Confucian', East Asia taking its place as a partner (or rival) with the West as one of the two dominant civilisation areas. Vogel is more inclined to stress the internationalising impact of the globalisation of communications and of short or longer term population movements as diluting the distinctiveness of the East, as well as the uncertain impact of a shift from labour intensive to service industries and the rise of demands for political liberalisation. He also argues, however, that East Asia as a source of investment capital and as a model for development has yet to reach the height of its international influence. But both would agree that the Confucian variable needs to be taken seriously. Here, perhaps, the influence of the 'contempt for America' school in Japan is a harbinger of trends elsewhere in the region.

Conclusions

Economic and political liberalisation in South Korea and Taiwan has undoubtedly diminished the capacity of the state to control these polities and economies. This diminishment, however, has been decidedly uneven, and for the present in the analysis of Korea and the Asian NIC phenomenon the 'state' requires the closest attention and scrutiny. In politics, Korea, in company with the NICs, has embarked upon the long road to pluralism; in economics, while some adjustments have been made towards a greater role for the market, Korea and the other NICs still practise some elements of an industrial policy. It is not an accident of market forces that there are no Japanese cars on Korean roads, and that no Japanese films may be screened in Korea outside Japan's cultural centre in Seoul.

There is a further point to make regarding the status and claims of the NIC state. If the NIC state's ambitions and capacities have been reduced as compared with the situation in the 1970s, the NICs themselves have grown meanwhile to be regional and even world actors. Both South Korea and Taiwan are ranked in the top twelve of the trading nations; the latter's external reserves are the world's largest and Singapore's are the world's largest per capita. Singapore, Taiwan and Hong Kong have overtaken the prosperity indices of the second tier of countries in Western Europe, and South Korea is poised to follow. As a phenomenon on the agenda of study in world politics, the NIC state with such resources at its disposal now looms as an immeasurably larger item. Just as Korea is now a major regional actor, so Korean foundations now have the resources to begin to shape the image of Korea abroad.

Notes

1 With reference to Korea, see for example Gavan McCormack and Mark Selden, eds, *Korea North and South*, New York: Monthly Review, 1978; cf. James Cotton, 'Understanding the State in South Korea', *Comparative Political Studies*, vol. 24 (1992), pp. 512–31.

2 Bela Balassa, *Economic Policies in the Pacific Area Developing Countries*, London: Macmillan, 1991.

3 Robert Wade, *Governing the Market*, Princeton: Princeton University Press, 1990.

4 See the discussion in Samuel P. Huntington, 'Will More Countries Become Democratic?', *Political Science Quarterly*, vol. 99 (1984), pp. 193–218.

5 See, for example, Thomas B. Gold, *State and Society in the Taiwan Economic Miracle*, New York: M. E Sharpe., 1986; Stephan Haggard, 'The East Asian NICs in Comparative Perspective', *Annals of the American Academy of Political and Social Science*, no. 505 (1989), pp. 129–41.

6 Linda Lim, 'Social Welfare', in Kernial S. Sandhu and Paul Wheatley, eds, *Management of Success. The Moulding of Modern Singapore*, Singapore: Institute of Southeast Asian Studies, 1989, pp. 171–97.

7 *The Straits Times* (Singapore), 25 August 1993, p. 1.

8 Frederic Deyo, ed., *The Political Economy of the New Asian Industrialism*, Ithaca: Cornell University Press, 1987.

9 Garry Rodan, 'Singapore: Emerging Tensions in the Dictatorship of the Middle Class', *Pacific Review*, vol. 5 (1992), pp. 370–81.

10 Alice Amsden, *Asia's Next Giant*, New York: Oxford University Press, 1989; Woo Jung-en, *Race to the Swift*, New York: Columbia University Press, 1991.

11 Chalmers Johnson, 'Political Institutions and Economic Performance: The Government–Business Relationship in Japan, South Korea, and Taiwan', in Frederic Deyo, ed., *The Political Economy of the New Asian Industrialism*, Ithaca: Cornell University Press, 1987, pp. 136–64.

12 Stephan Haggard, *Pathways from the Periphery*, Ithaca: Cornell University Press, 1990.

13 Winston Davis, 'Religion and Development: Weber and the East Asian Experience', in Myron Weiner and Samuel P. Huntington, eds, *Understanding Political Development*, Boston: Little, Brown, 1987, pp. 221–80.

14 Lucian W. Pye, *Asian Power and Politics*, Cambridge: Harvard University Press, 1985.

15 Bae Sun-kwang and James Cotton, 'Regionalism in Electoral Politics', in James Cotton, ed., *Korea under Roh Tae-woo*, Sydney: Allen & Unwin, 1993, pp. 170–84.

16 Ahn Chung-si, 'Economic Development and Democratization in South Korea — An Examination of Economic Change and Empowerment of Civil Society', *Korea and World Affairs*, vol. 15 (1991), pp. 740–54.

17 Cheng Tun-jen and Stephan Haggard, eds, *Political Change in Taiwan*, Boulder: Lynne Rienner, 1992.

18 Garry Rodan, ed., *Singapore Changes Guard. Social, Political and Economic Directions in the 1990s*, Melbourne: Longman Cheshire, 1993.

19 Gilbert Rozman (ed.), *The East Asian Region*, Princeton: Princeton University Press, 1991; Ezra Vogel, *The Four Little Dragons*, Cambridge: Harvard University Press, 1991.

Index